IMAGES
of America

PLYMOUTH REVISITED

On the Cover: In this 1910 photograph taken in Terryville, boys riding bicycles pose on Prospect Street, the site of the Eagle Lock's employee lodging as well as Prospect Street School. Prospect Street's proximity to the Eagle Lock and the center of Terryville, businesses, and churches made it a popular place to live. (Courtesy of Plymouth Historical Society.)

IMAGES
of America

PLYMOUTH REVISITED

Judy Giguere

ARCADIA
PUBLISHING

ISBN 978-0-7385-7591-9

Published by Arcadia Publishing
Charleston, South Carolina

Printed in the United States of America

Library of Congress Control Number: 2011922957

For all general information, please contact Arcadia Publishing:
Telephone 843-853-2070
Fax 843-853-0044
E-mail sales@arcadiapublishing.com
For customer service and orders:
Toll-Free 1-888-313-2665

Visit us on the Internet at www.arcadiapublishing.com

To my Uncle Norman,
the best uncle anyone could ever have

In memory of MaryAnn Evans,
who recently lost her battle with cancer,
for her kindness, spirit, love of Belgian Malinois dogs and all creatures

CONTENTS

ACKNOWLEDGMENTS

I would like to acknowledge the help and support of my friend Paula Ciarmella and the invaluable assistance of Peter Bugryn, whose patience and computer skills were instrumental in this project. My friends Bob and Ingrid Breikreutz, Dawn Leger, Jan Lewis, Lori Ciarmella, Bea Hubert, Jim and MaryAnn Evans, Patrice Dumond, and Burlington town historian Len Alderman for their friendship, patience, and encouragement. Special thanks to Matt Malley, president of Plymouth Historical Society, for his assistance in sharing his knowledge for this book. My thanks to everyone who took time to talk with me about their experiences in Plymouth.

Thank you to the American Clock & Watch Museum for its contribution and assistance with materials and photographs of the genius of Eli Terry. Ives Toys information appears courtesy of historian Dave McEntarfer with the Ives Train Society. Ruth Quick of the Ashtabula County Historical Society provided information and photographs of the Blakeslee Log Cabin. Ken and Joyce Wood of Wood Acres Farm provided images and information about the farm and its history. A generous thanks goes out to the Plymouth Historical Society for the loan of many of the photographs in this book.

INTRODUCTION

In early days, the hills, rocks, and trees of the rough region that came to be Plymouth were pristine. Native Americans rarely frequented the area, and the land was largely undisturbed. An encampment of Tunxis Indians was in Farmington along the Farmington River. Other than hunting, few had reason to travel to Plymouth. Some portions of the community are credited with Native American names, such as "Fall" Mountain, whose Native American name sounded like the word "fall" to the newly arriving white settlers, and Chippen's Hill, which was named for the Indian "Cochipianee" (the name was later shortened to Chipppeny or Chippen's Hill).

New settlers came to the area in search of a lead mine. The Tunxis Indians granted settlers the right to search. Parties scoured the hills and woodlands for the rumored mine, which, even today, remains elusive. Many locations show rocks that have been drilled or chipped in search of lead, yet it is unknown if a mine ever even existed. While hiding from the Sons of Liberty, local Revolutionary War British sympathizer Capt. Moses Dunbar is reported to have found a cave with a large vein of lead. However, he never had a chance to return to the cave. He was captured, tried for treason, and executed as a traitor in Hartford in 1777.

Plymouth was originally part of the Mattatuck Plantation called Northbury. In 1747, the land was given to the Society of Northbury by the Town of Waterbury as a parade and burial ground. A road originally ran through the parade ground. Later, when the Congregational Church was erected, the area was enclosed by a fence and the road discontinued.

The earliest burial in the cemetery known as the Old Plymouth Cemetery is recorded as 1749. The cemetery contains approximately 300 markers and is the final resting place of many Plymouth Revolutionary War soldiers, as well as soldiers from the French and Indian War, War of 1812, and the Civil War. Many graves are marked with brownstones carved with classic death's heads imagery, some of which are still legible. An additional burying ground, the West Cemetery, is a short distance away on Carter Road and dates from 1796. A stone wall along Carter Road is dominated by huge evergreens and several burial vaults.

Plymouth Center is home to the first of two historic districts in Plymouth: Plymouth Green and East Church. The focus of Plymouth Green was the Plymouth Congregational Church, and the present structure was built in 1838. The large clock and wooden clock movement that dominate the steeple of the church were donated by Eli Terry, Plymouth resident, inventor, clock maker, and generous industrialist. The Reverend Andrew Storrs House on Plymouth Green was built in 1766. Reverend Storrs planted many trees on the Green, only one of which, a sycamore, remains today. Plymouth Green is also host to one of Connecticut's first Civil War memorials. The memorial is elegantly carved in a simple style by local store owner and stone cutter Daniel Mattoon. Inscribed on the monument are the words "War of 1861," "Abraham Lincoln," and a list of the names of several Civil War soldiers from Plymouth.

In the corner of Plymouth's historic green and churchyard is Plymouth's Constitution Oak Tree. The tree is named for the 1902 Connecticut Constitutional Convention. Each representative of the 1902 Connecticut Constitutional Convention received a tiny pin oak (*Quercus palustris*) tree from the US Department of Agriculture in Washington, DC, to commemorate the event. Plymouth's tree was planted on the Green, near the Plymouth Congregational Church. The community focus of Plymouth Green makes it a perfect place for this historic beauty.

There have been many historic structures in Plymouth. St. Peter's Episcopal Church on North Street is a charming chapel constructed of fieldstone. The original church was lost to fire. The Plymouth Post Office was originally built in 1782. The building next to the post office was the Grange Hall, and, prior to that, the Ives Toy Factory. Ives Toys earned an international reputation as a toy maker. Ives originally manufactured buttons for Union soldier's uniforms during the Civil War but moved on to toy manufacturing using clockwork mechanisms.

The Beach & Blackmer structure dates from 1780 and still exists as an antique shop. Next door to it is a small brick building that was once the town clerk's office. A.C. Shelton & Tuttle carried on a successful carriage-making business near Plymouth Center. A bit farther north is the former home of David Smith, an officer during the Revolutionary War. The house was built in 1766. According to certain accounts, George Washington was Smith's guest. Unfortunately, the actual register with Washington's signature was lost in a fire.

Numerous private homes date from the mid-1700s and 1800s, two of which were sites on the Underground Railroad. One is the Maple Street home of ardent abolitionist Joel Blakeslee. Another home on North Street, built by Henry K. Terry and later owned by the Taylor family, had a tunnel leading to the woods. The tunnel was used for slaves to continue on their journey to freedom.

Plymouth's second historic district, East Church, is located at the shared boundary of Bristol, Plymouth, and Harwinton. It became its own distinct section of Plymouth largely because of disputes with England and the original 13 colonies: most East Church residents maintained their loyalty to the King of England, much to the chagrin of Captain Wilson and the local branch of the Sons of Liberty. The woods of East Church contain a cave known as "Tories Den," which is historically recognized as the hiding place for Loyalists or Tories when the Sons of Liberty were on the prowl.

The center of East Church is St. Matthew's Episcopal Church, which was consecrated in 1795. Surrounding a small triangular green in front of St. Matthew's Church are several historic homes dating from the early 1700s. St. Matthew's burying ground was first used in 1795 and contains more than 500 interments of both Tories and Revolutionaries.

Records indicate economic growth followed the tenacious little community of East Church. Lyman Preston operated a carding mill on the Old Marsh stream. Preston built a business of spinning, weaving, and dressing of cloth. Josiah Kimberly operated a tannery. Randall Matthews made nails. Willis Hinman had a shop to manufacture clock cases. William Yale and his sons made toy wheelbarrows. As the Industrial Revolution progressed, better industrial opportunities were created in other parts of town and East Church returned to the quiet dignity of village life.

Ingenuity and creativity were the means to stimulate Plymouth's industrial firsts. Eli Terry is credited as initiating interchangeable parts. Andrew Terry was one of the first in the new United States to bring about production of quality malleable iron. The Eagle Bit & Buckle, later known as Eagle Lock, was one of the first companies in the United States to manufacture cabinet locks and patented locks for mail bags. Cooper Oven Thermometer created the first baking thermometers. The culturing of silkworms was attempted by James Terry, son of Eli Terry Jr. The silk process was a good choice for a supplemental income but was so labor intensive that Terry ultimately turned his ingenuity to other ventures after selling his silk business to the Cheney brothers of Manchester, Connecticut.

As new people came into Plymouth to work in businesses and factories, they found a sense of community. They organized and built churches in their new home through togetherness, hard work, and sacrifice. They actively gave of their labor to build the physical structures, and energies to formulate their congregations and generously gave up a portion of their incomes and labor for the common good.

Over the years, large and small businesses claimed Plymouth as their home. Generations of immigrants have settled here to work in local industries and continue to contribute to their home town. Plymouth maintains its small-town flavor and history while moving quietly into the 21st century.

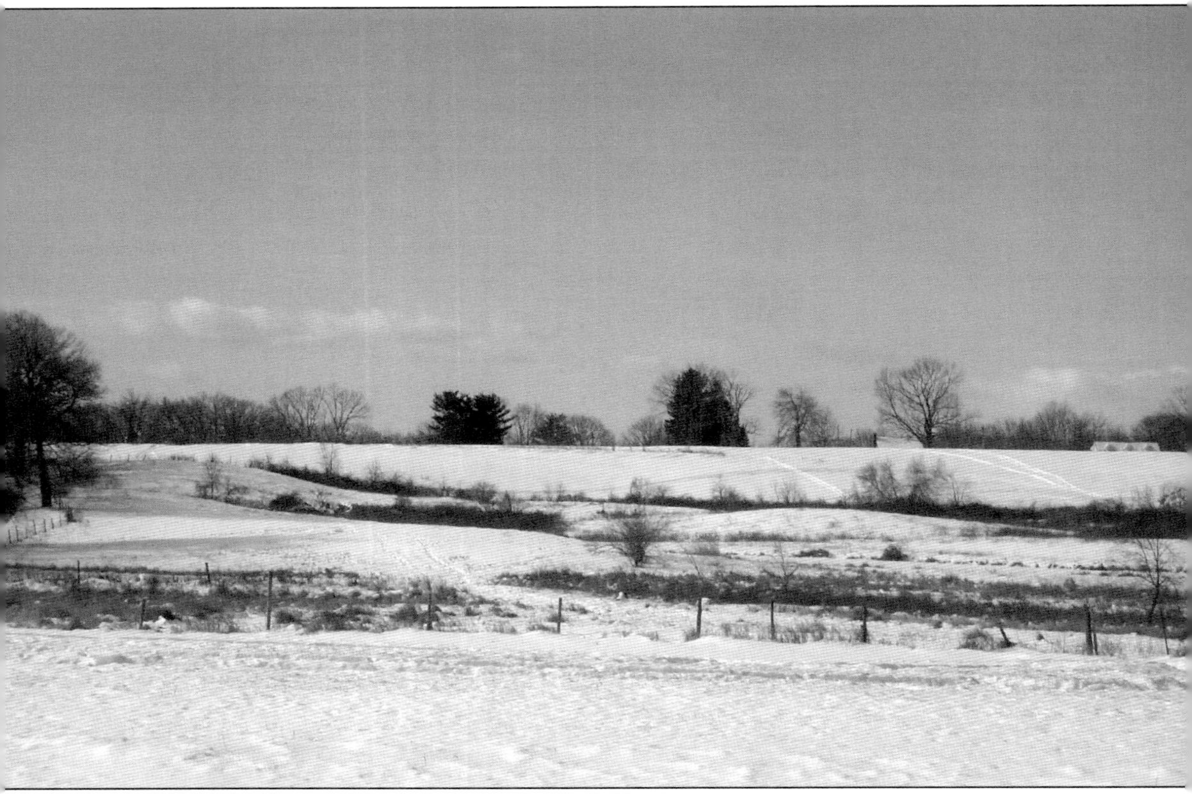

Plymouth was a stop on the Underground Railroad. For those escaping slavery, the route was long and treacherous. It took months to walk to safety traveling from one conductor to the next. (Photograph by Judy Giguere.)

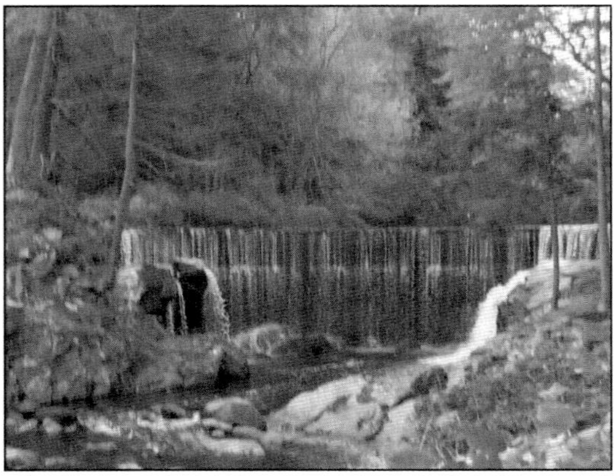

The year 1900 dawned brightly as Plymouth moved toward the forefront in industrialization. New growth in science, medicine and manufacturing gave rise to new discoveries and new confidence for new and better times. Horseshoe Falls was one of many retaining ponds built to create water sources for newly created industries. (Photograph by Judy Giguere.)

One

Early Plymouth

The Town of Plymouth, formerly Northbury, was incorporated in 1795. The Plymouth Hollow section later became Thomaston in 1875 when it was incorporated. The first churches were formed in Plymouth Hollow and Plymouth Center. The early town hall building was next to the Beach & Blackmer store. The town hall building was constructed of bricks manufactured within the town and remained the site of town official business until 1890 when the town offices moved to Terryville.

Plymouth was the center of the Underground Railroad in this area. Joel Blakeslee was a known conductor, historically known for a cordial welcome and hearty meal at his home for those in need. The ones who lost their way on the path northward could expect Joel or one of the other conductor's watchful eyes to find them and to set them back on the right path as soon as it was safe to continue. Other conductors in Plymouth were William Bull, Joel Blakeslee, and Ferrand Dunbar.

Town Hill, the site of the Terryville fairgrounds and surrounding area, was intended to be the center of town, but it lacked sufficient waterpower and became a farming community.

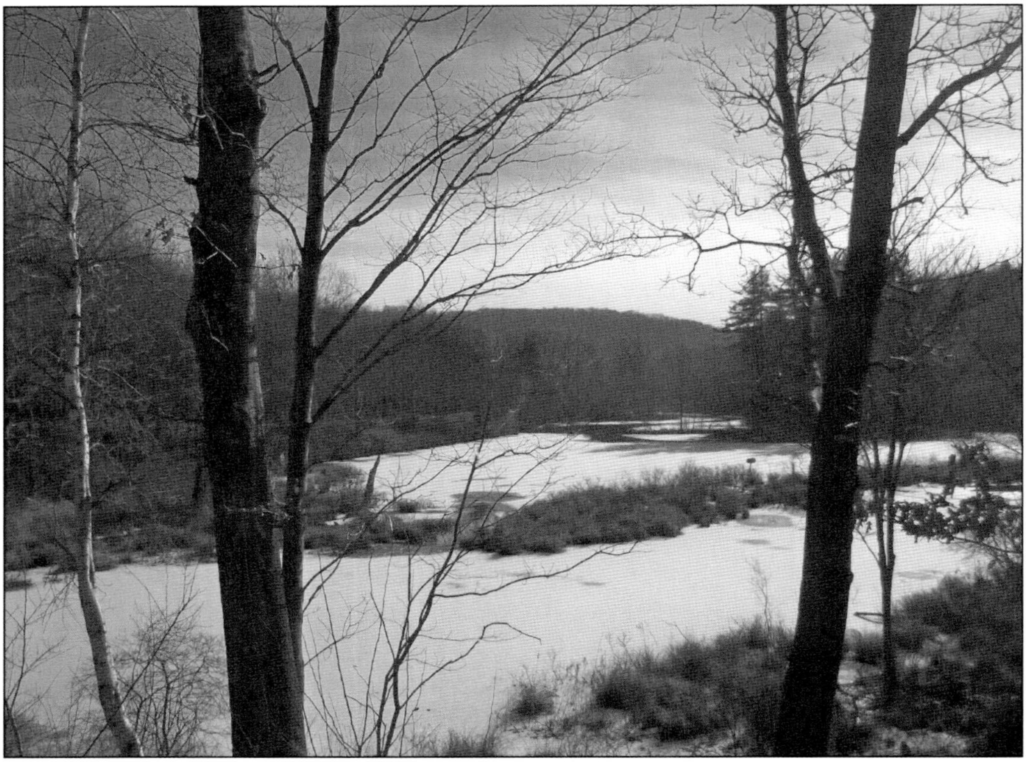

Pictured here is a view of Hancock meadows. This beautiful area was along the path of the first visitors to Plymouth. Early explorers entered from Waterbury, as Plymouth was initially part of Waterbury. Even today, parts of it have not changed significantly; it is easy to imagine why early explorers were impressed with the area. (Photograph by Judy Giguere.)

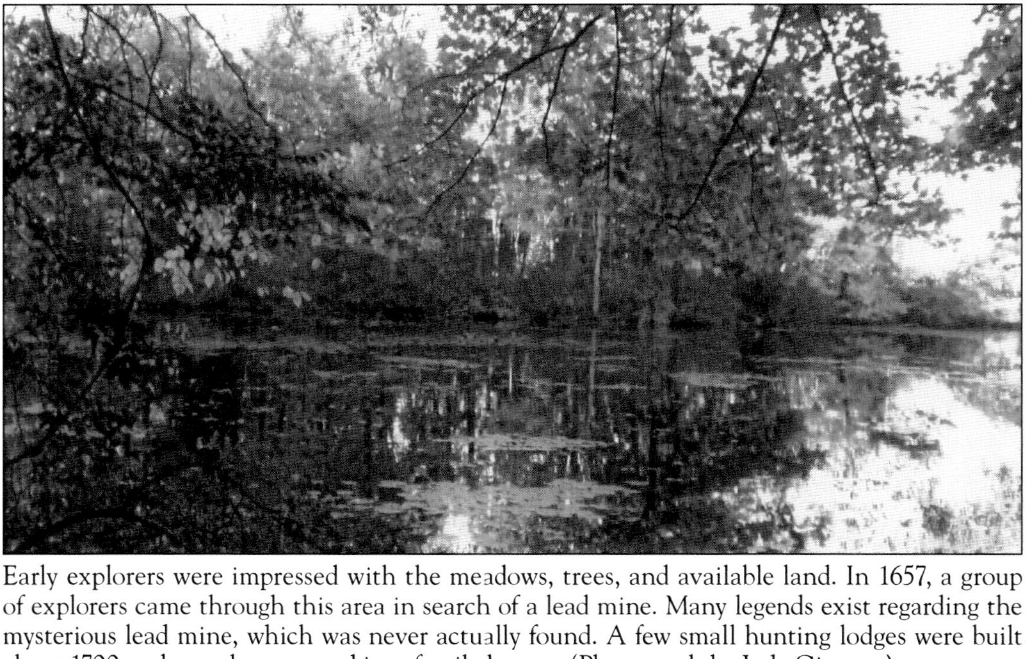

Early explorers were impressed with the meadows, trees, and available land. In 1657, a group of explorers came through this area in search of a lead mine. Many legends exist regarding the mysterious lead mine, which was never actually found. A few small hunting lodges were built about 1700 and were later turned into family homes. (Photograph by Judy Giguere.)

This is a collection of arrowheads found on South Eagle Street. Although a significant Native American presence did not exist, a few individuals ventured into the area for hunting. The Allentown section of Fall Mountain was noted for its fields of corn planted by Native American women. Many place names in Plymouth have been taken from Indian languages. (Photograph by Judy Giguere.)

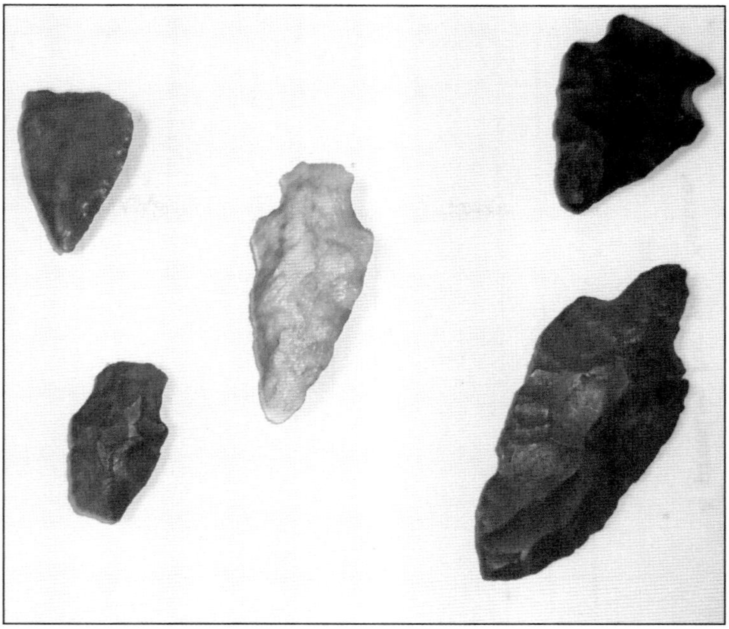

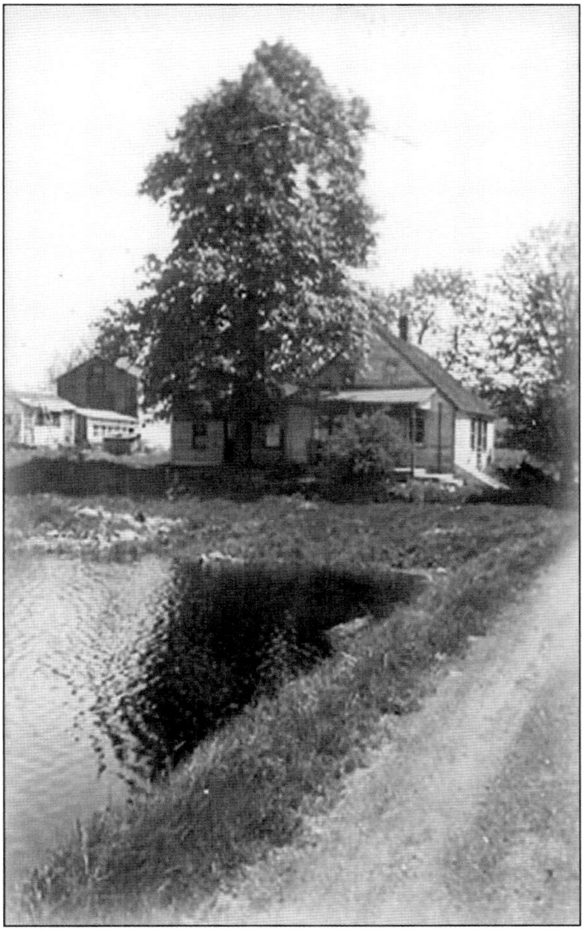

This home was constructed in the mid-1700s and has belonged to the Woods family for 250 years. It is one of the few continuously owned and operated farms remaining in Plymouth. Today, it is the site of Wood Acres Farm and continues the tradition of hayrides, sleigh rides, and carriage rides. (Courtesy of Wood Acres Farm.)

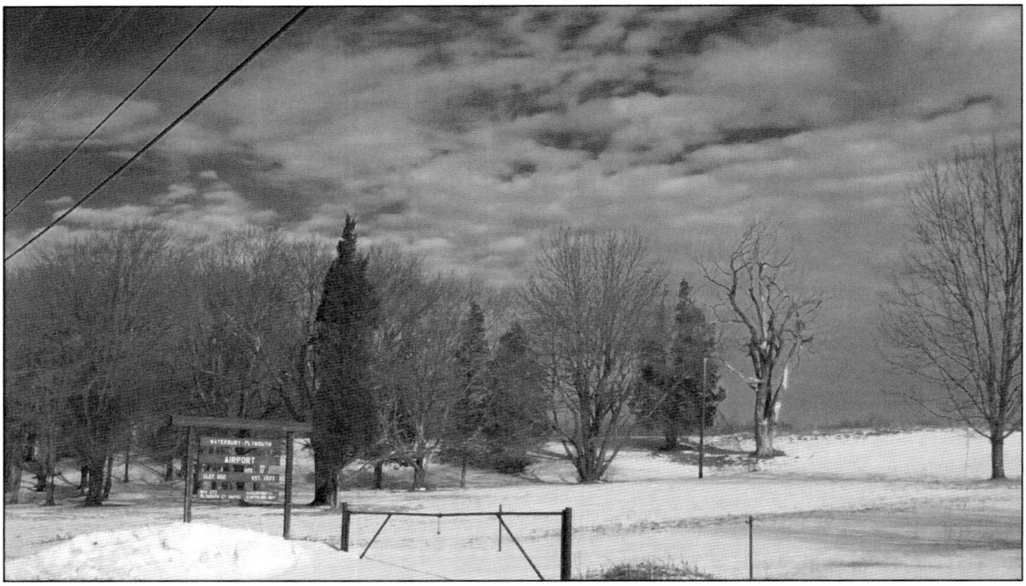

The former Mount Tobe airport, also known as the Waterbury Airport was located here on this high flat land. Mount Tobe is home to the Mattatuck Boy Scout Camp, which maintains the meadows, ponds, and forests as they once were in the early days. (Photograph by Judy Giguere.)

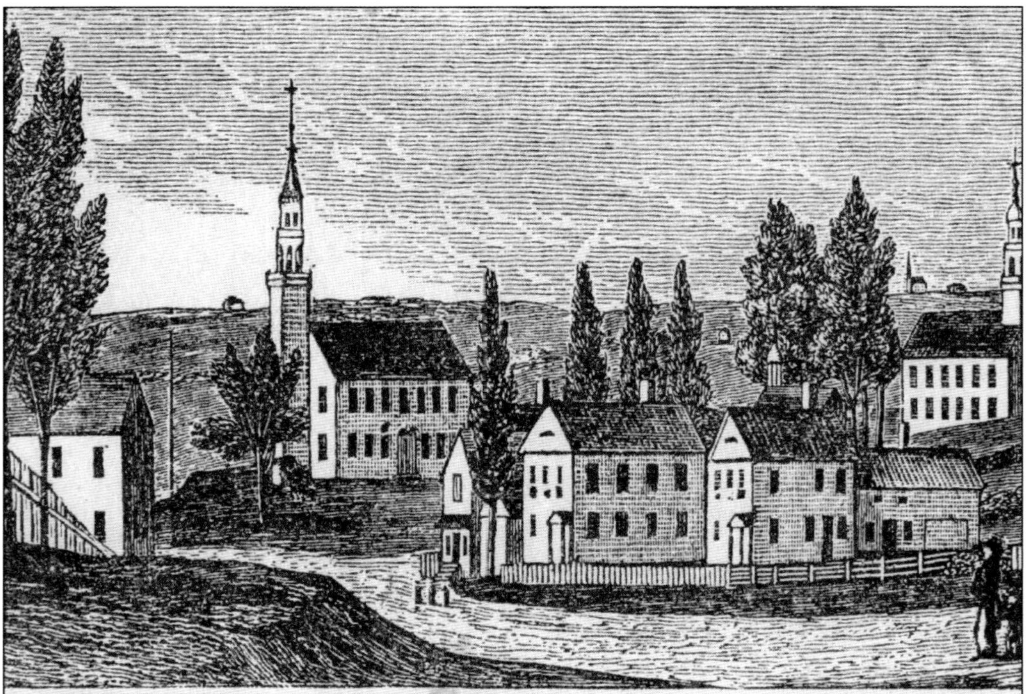

East view of the central part of Plymouth.

This early woodcut displays the center of Plymouth as it looked in Revolutionary War times. Note the Episcopal church's spire on the right and the early meetinghouse on the left that belonged to the early Plymouth Congregational Church. The Plymouth Congregational Church, as it is seen today, was built in 1838. (Courtesy of Plymouth Historical Society.)

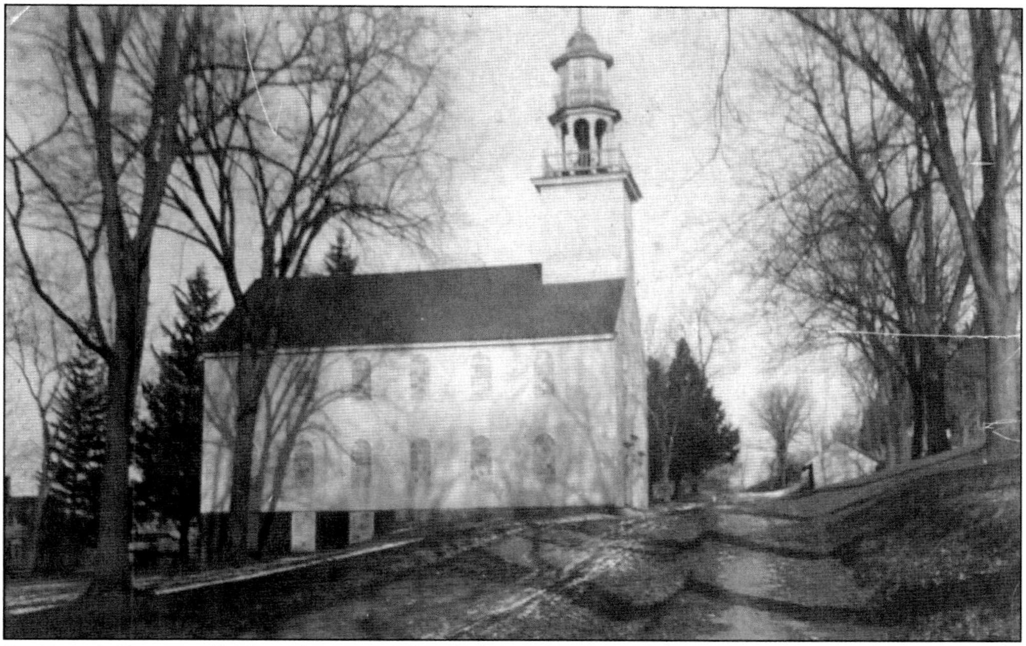

St. Peter's Episcopal Church, pictured, was located along the far end of Plymouth Green. At the time of this photograph, North Street was a dirt road. This structure was destroyed by fire in 1915 and later replaced by a new church on the south end of Plymouth Green. (Courtesy of Plymouth Historical Society.)

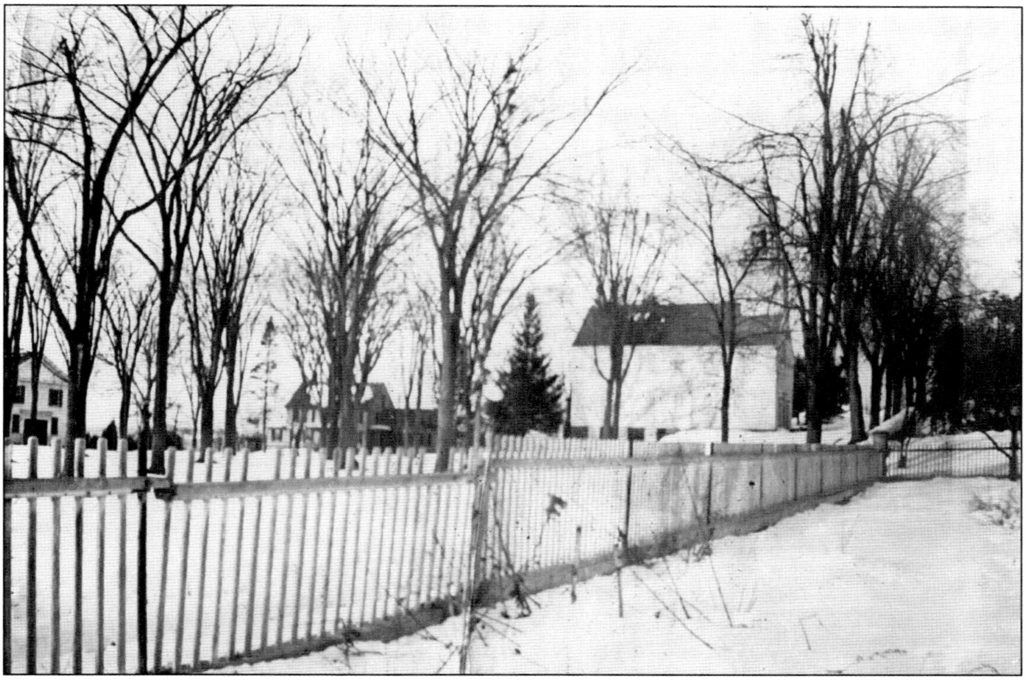

This is the eastern side of Plymouth Green, including St. Peter's Episcopal Church. Plymouth Green was once covered with trees and enclosed by a fence. Many of the trees were planted in the late 1700s by the Reverend Storrs. Only one elm remains in the northwest corner near the cemetery. (Courtesy of Plymouth Historical Society.)

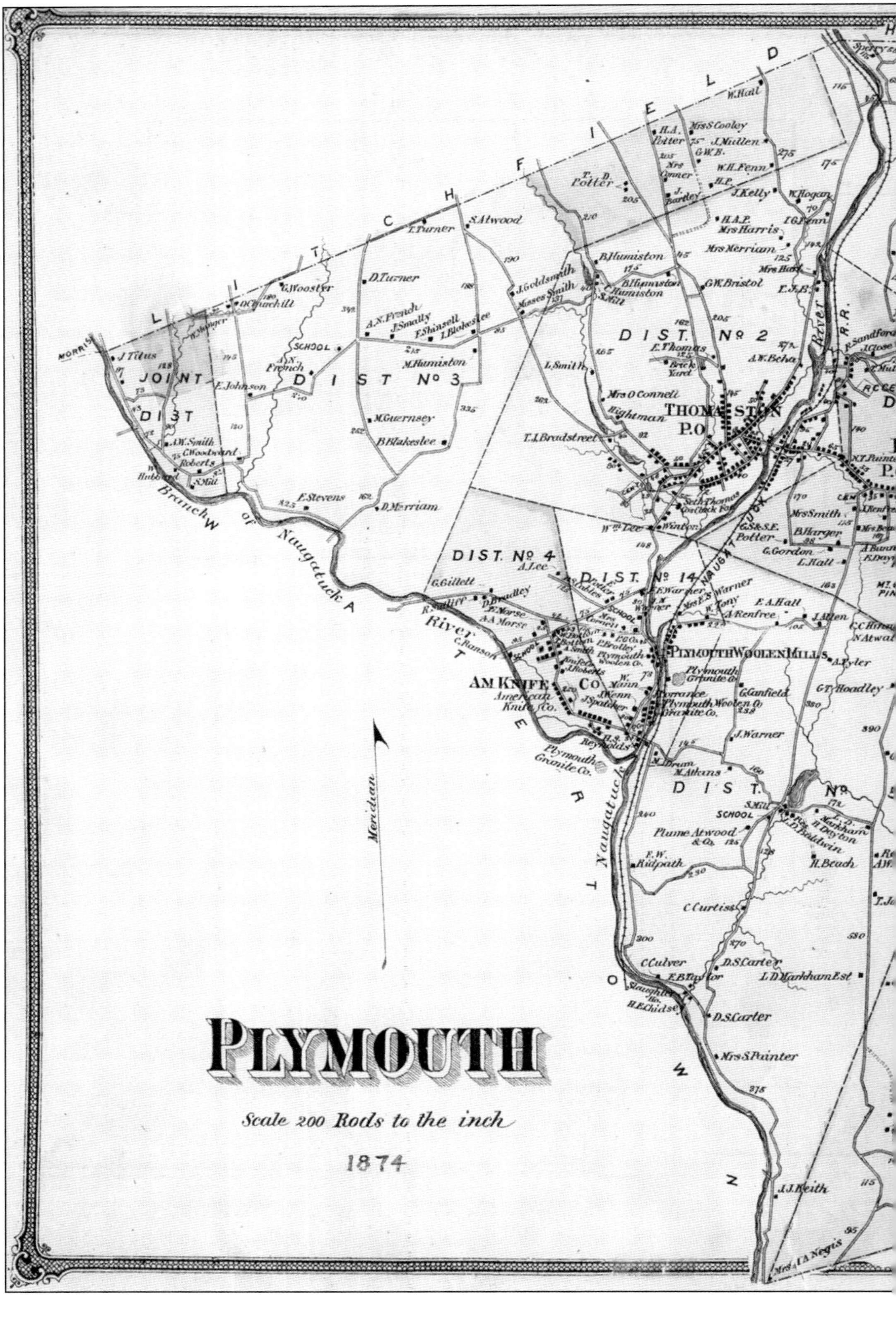
PLYMOUTH
Scale 200 Rods to the inch
1874
LITCHFIELD
WATERTOWN
DIST. Nº 2
DIST Nº 3
DIST. Nº 4
DIST. Nº 14
JOINT DIST
THOMASTON P.O.
PLYMOUTH WOOLEN MILLS
AM KNIFE CO
Meridian
Naugatuck River
Branch of Naugatuck River

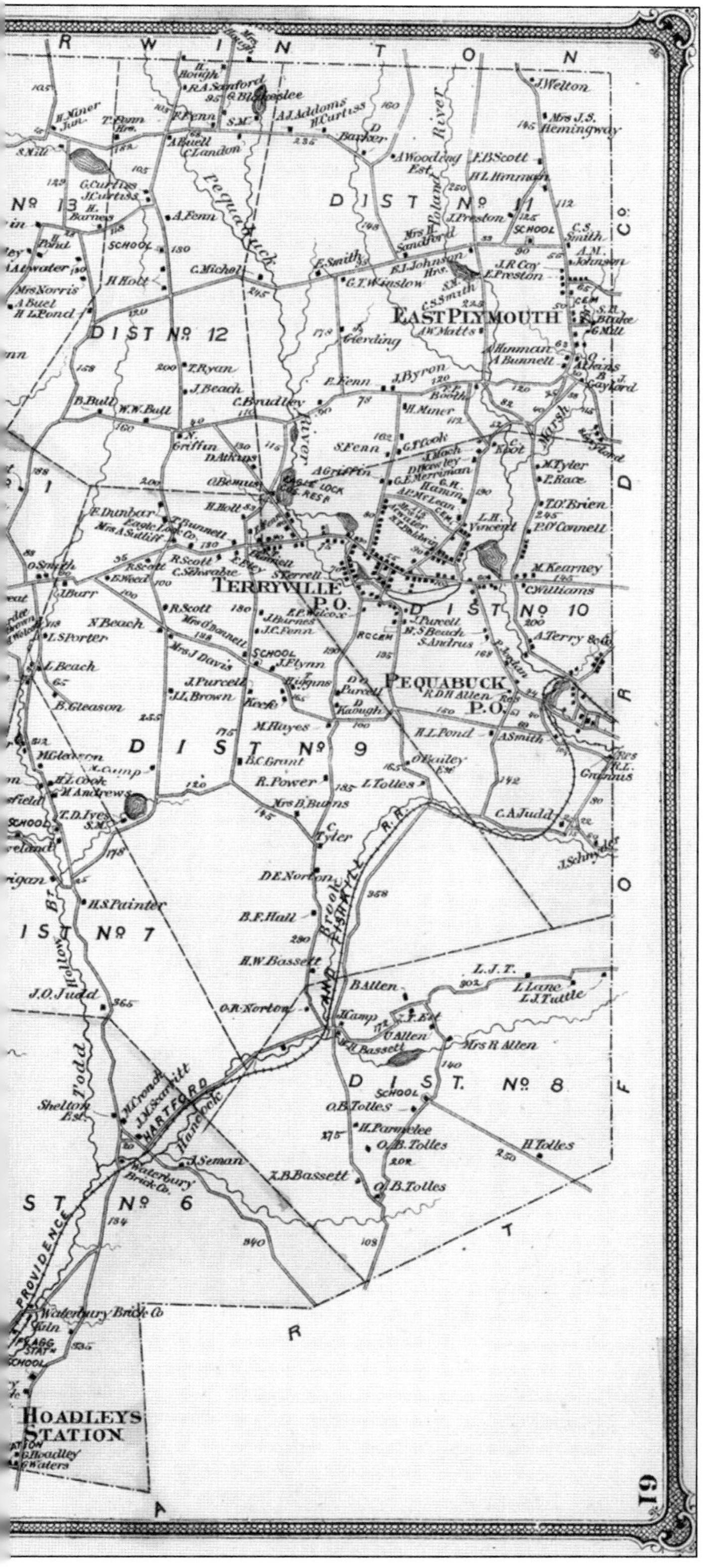

This is an 1874 district map of Plymouth. Originally, Plymouth was called Northbury. It was set aside as its own distinct society in 1780. Plymouth Center, now a historic district, was intended as the center of town. This map includes Plymouth Hollow, which was part of Northbury until it broke away in 1875 to become its own community called Thomaston. Plymouth was incorporated in 1795. Early incursions into the area began as early as 1657, when prospectors came in search of a lead mine. The source of the much hoped for wealth was never identified; even today it is the topic of many legends. Henry Cook is recorded as the first settler, around 1728. He was followed by John Sutliff, Thomas Blakeslee, Isaac Castle, Barnabas Ford, and others. (Courtesy of Plymouth Historical Society.)

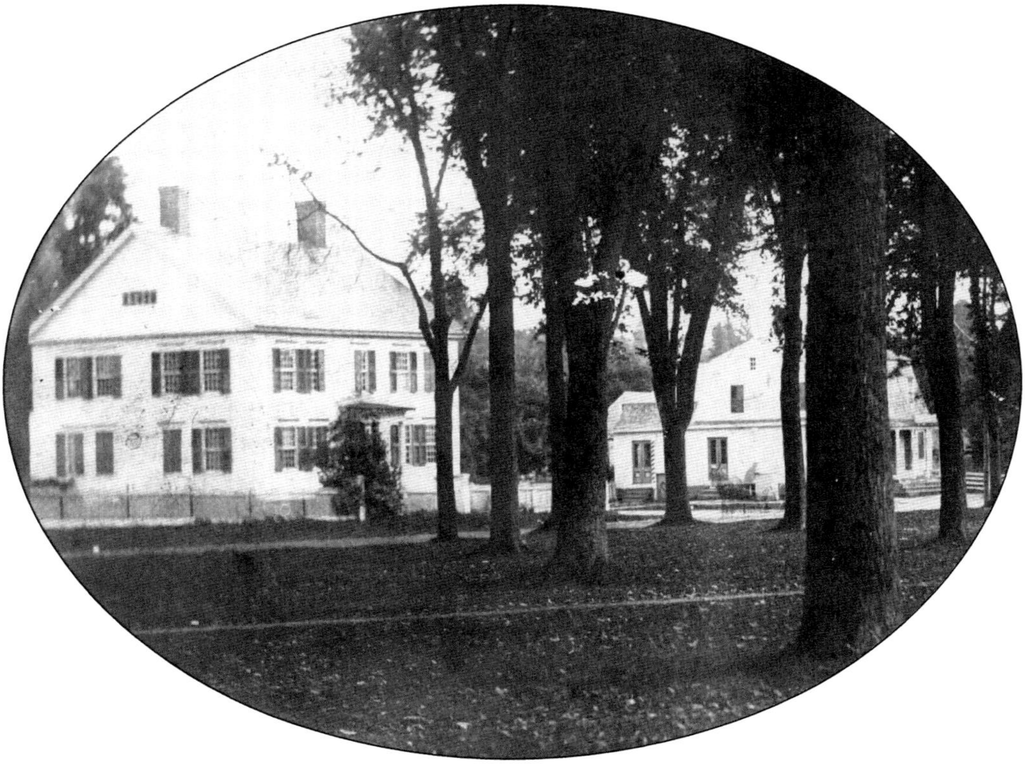

Formerly the Red Tavern, this building became St. Peter's Church Parsonage. Located on the corner of Main and North Streets in Plymouth, it is part of the historic district. This c. 1800 Georgian Colonial has twin interior chimneys, gable overhangs, and a flat-roofed portico. Today, it serves as the First Baptist Church of Plymouth. (Courtesy of Plymouth Historical Society.)

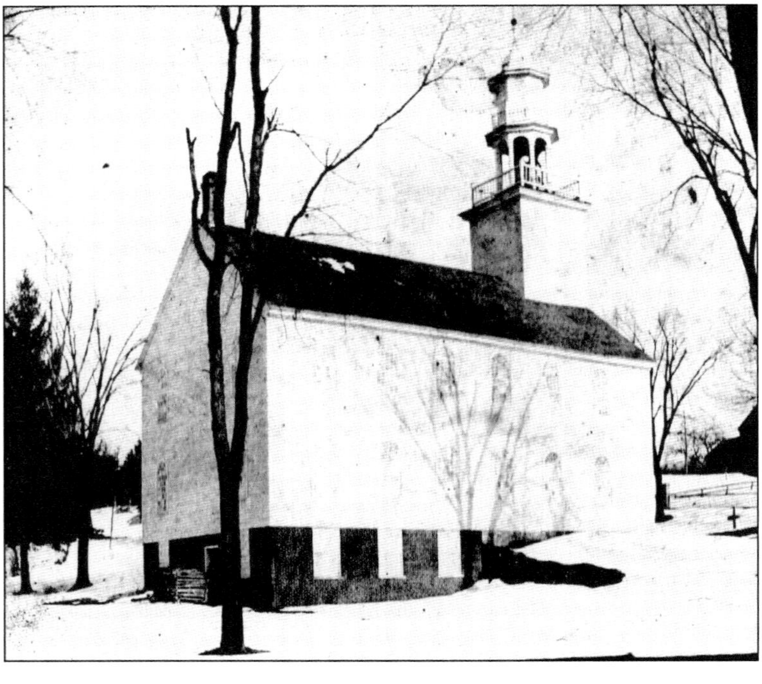

St. Peter's Episcopal Church is pictured before it was totally destroyed by fire in 1915. The first service was held in this building in November 1796 and was consecrated by Bishop Jarvis. In 1823, a bell was hung in the belfry. The first church school began in 1829. A pipe organ was installed in 1838. (Courtesy of Plymouth Historical Society.)

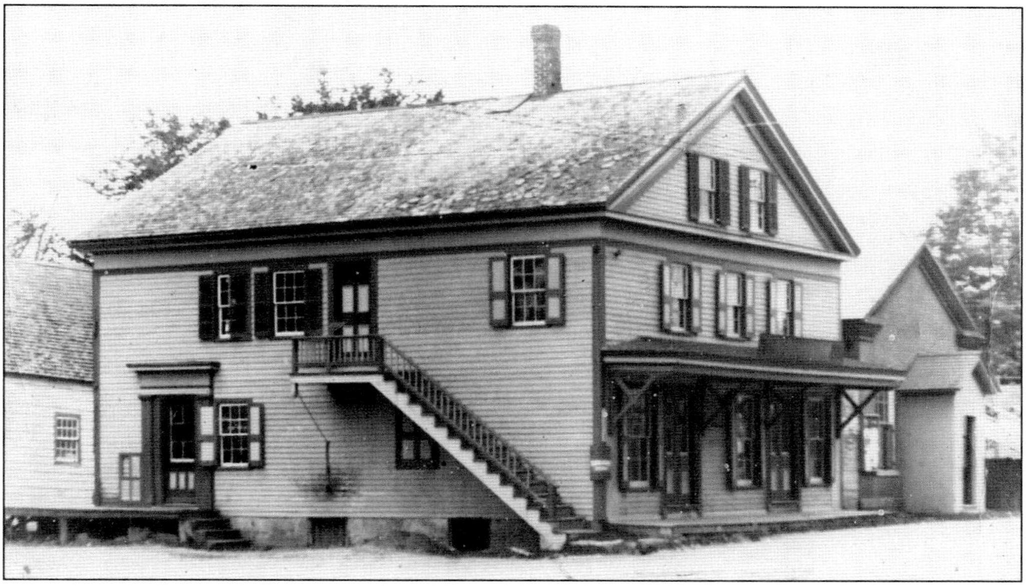

Beach & Blackmer's Store was known for its honesty and complete stock of dry goods, groceries, hats, caps, boots, shoes, hardware, crockery, hay, and feed. The early town hall building was next to it with a small attached entranceway. Beach & Blackmer's dates back to 1780. The building has undergone some transitions but is basically the same as it was during the early days. (Courtesy of Plymouth Historical Society.)

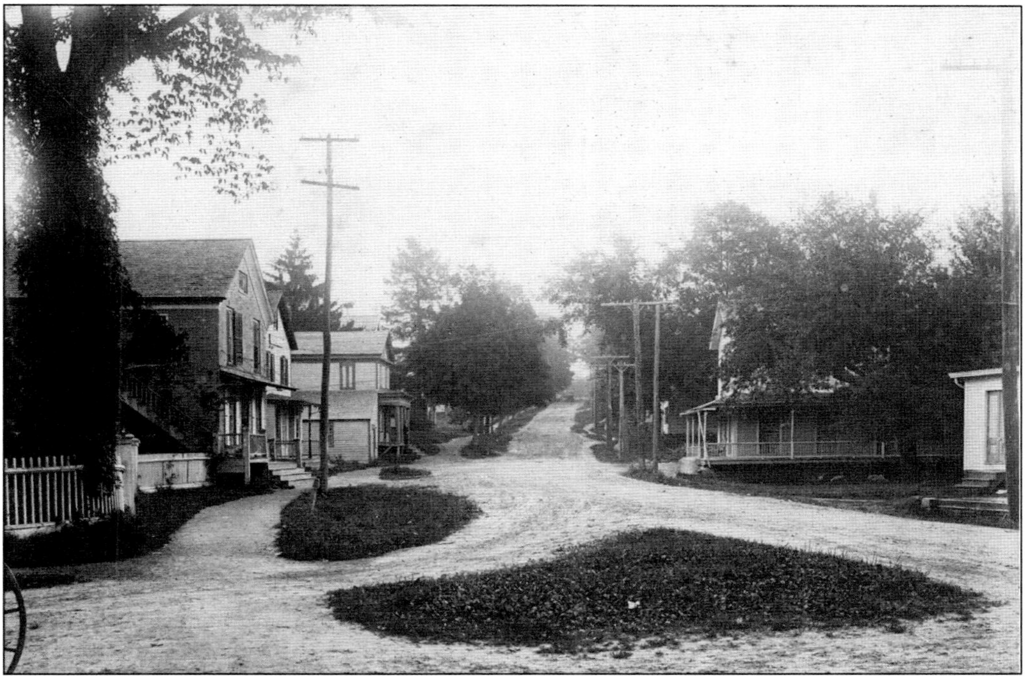

Pictured here is the main road in Plymouth Center, looking east toward Terryville. Early roads were initially intolerable. Work crews cleared and smoothed the roads with teams of oxen. Local citizens were unwilling to pay for road improvements. Therefore, each citizen was required to do his share to maintain local roads. Around 1800, a network of turnpikes developed throughout New England. This road was one of the early toll roads. (Courtesy of Plymouth Historical Society.)

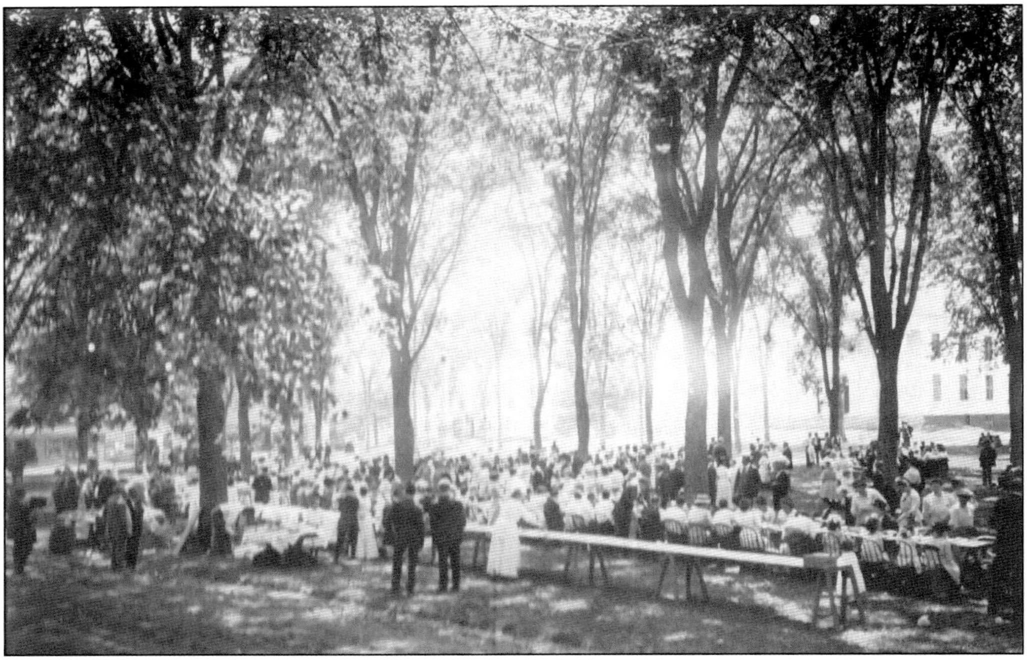

Plymouth Green was often the site of many community gatherings, from drilling grounds for soldiers to local functions. This gathering took place in 1910. Old Home Day was a special day dedicated to picnics, friends, community, and showing off one's very best clothes. (Photograph by Arthur Gordon, courtesy of Plymouth Historical Society.)

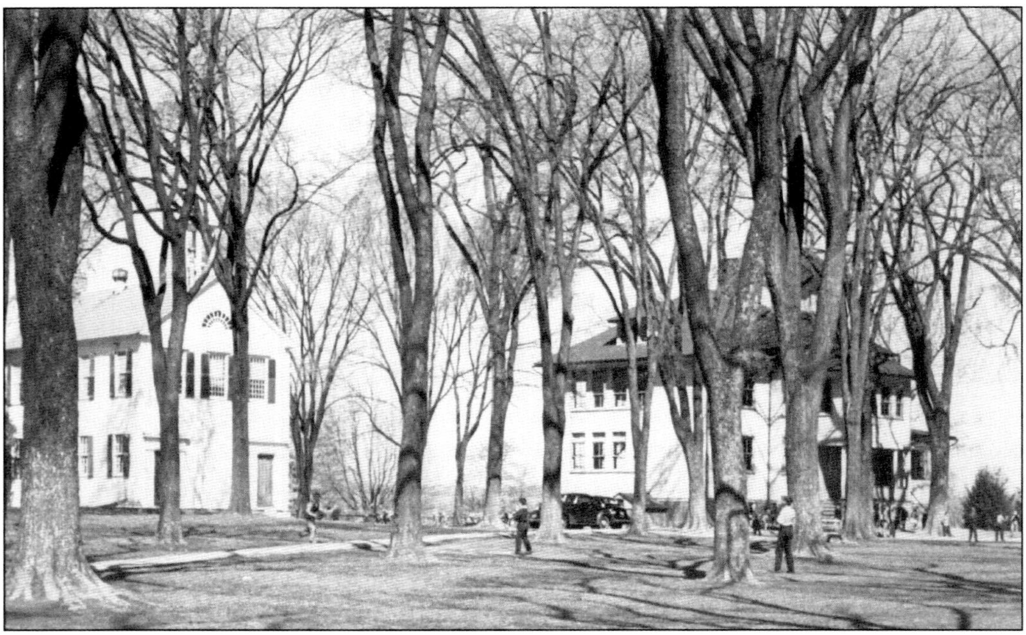

This is a later picture of the north end of Plymouth Green when it was covered in trees. The building on the left is the c. 1840 Stoughton Building, which was moved to this location. The bell tower, gable fanlight, and south wing are later additions. On the right is the Reverend Andrew Storrs House, built in 1766. It is a five-bay Colonial with a double overhang and once had a large center chimney. (Courtesy of Plymouth Historical Society.)

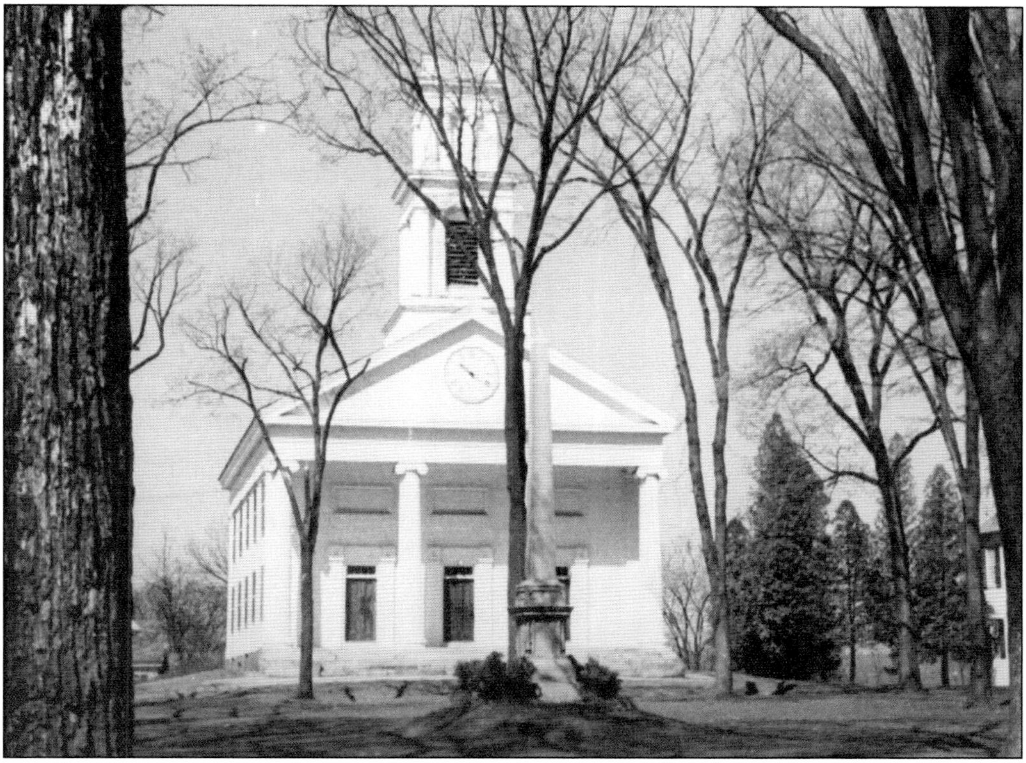

The Plymouth Congregational Church was constructed in 1838 to replace the two earlier versions of wooden structures that served as church meetinghouses. Eli Terry, clockmaker, donated the large wooden clockworks in both Plymouth Congregational Church and the Terryville Congregational Church. The original Terryville Congregational Church building was similar and was built as the center of Plymouth moved eastward with manufacturing. (Courtesy of Plymouth Historical Society.)

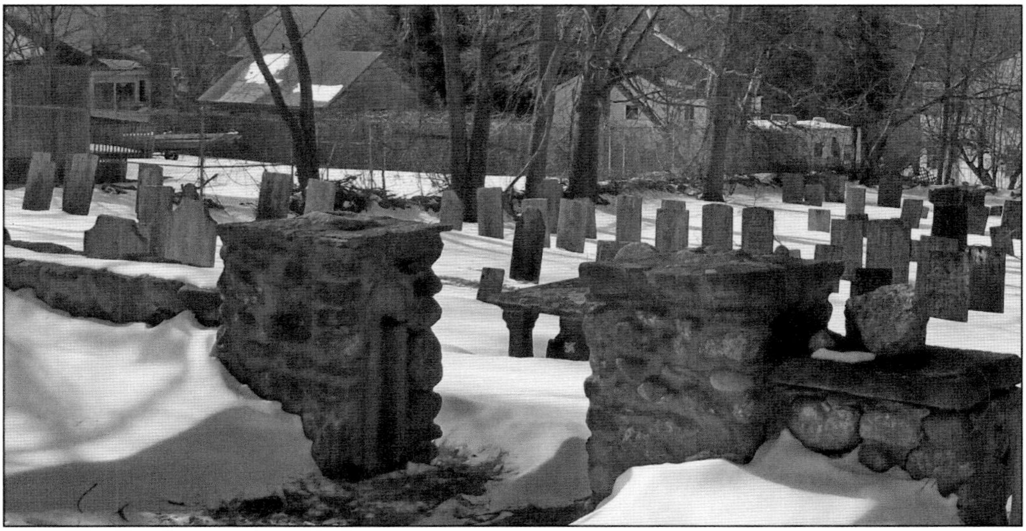

The Plymouth Burying Ground was given to the Town of Northbury in 1740. The cemetery is the final resting place of many soldiers of the French and Indian War, the Revolutionary War, the War of 1812, and the Civil War. (Photograph by Judy Giguere.)

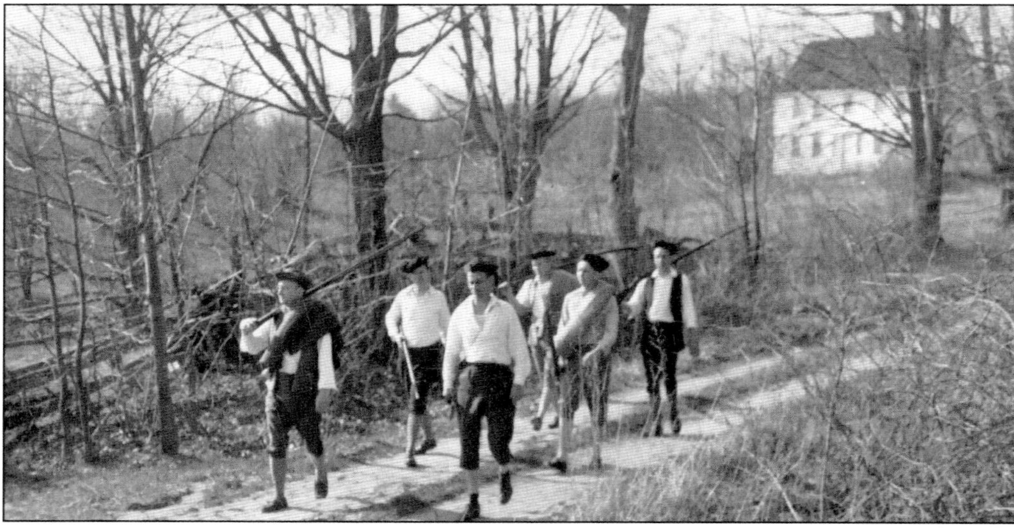

Present-day Route 6 was formerly a stagecoach road to Hartford. Travel was by turnpike roads and post roads. Later, public transportation was by stagecoach. Generally, a stage was drawn by six horses and horses were changed every 15 miles. Two taverns or hotels were located in Plymouth. One inn belonged to Revolutionary War veteran David Smith and his wife. Serving as captain at the time, Smith was with George Washington's army at Valley Forge. Washington traveled through this area in September 1780 and March 1781, varying his route to prevent British soldiers from finding him. Washington was a guest of the Smiths on at least one occasion, though the register containing his signature was lost in a fire. (Both images courtesy of Plymouth Historical Society.)

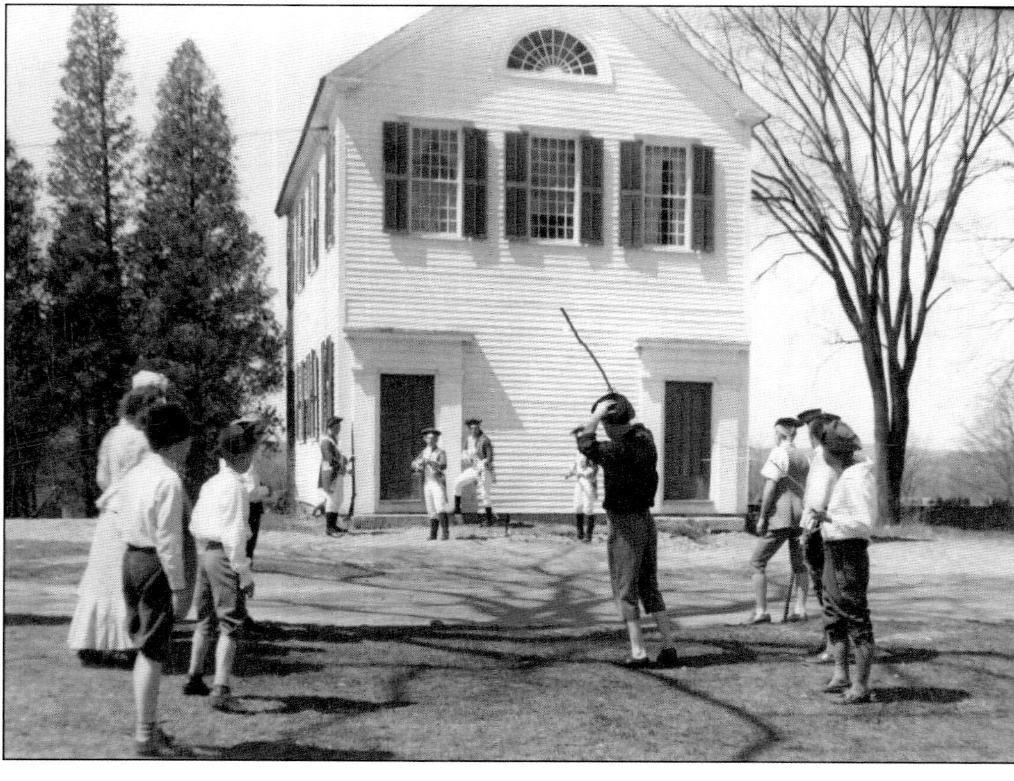

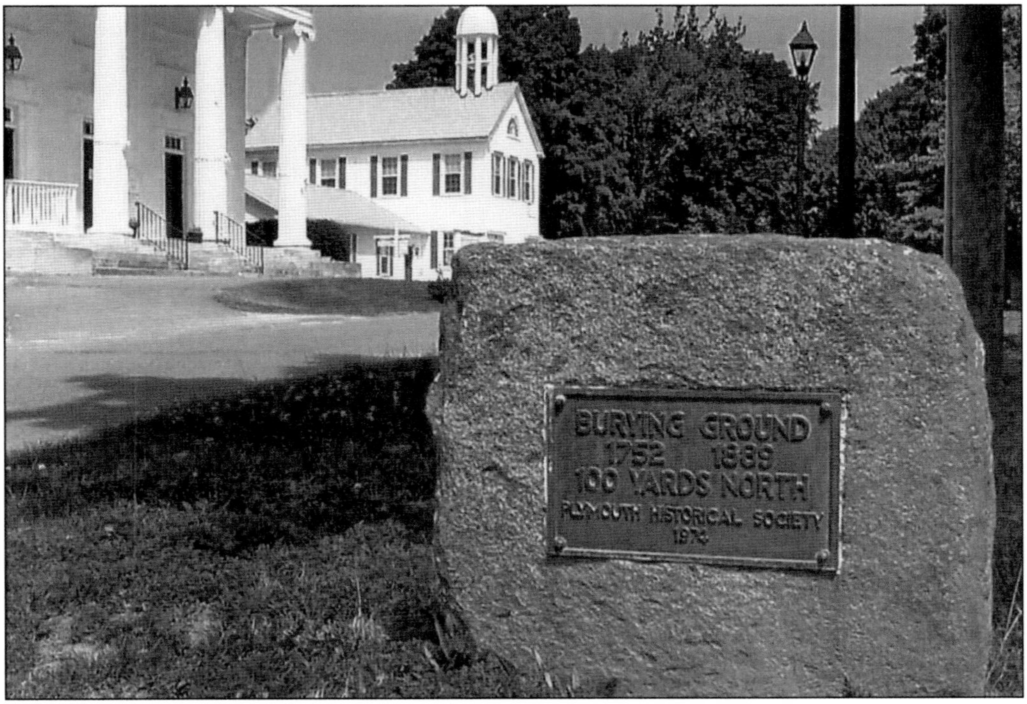

This plaque was placed by the Plymouth Historical Society and marked the historical significance of the Plymouth burying ground. The land was initially swamp and was drained. It is the site of the first and second Plymouth Congregational meetinghouses and the Episcopal Church in the upper northern corner of the site. A plaque also marks the site of the early Episcopal Church. (Photograph by Judy Giguere.)

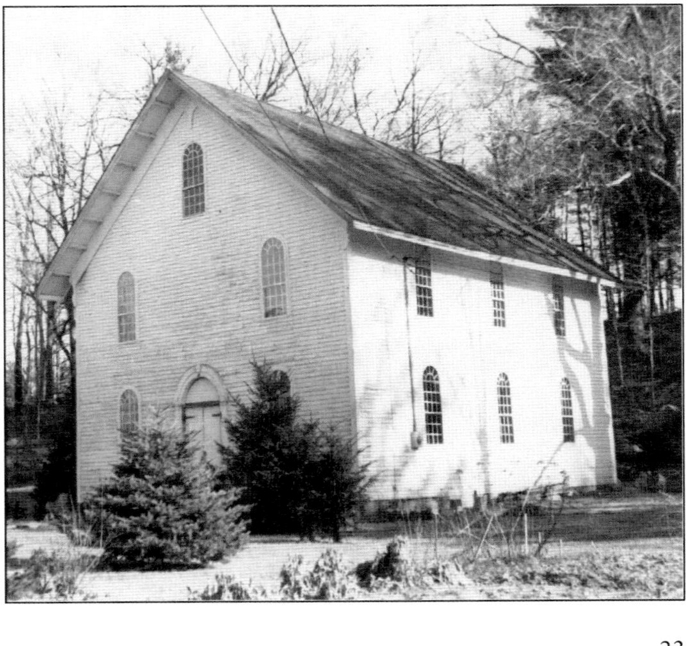

St. Matthew's Episcopal Church is the center of the East Church Revolutionary War historic district. In 1747, an internal dispute within the New Cambridge Church of England divided the congregation. Many retained their sympathies to England even after the Revolutionary War, and the little community maintained the quiet dignity of a close-knit village. Generations later, the small East Church community was still spoken of in whispers. (Courtesy of Plymouth Historical Society.)

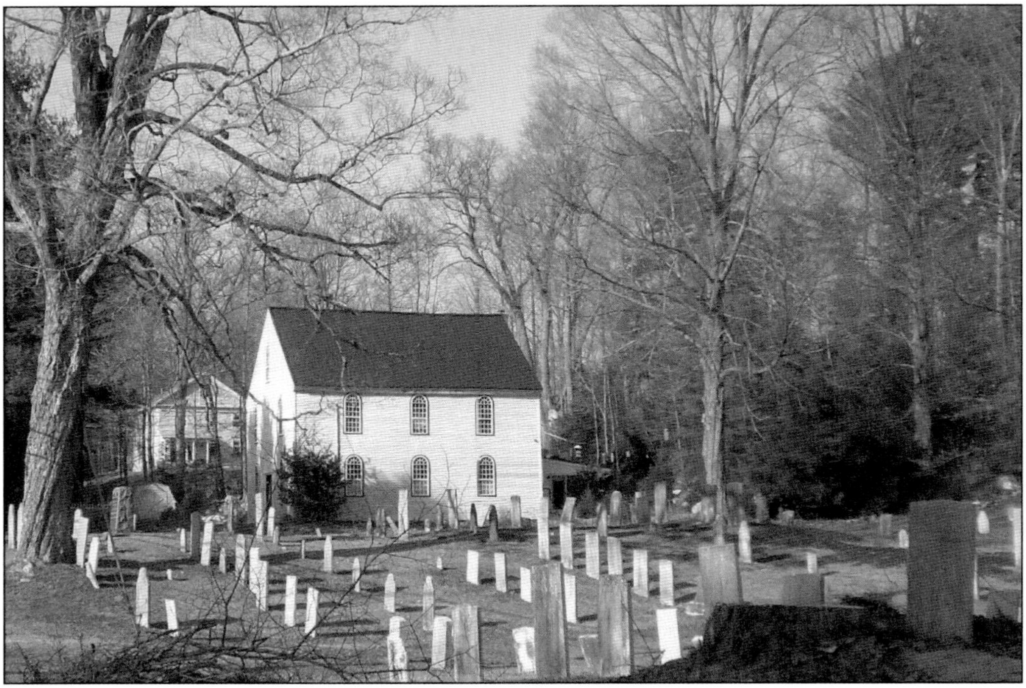

This is a northward view of St. Matthew's Episcopal Church and burying ground. The Revolutionary War disrupted the New Cambridge Church factions. It was not until October 21, 1795, that St. Matthew's Episcopal Church was consecrated by Bishop Samuel Seabury. Many early graves were unmarked and have been lost to time. It is believed that more 500 were interred here. (Photograph by Judy Giguere.)

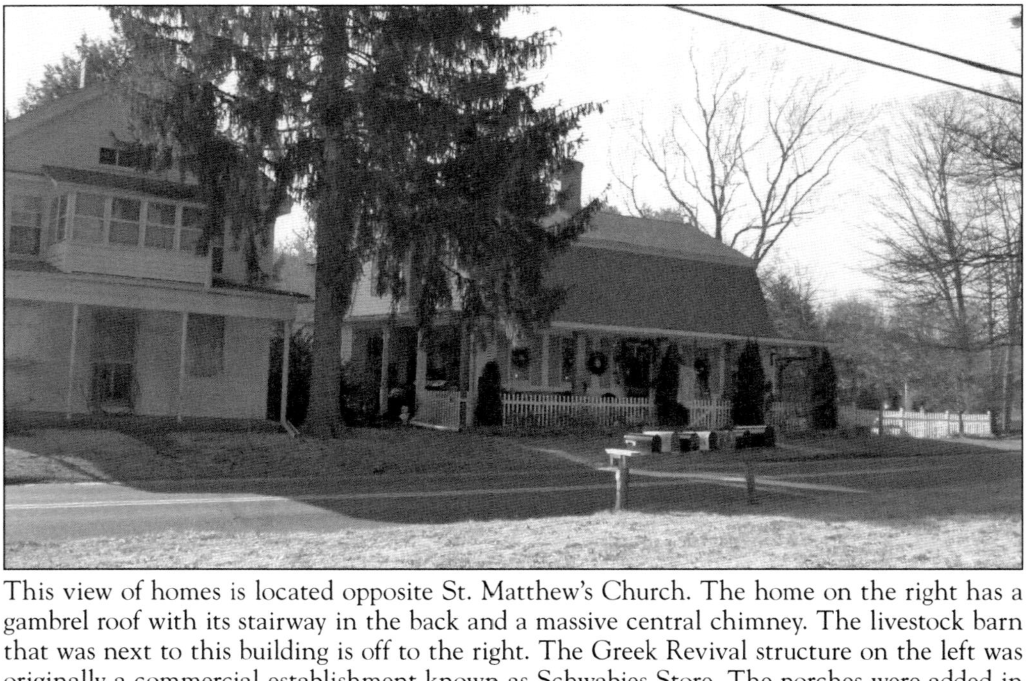

This view of homes is located opposite St. Matthew's Church. The home on the right has a gambrel roof with its stairway in the back and a massive central chimney. The livestock barn that was next to this building is off to the right. The Greek Revival structure on the left was originally a commercial establishment known as Schwabies Store. The porches were added in the 20th century. (Photograph by Judy Giguere.)

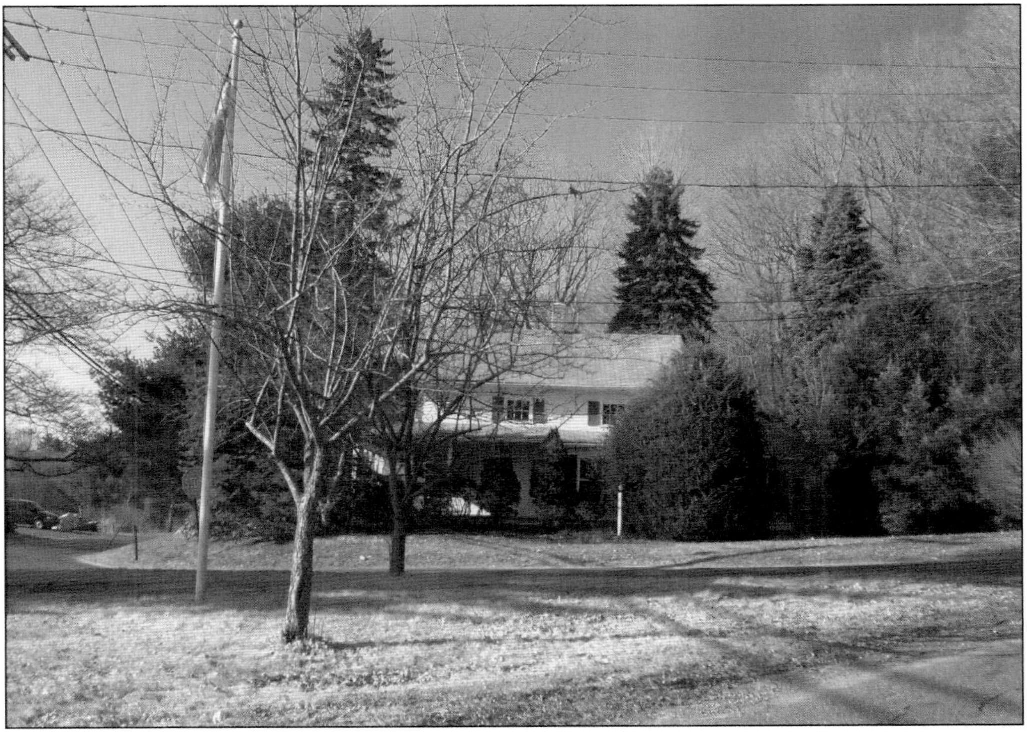

East Church Green is a small triangular parcel of land in front of the church. Other homes date from 1700 onward. One home built in 1732 has three fireplaces and a bake oven. The attic contains a crawl space above the kitchen used as a hiding place for Tories, or Loyalists, during Revolutionary times. (Photograph by Judy Giguere.)

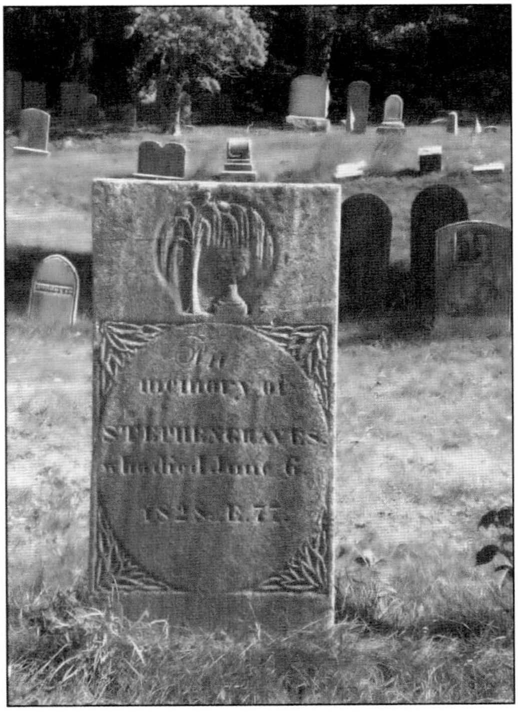

This is the site of the final resting place of Stephen Graves in St. Matthew's Church and burying ground. Graves hired a substitute to serve in his place in the Revolutionary army, but when he was called again he did not hire another. He remained loyal to England in spite of numerous attempts by Captain Wilson's Sons of Liberty to change his mind. (Photograph by Judy Giguere.)

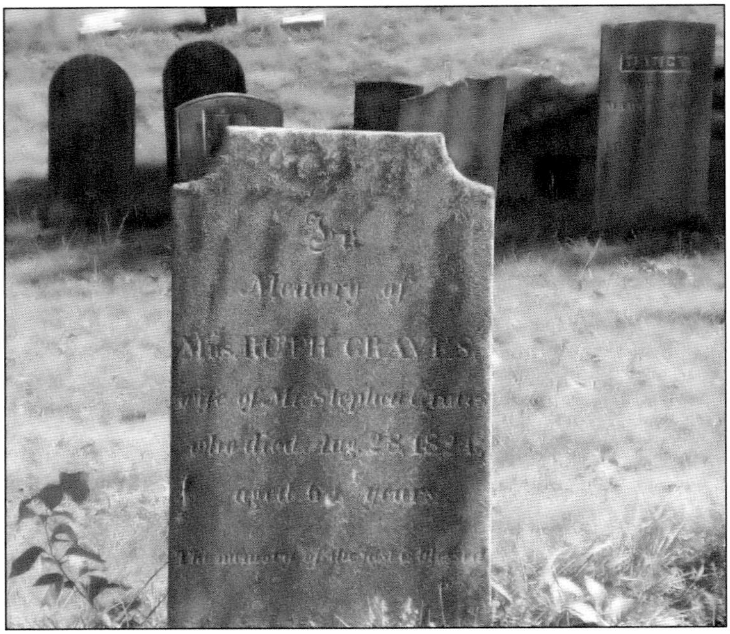

Ruth Graves, wife of Stephen, was adamant in the face of Captain Wilson, leader of the Sons of Liberty. Captain Wilson demanded at gunpoint the conch shell that she used to warn neighbors of the approach of the Sons of Liberty. She reluctantly gave up her treasured conch shell. Upon learning of the death of Captain Wilson, Mrs. Graves remarked that he never returned her conch shell. (Photograph by Judy Giguere.)

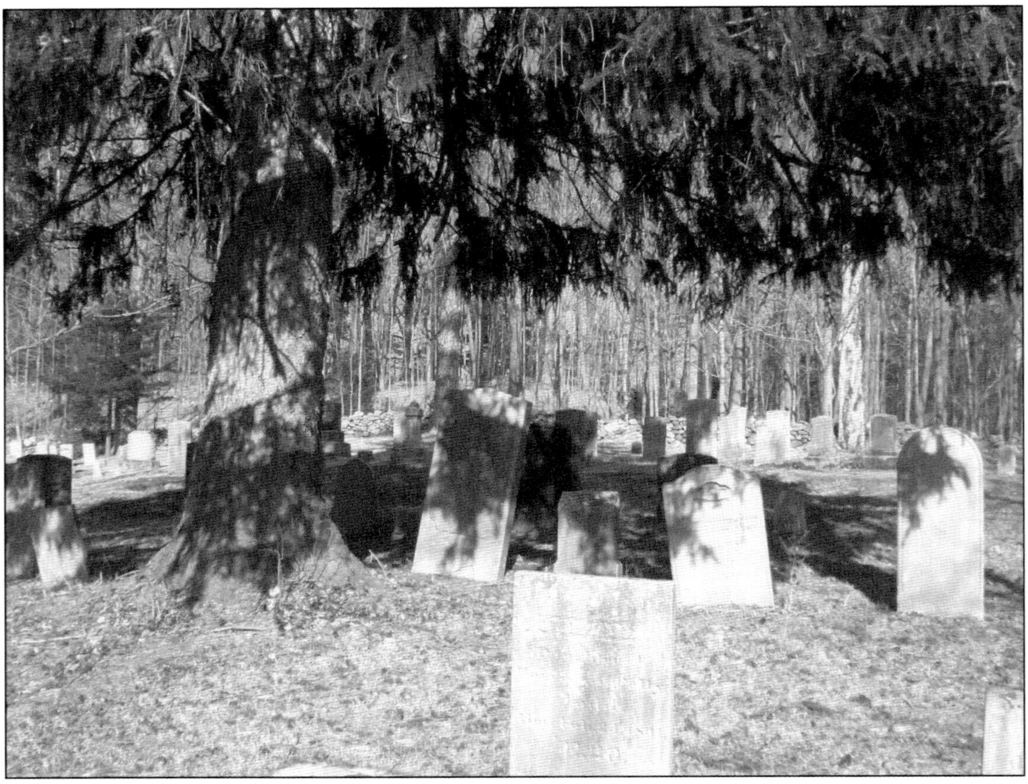

This photograph shows a section of St. Matthew's burying ground. There are 23 small stones marking pauper's graves. Names are recorded for 22 of the 23 markers. Peter Primus is recorded as a former slave who was once sold for 30 bushels of rye. Two of the graves here belong to former slaves. (Photograph by Judy Giguere.)

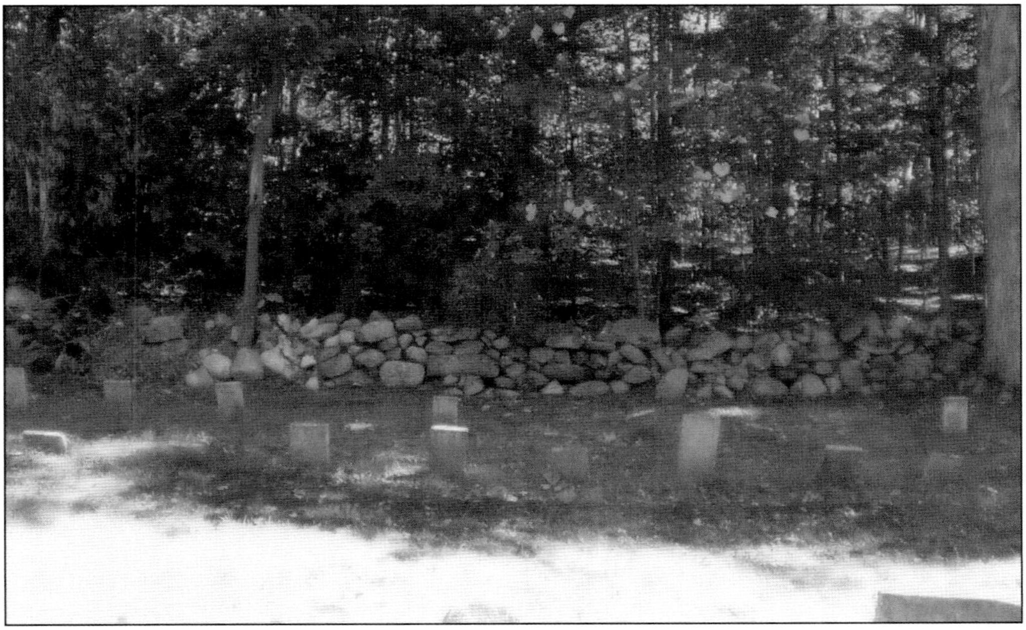

Moses Dunbar, loyalist, was executed on March 18, 1777 for crimes against the new nation. He was buried in an unmarked grave in Hartford, but rumors persist that his family and friends removed Dunbar's body and buried it in this cemetery. Plot 23 may be Moses Dunbar, but the legend is unconfirmed. (Photograph by Judy Giguere.)

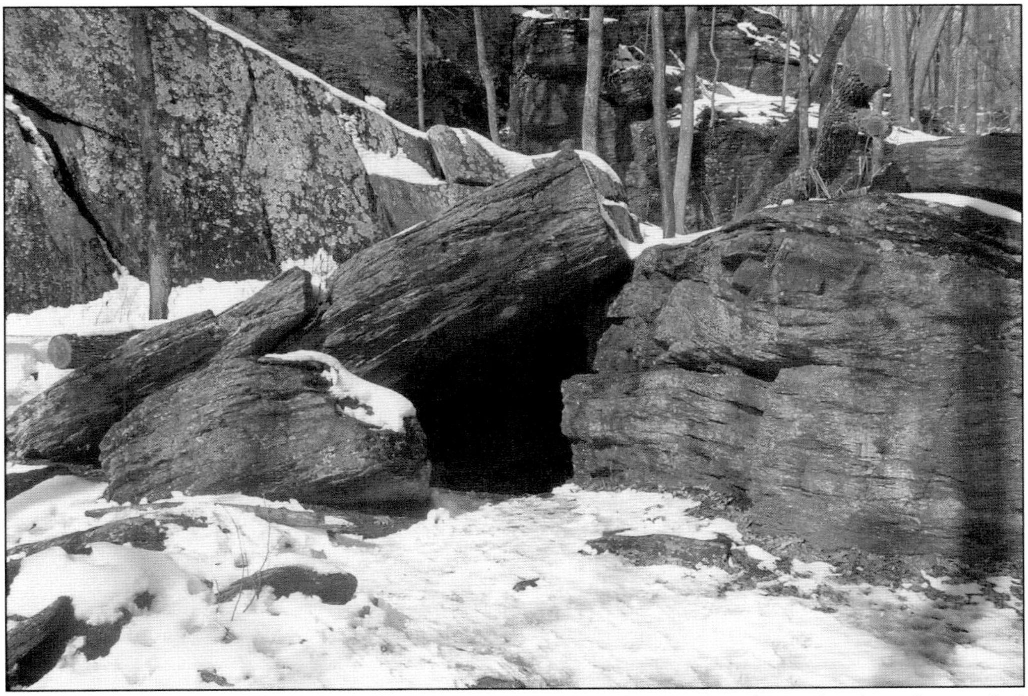

Tories Den is located about two miles north of St. Matthews Church in the densely wooded ledges of East Plymouth. It was the hiding place of Stephen Graves as well as other Tories during Revolutionary War times. Tories Den is located about a quarter of a mile in the woods. (Photograph by Brian Armbruster.)

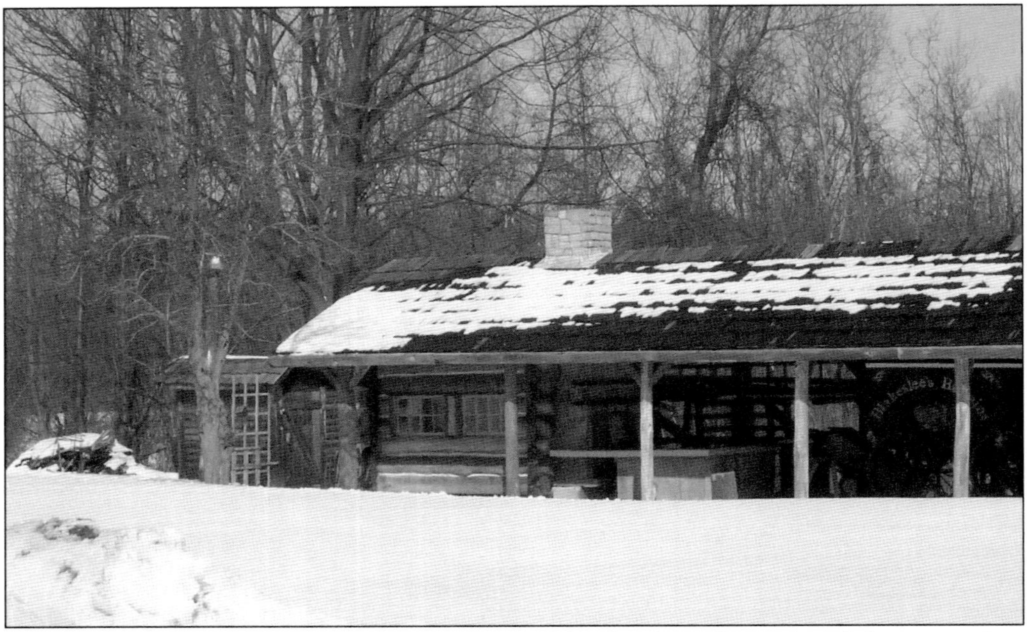

After the Revolutionary War, but before 1810, several families from Plymouth and the surrounding area left their New England homes to make a new life in the Western Reserve, which became Ohio. Their common bond was membership of St. Peters Episcopal Church in Plymouth. One was Sala Blakeslee of Plymouth. The journey was a long and arduous trek into wilderness. The Blakeslee cabin site was selected for the quality of the land, steams, timber, and water sources. The cabin served as a home as well as the first church for the homesteaders. The cabin still stands today and is listed in the National Register of Historic Places. (Both images courtesy of Ashtabula County Historic Society and Blakeslee Log Cabin historic site.)

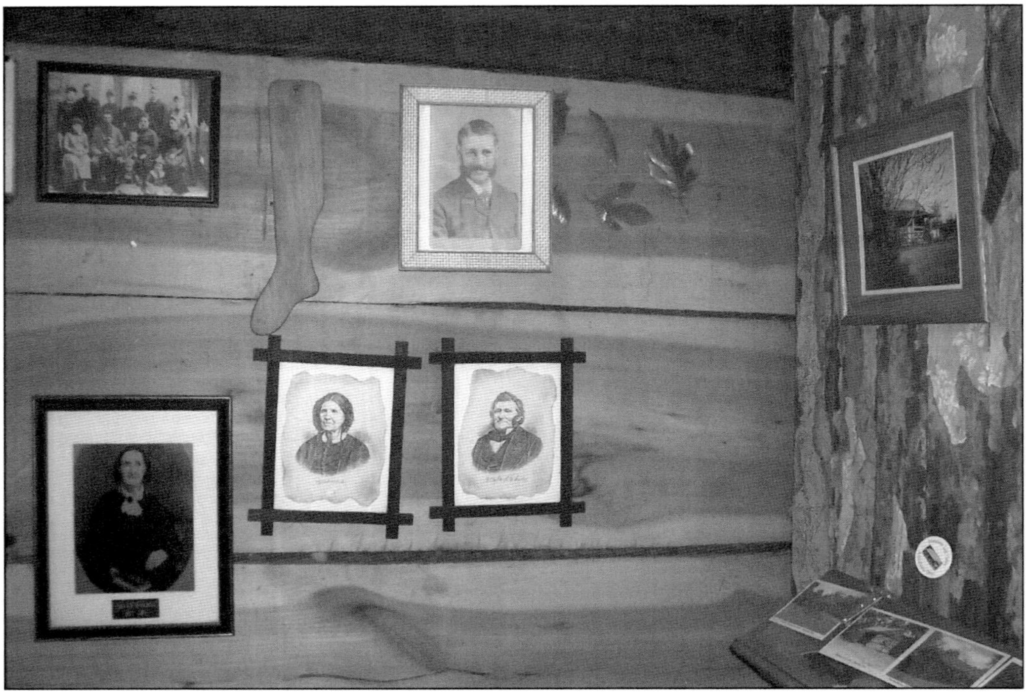

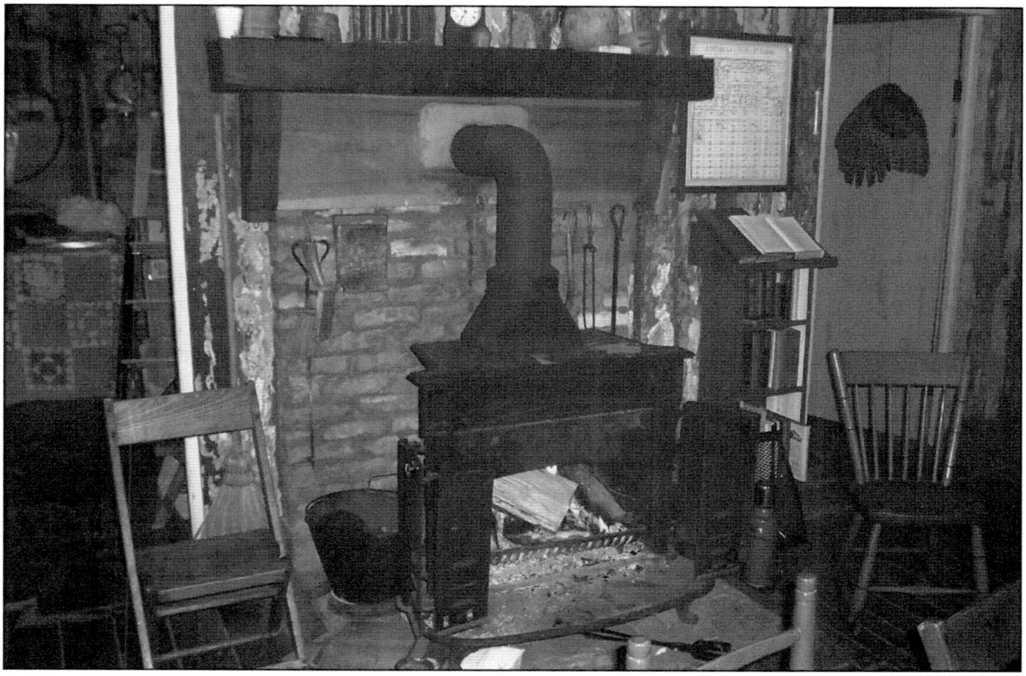

A Franklin stove is located in the interior of the Blakeslee cabin. The cabin was built about 1810 and sits on a high spot with a small wooded area and native trees. A free-flowing spring is laid with rocks and enclosed by a log-built spring house. It is preserved as it appeared in its early-19th-century pioneer days. (Courtesy of Ashtabula County Historic Society and Blakeslee Log Cabin historic site.)

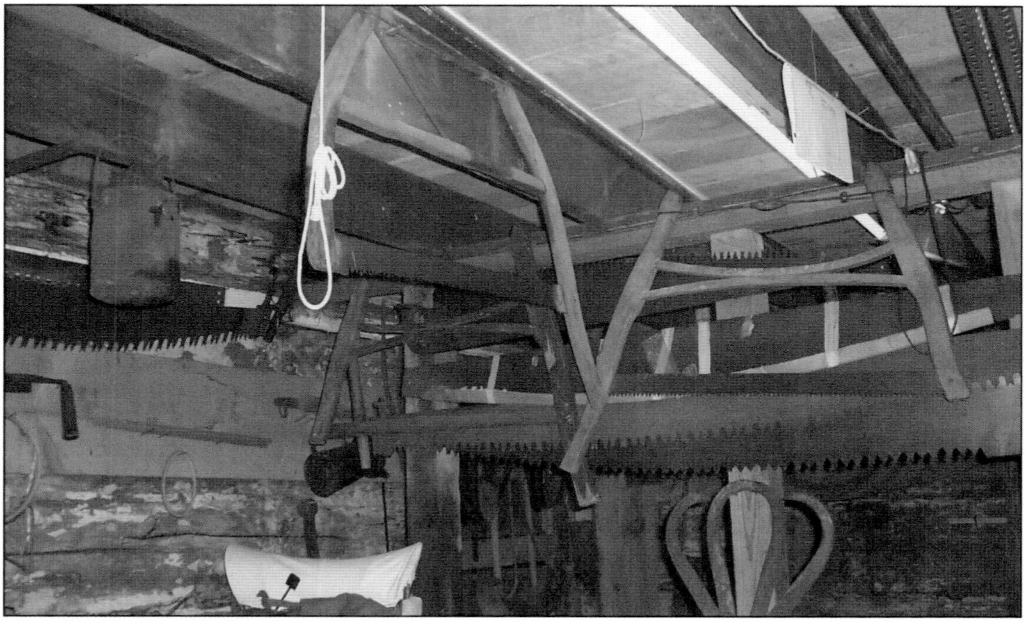

The cabin sits on its original cornerstones and is constructed of 16-foot split white logs with half dove corner notches. All logs and roof rafters are stabilized with wooden pins. The original boards are believed to have been cut at a nearby sawmill built in 1808, about one mile from the cabin. (Courtesy of Ashtabula County Historic Society and Blakeslee Log Cabin historic site.)

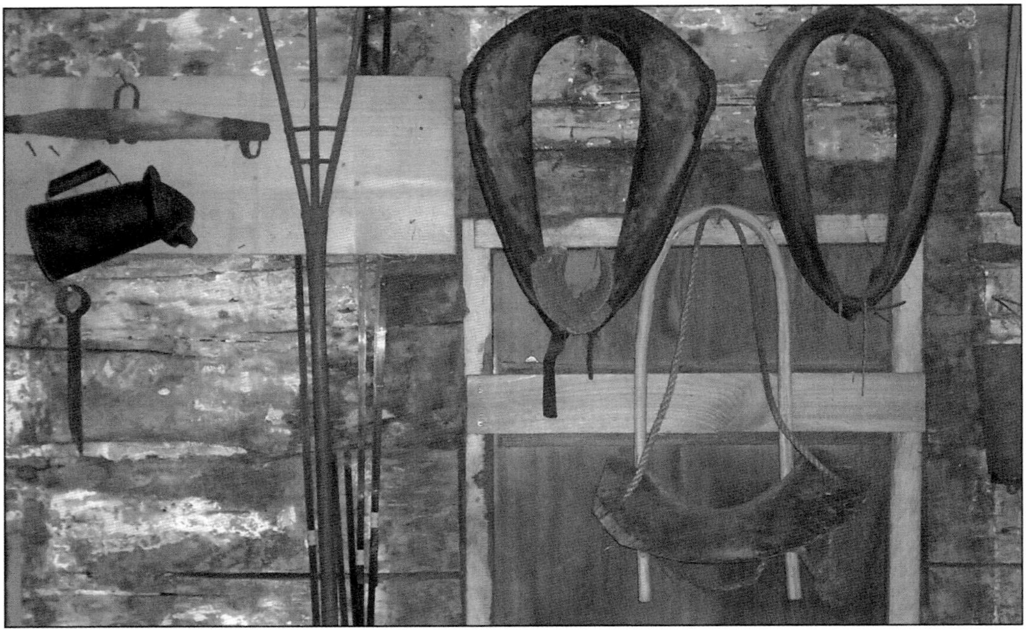

Tools and horse collars are stored in the rafters of the cabin. The dimensions of the cabin are 21 feet by 28 feet. It is 1.5 stories tall with a gabled roof at the north and south ends and two separate rooms partitioned by a wall of vertical boards. It was typical of frontier cabins of its day. (Courtesy of Ashtabula County Historic Society and Blakeslee Log Cabin historic site.)

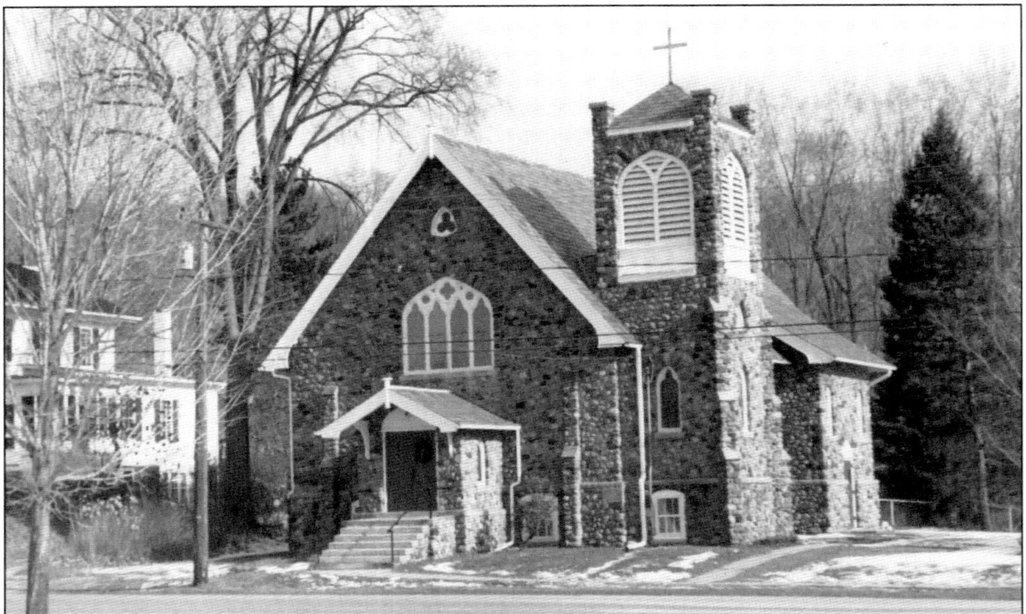

This is St. Peter's Episcopal Church, which replaced the original one that was on the northern section of Plymouth Green. This church is constructed of local fieldstone. The original church of wood construction was destroyed by fire on Saturday afternoon, February 27, 1915. The parish accepted the invitation of the Plymouth Congregational Church facilities for worship services until the new church opened in June 1916. (Courtesy of Plymouth Historical Society.)

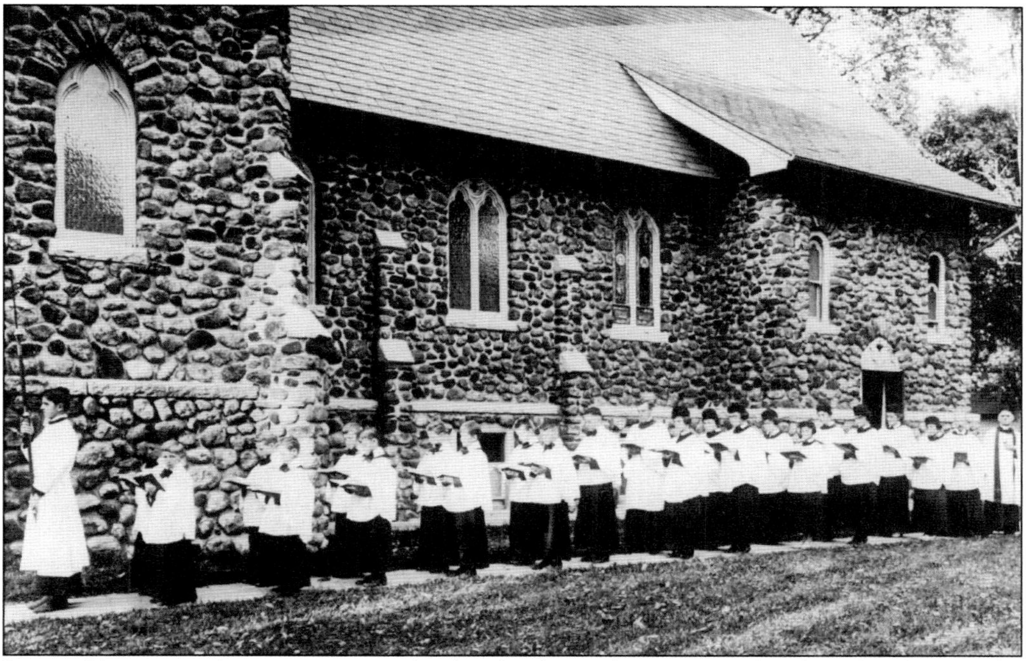

Pictured here is a religious procession by the altar boys of St. Peter's Church. After the fire, the church was immediately voted to be rebuilt next to the rectory. Friends donated the stones, even sacrificing their stone walls so that stones of the proper shape, size, and color would be available for use in the new structure. The stonework was done by Ard Welton, assisted by Fred Roselle, Andrew Consetti, and Ammi Tomlinson. (Courtesy of Plymouth Historical Society.)

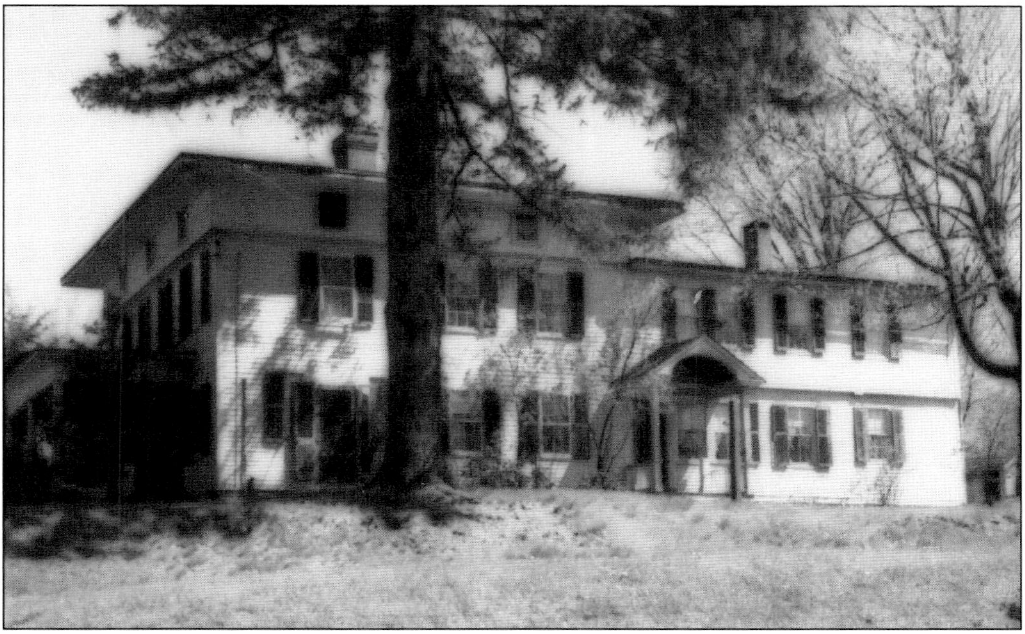

This home was built in 1850 by Henry K. Terry. It has a tunnel leading into the woods for use by runaway slaves. It was a documented station on the Underground Railroad, as was the Blakeslee home. Others who were known conductors on the Underground Railroad were the Blakeslee family, William Bull, Daniel Dunbar, and Ferrand Dunbar.

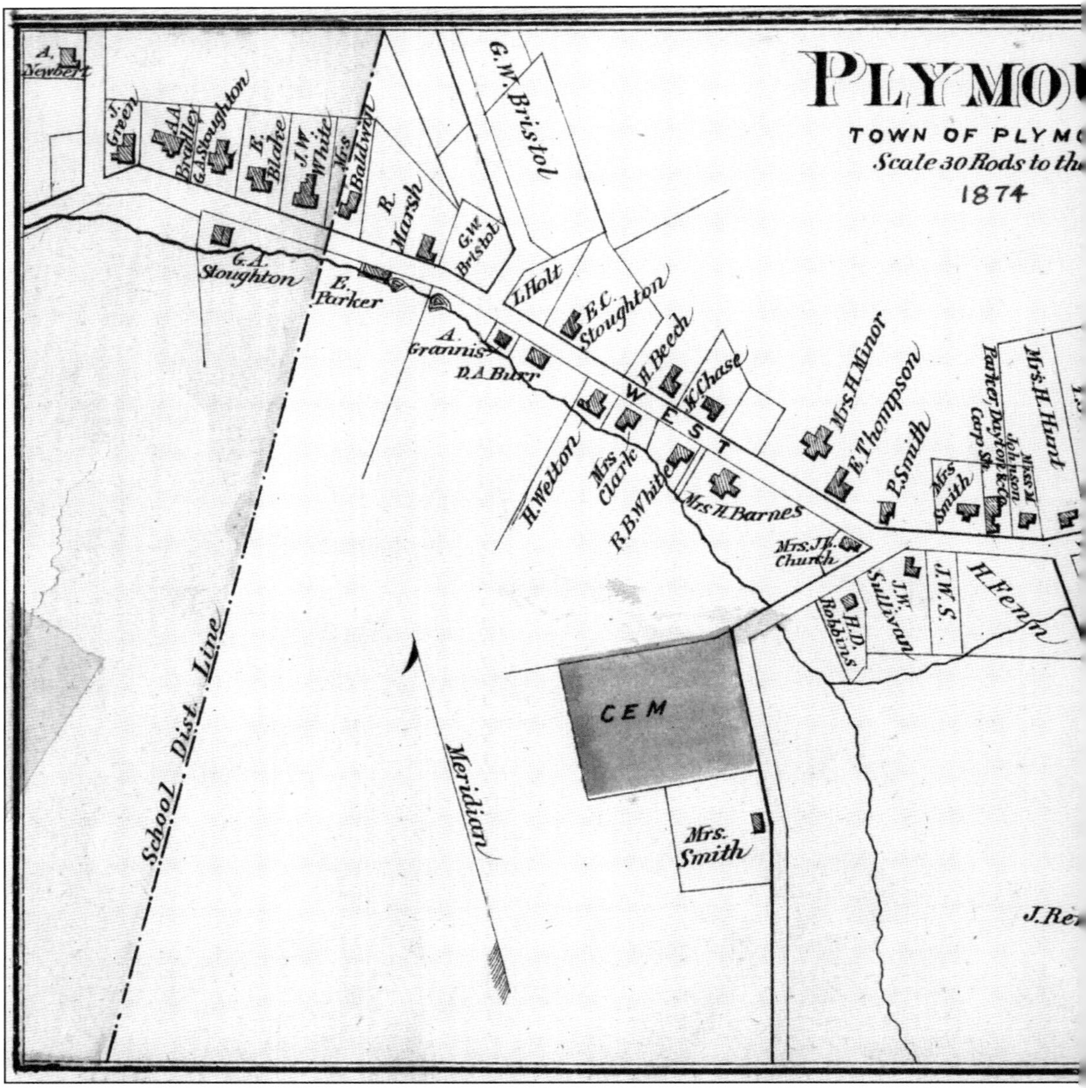

A map of Plymouth details various home sites, business, and locations prior to Plymouth Hollow breaking off to become its own community of Thomaston. The map is dated 1874. First community organizations were ecclesiastical with the churches being the predominant governing body. Settlers made several attempts to form their own churches, because travel to the nearest church was seven miles and more, requiring the crossing of the often treacherous river many times. In 1746,

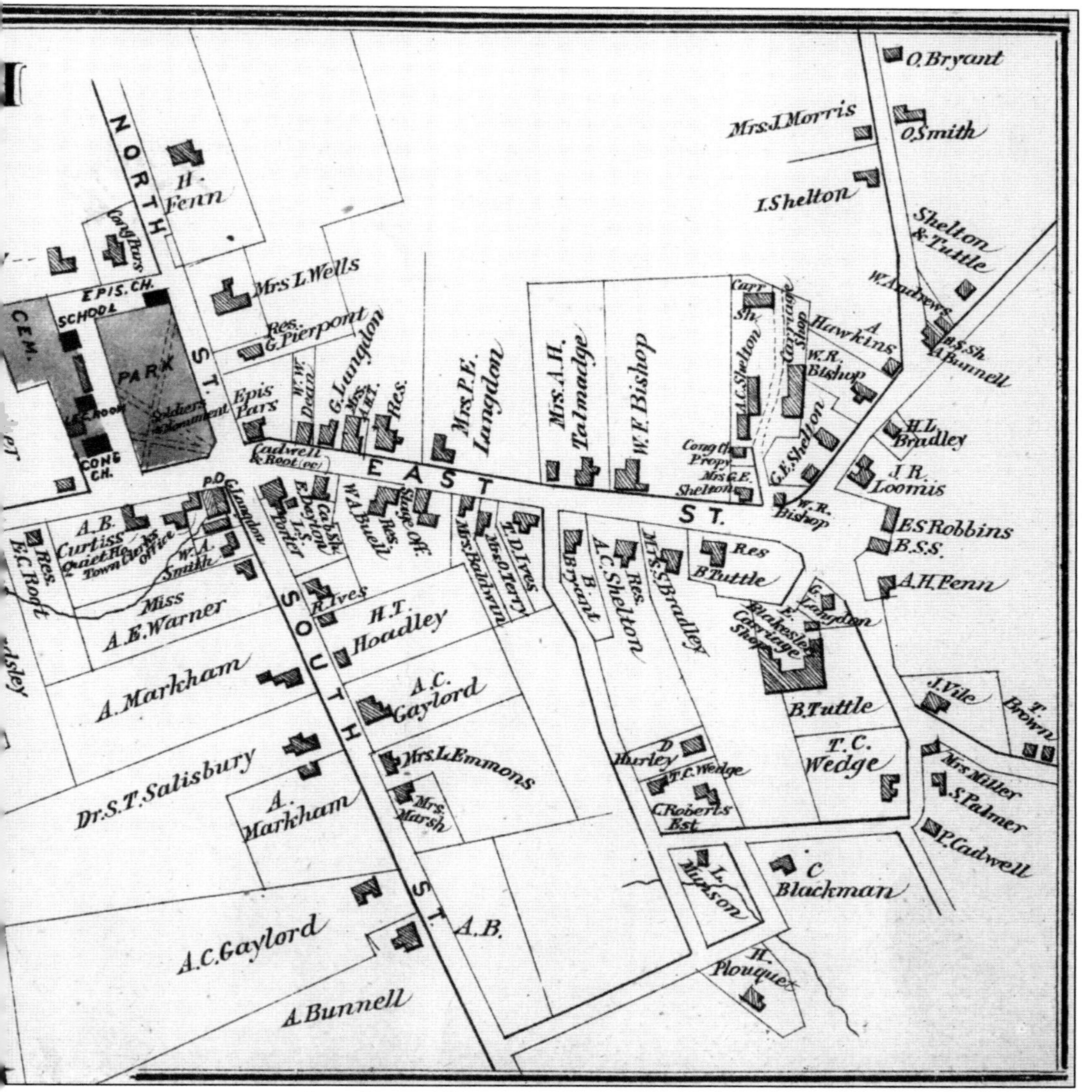

a compromise was voted on that resulted in residents meeting half of the year on each side of the river at the homes of Phineas Royce and Caleb Weed. Many of these early homes, churches, and early industries are encompassed in the Plymouth Center historic district located along intersections of North and South Street and Route 6. (Courtesy of Plymouth Historical Society.)

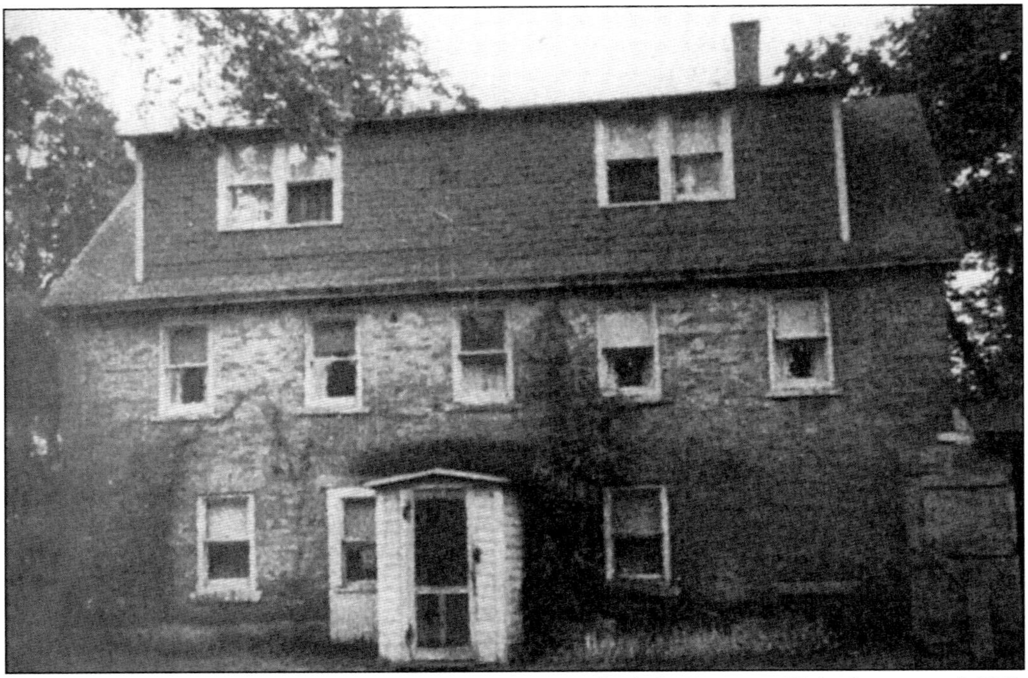

The brick Blakeslee building is pictured in 1945. It was built by Ransom Blakeslee around 1775. Blakeslee was the first selectman between 1822 and 1826. The Blakeslee Carriage works was operated by Ransom's son Joel, who later became famous as a toy manufacturer. His brother Enos continued the carriage works. (Courtesy of Plymouth Historical Society.)

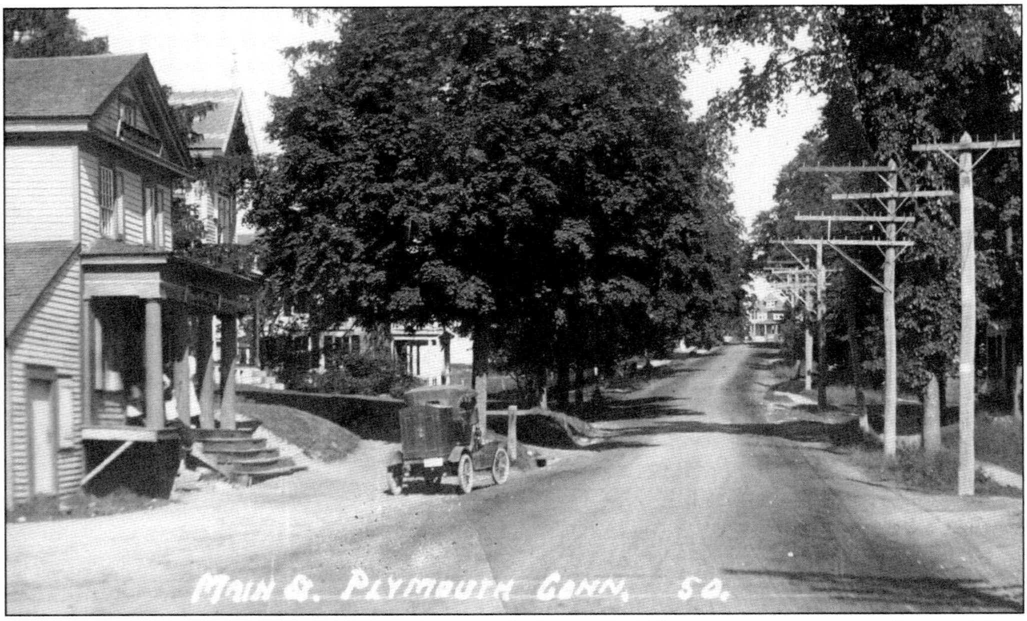

Main Street in Plymouth headed easterly toward Terryville. This route was a major thoroughfare to Hartford. Travelers stayed at the Red Tavern. Later, A.B. Curtiss converted General Smith's 1765 house into a tavern and inn. After Curtiss died, his wife and an Irish servant ran the hotel, instituting temperance and renaming the facility the Quiet House. (Courtesy of Plymouth Historical Society.)

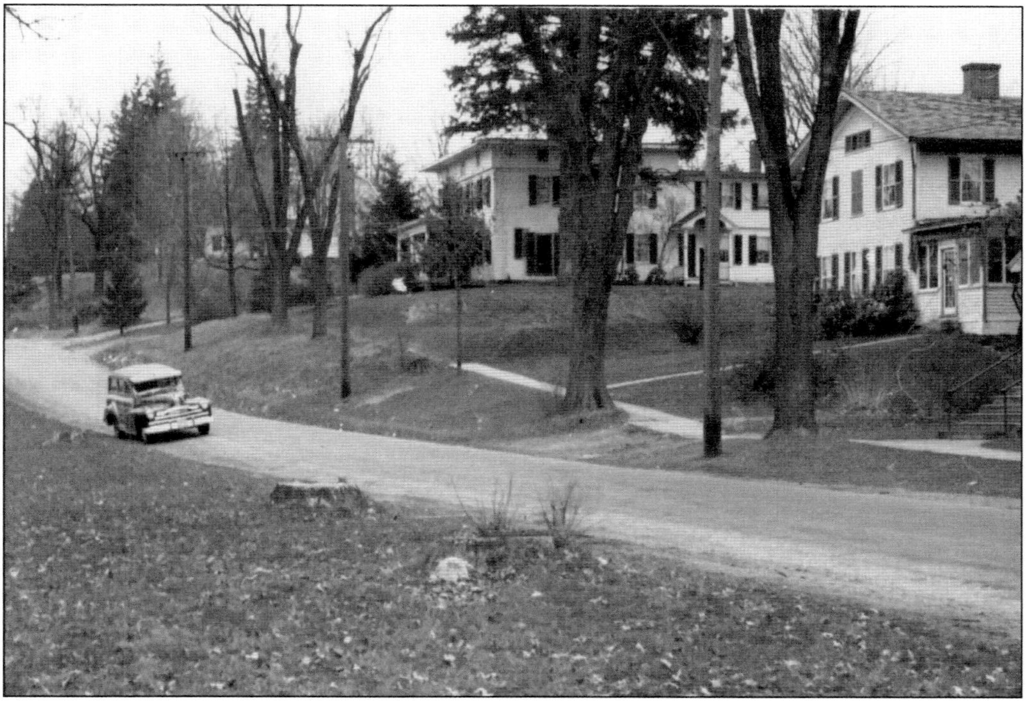

A paved North Street in Plymouth is pictured in the mid-1900s. The 1870 federal census identified 40 heads of households as residents of Plymouth Center. They were industrialists, professionals, tradesmen, farmers, and skilled workers. Some also were able to afford live-in domestics, many of whom were of Irish origin. (Courtesy of Plymouth Historical Society.)

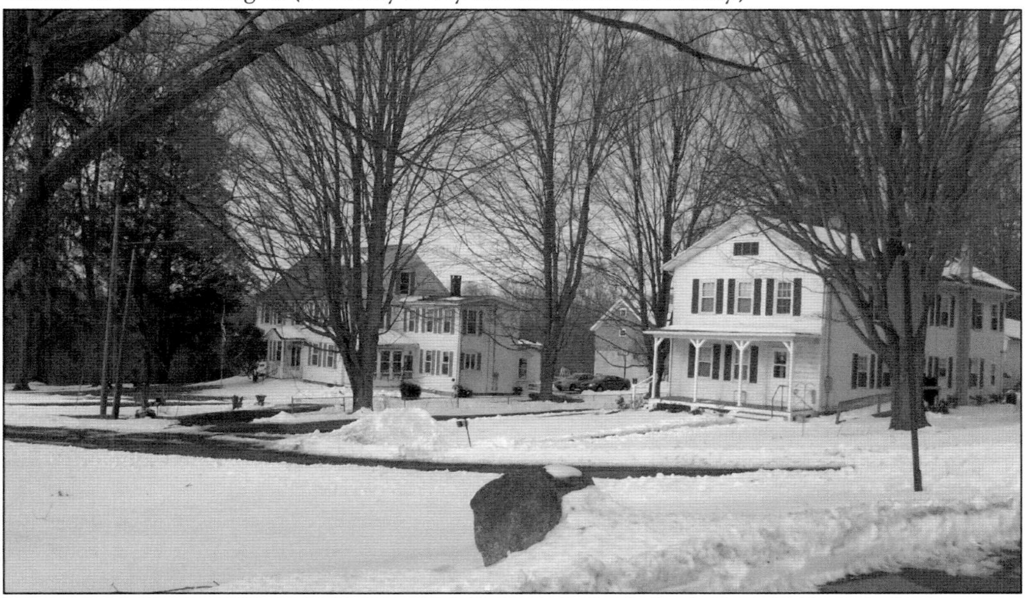

The houses at the north end of Plymouth Green are pictured here. One was built by the Reverend Andrew Storrs in 1766, and the other was formerly the Hart Female Seminary, or school for young ladies founded by Reverend Isaac Warren in 1853. The school closed in 1857. The wing that had been added to the Storrs home was detached and served as the congregational parsonage until 1865. (Photograph by Judy Giguere.)

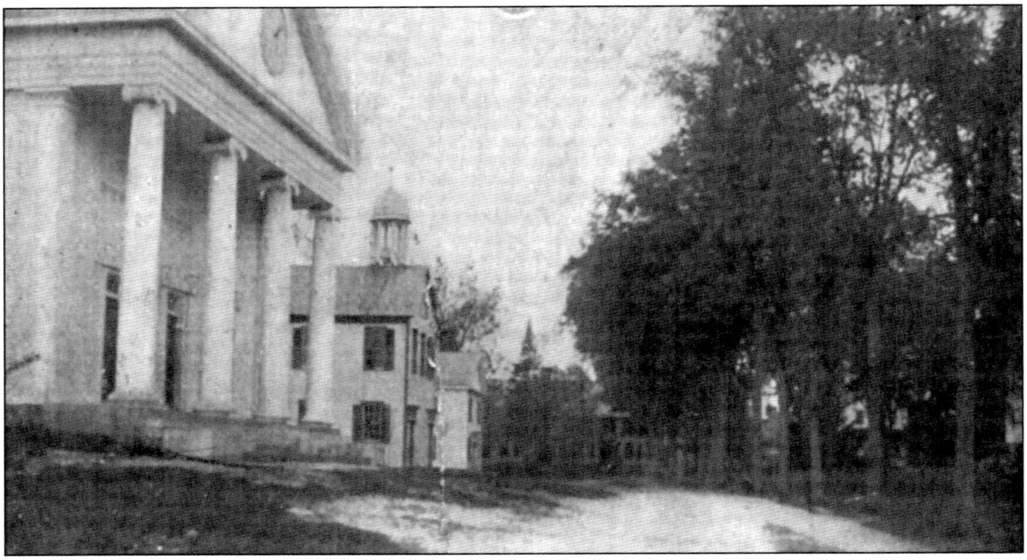

The dirt road and trees that were once in front of Plymouth Congregational Church are pictured here. The stone steps of the Plymouth Congregational Church were quarried from the woods of the Holt District, presently the vicinity of North Harwinton Avenue. The Green was mowed once a year by hand scythes, and sometimes a resident would pay a small sum for the hay. (Courtesy of Plymouth Historical Society.)

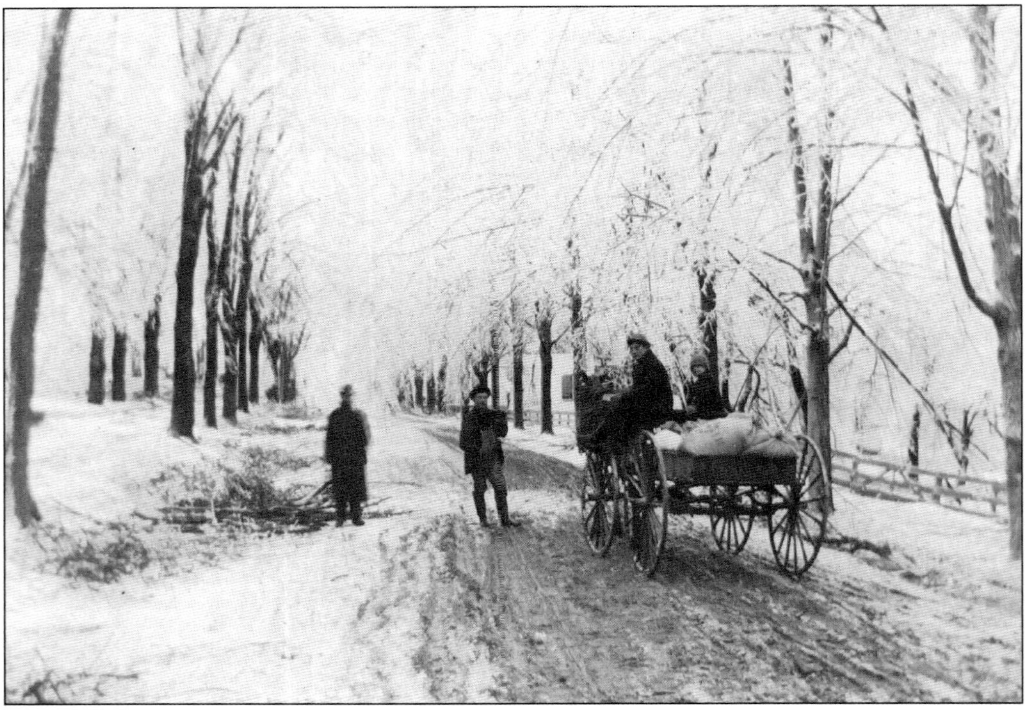

The carriage-making business began with Zalmon Coley in 1836. It was not long before other carriage makers went into business. Augustus C. Shelton apprenticed as a wheelwright and later set up his factory. Byron Tuttle was also in the carriage making trade and their companies merged into A.C. Shelton & Tuttle. Stonework from the foundations of the factory remains in the wooded area belonging to the Plymouth Land Trust. (Courtesy of Plymouth Historical Society.)

Two

The Genius of Eli Terry

Eli Terry was one of the most important figures in American history. Although he was "just" one of many clockmakers in Connecticut early in the 19th century, his inventive ideas ended up changing the Terryville area, America, and the entire industrialized world. He is recognized as the person who designed and built the first truly modern factory in America and starting the American Industrial Revolution. Born April 13, 1772, Terry served an apprenticeship under Daniel Burnap and learned to make the standard brass tall case movement. These clocks were very time-consuming to make. The account book shows that in one of the more productive years, a total of just six clocks were constructed. It took about one month to make one movement and a brass dial. In addition, a joiner or cabinet maker would be required to make the case. This made clocks very expensive. Eli Terry is likely to have received some training in wooden gear clocks from the Cheney brothers in East Hartford Connecticut. Wooden gear clocks were less expensive, as they used limited amounts of metal but were still made one at a time. They were affordable only to relatively well-to-do clients.

Terry proved to be an able student and completed his apprenticeship one year early. After his apprenticeship, from 1792 to 1800, he continued to make eight-day brass clocks. By 1795, he was making wooden-gear, 30-hour tall case clocks as well. It was a very difficult business in which to make a profit, as production was limited and selling was done door to door. This took time away from the manufacturing of the clocks.

Obviously, Eli Terry had been thinking about how these clocks could be made in larger quantities. Lowering costs and production time could expand sales and increase profits. In 1806, he hired two local joiners, Silas Hoadley and Seth Thomas, to help him build a new type of factory. He also signed a contract with two sales agents to sell clocks. This new factory raised production to roughly 3,000 clocks—in 1809! This was an astounding accomplishment. The price dropped, sales expanded, and a whole new industry was established. What made this possible?

For the first time, mass production of clock parts was done by machinery; the parts were interchangeable, made possible by quality gauges; outside power was used to run the machinery; and the parts could be made by unskilled labor.

By the late 1830s, these manufacturing techniques were used to produce cheap brass movement clocks, which then for the first time could be exported across the world. They were a huge international success—so successful that many foreign clock industries were hurt, as they could not compete. By 1850, the Bristol clock makers had made and sold many tens of thousands of clocks all over America and the world, all based on the concepts and ideas generated by one industrial genius named Eli Terry.

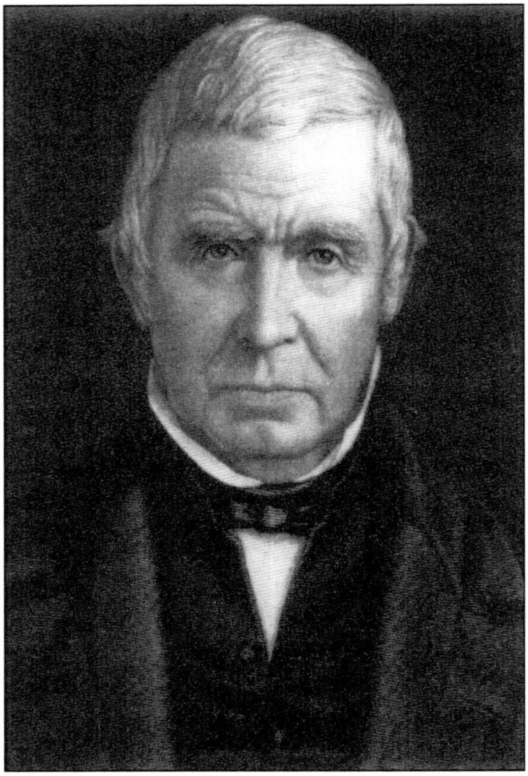

Eli Terry is pictured in his later years. The father of the American Industrial Revolution, Terry was a highly successful inventor and businessman who forever changed the way goods were manufactured, making goods affordable to the common man in the United States. (Courtesy of American Clock & Watch Museum.)

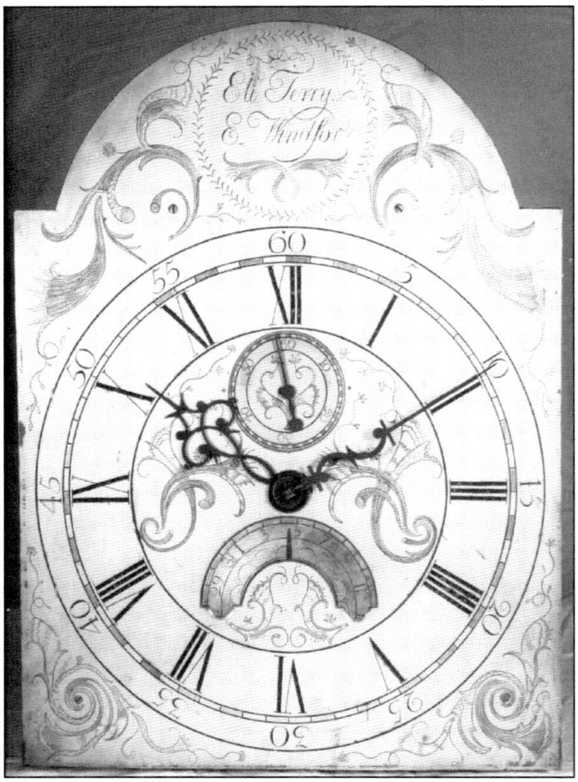

This is the dial of a very early Eli Terry grandfather clock from when Terry worked in East Windsor. The silvered dial is of the highest quality usually found in expensive clock cases with eight-day brass movements. There are no holes in the dial that would have been to insert a key for winding. Previously, winding was the common mode of powering clocks. (Courtesy of American Clock & Watch Museum.)

The inner workings of an early Eli Terry Grandfather clock, it is likely that Mr. Terry learned to make wooden gears from the Cheney Brothers of East Hartford. A key is needed to wind this clock. It works on a 30-hour crude wooden gear movement that works by pulling a cord from inside the case instead of a high quality brass movement. This is the precursor to mass production. (Courtesy of American Clock & Watch Museum.)

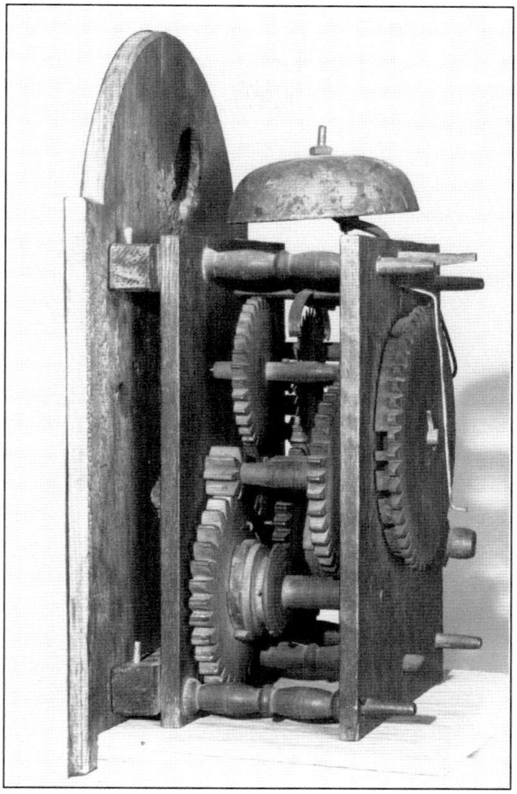

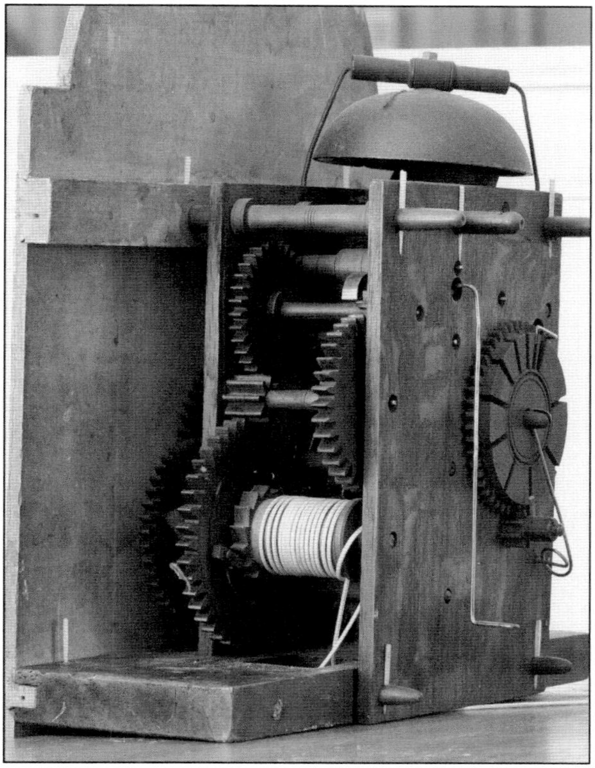

Eli Terry's first major contract was called the 1808 Porter Contract. The contract called for 4,000 thirty-hour wooden gear movements to be produced at Terry's factory in the Hoadleyville, or Ireland district of Plymouth. The contract was with the Levi G. and E. Porter Company of Waterbury. Payment was $4 per clock movement, with the materials being supplied by the Porter Company. The factory was built by Eli Terry, Seth Thomas, and Silas Hoadley. (Courtesy of American Clock & Watch Museum.)

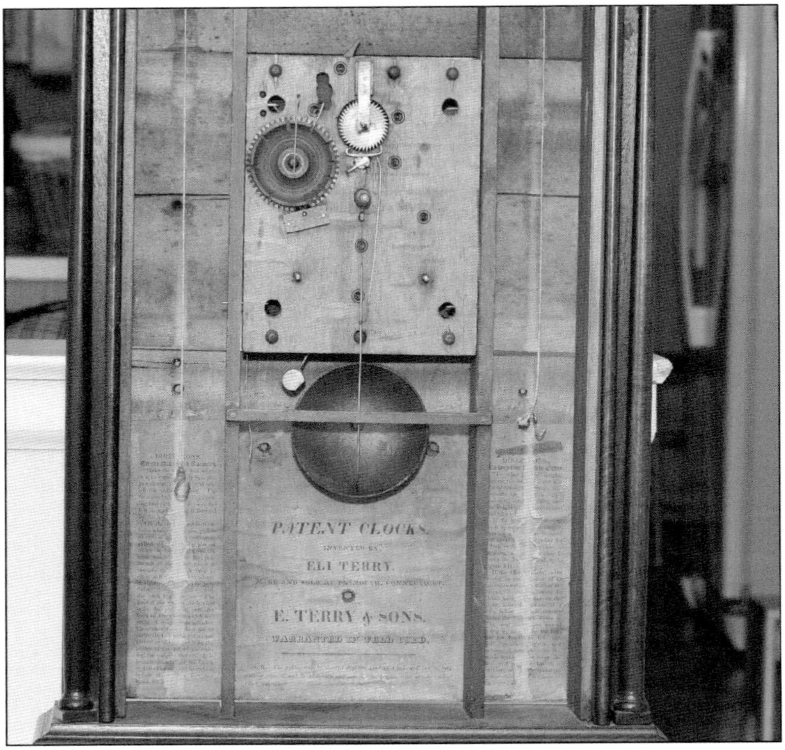

Eli Terry's factory successfully produced the 4,000 units in less than three years. This event was the start of the American Industrial Revolution. The clock movement itself is well finished and relatively more sophisticated than the early Eli Terry grandfather clock. (Courtesy of American Clock & Watch Museum.)

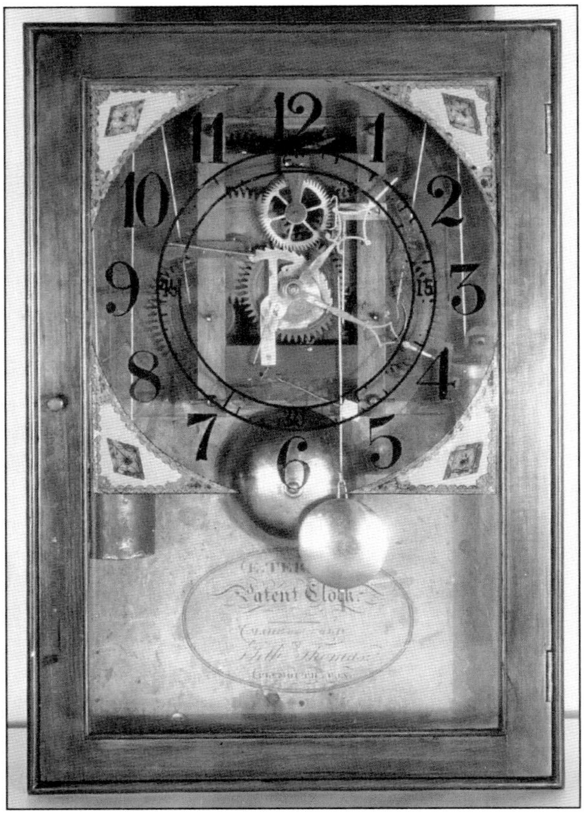

In 1813, Eli Terry developed a prototype shelf clock commonly referred to as the Box Clock. It is believed all the movements in the Box Clock were made by Eli Terry. Seth Thomas made some of the cases with the Seth Thomas label and sold them. Numbers are painted on the door glass and the case is not embellished. This is the first Connecticut wooden gear shelf clock with interchangeable gears. (Courtesy of American Clock & Watch Museum.)

This close-up shows the internal working of the Eli Terry Box Clock. The movement design uses a wood strap to hold the gears. The sawtooth rack and brass snail on the hour gear controls the striking of hours. This clock's running time was less than one day. (Courtesy of American Clock & Watch Museum.)

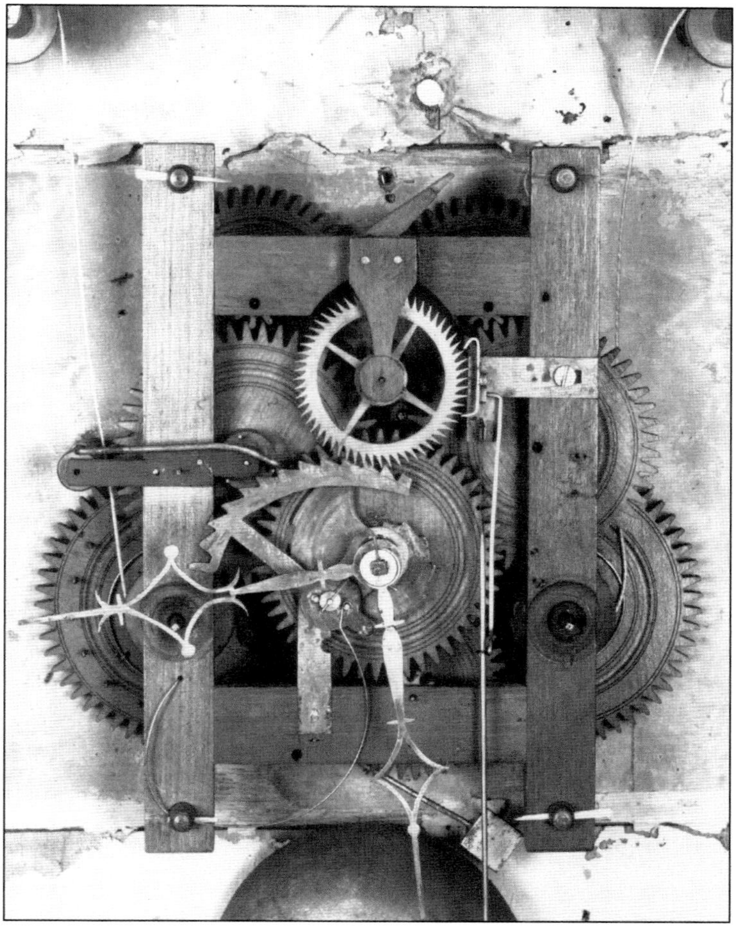

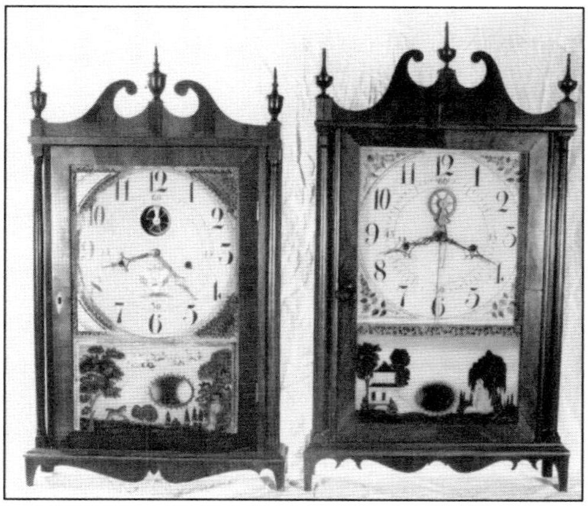

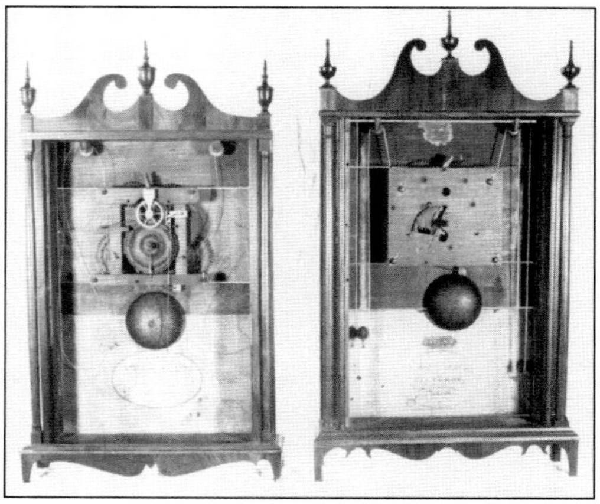

These two images compare a Seth Thomas Clock (on the left of each image) and an Eli Terry Pillar & Scroll shelf clock (on the right of each image). The Pillar and Scroll Shelf Clock was developed by late 1814 or early 1815. The Seth Thomas version has short feet and low scrolls and was considered not as pleasing to the eye as Eli Terry's more sophisticated version. Both movements were designed by Terry. The left one is the inner workings of the Seth Thomas clock, and the right is the Eli Terry. Terry sued Thomas for patent infringements on his movement designs and won. (Courtesy of American Clock & Watch Museum.)

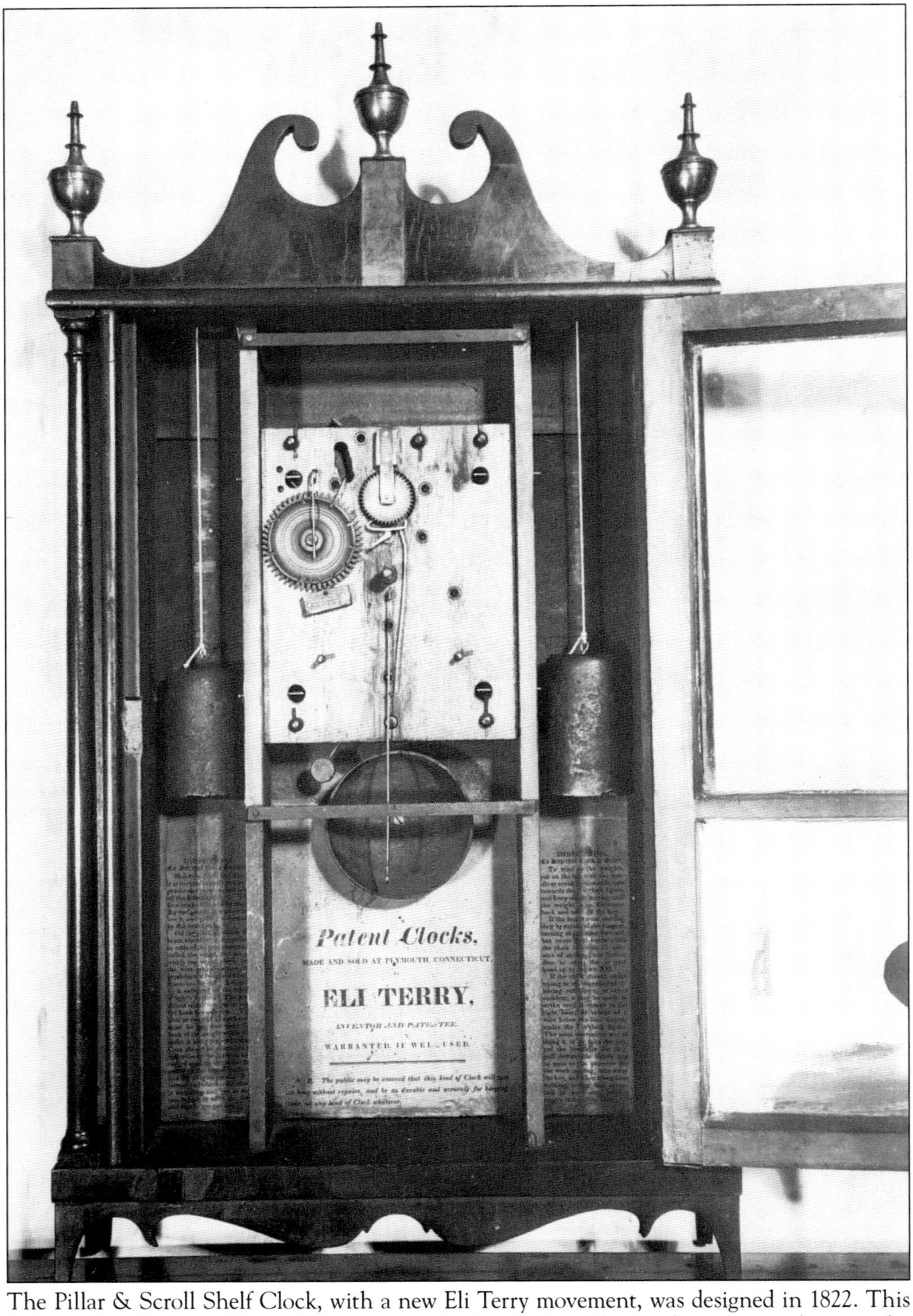

The Pillar & Scroll Shelf Clock, with a new Eli Terry movement, was designed in 1822. This high-quality clock could run 30 hours on a single winding. The clock movement became the standard movement used by Eli Terry and many other clockmakers for the next two decades. (Courtesy of American Clock & Watch Museum.)

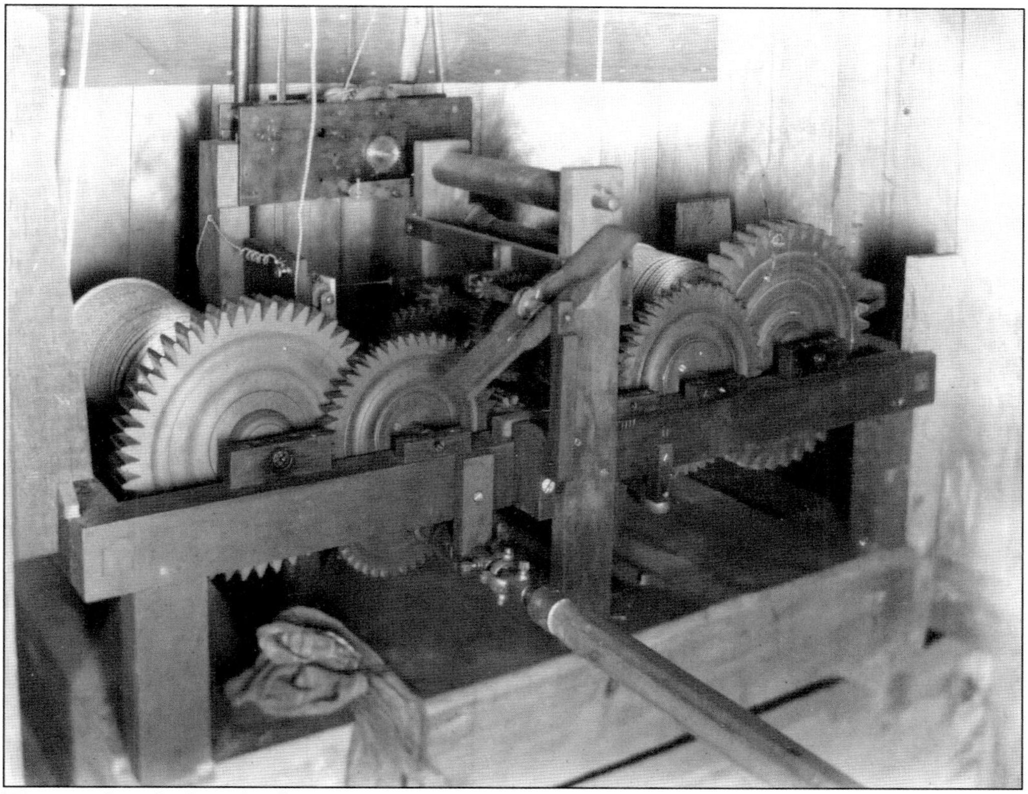

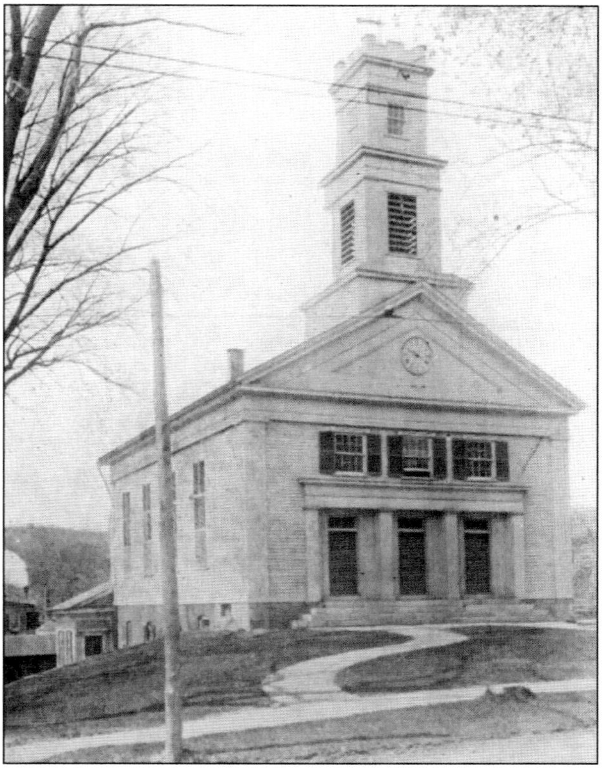

The wooden clockworks shown in the tower of the original Terryville Congregational Church were made and donated by Eli Terry, who was very generous to the church and donated clockworks to the Terryville and Plymouth Congregational Churches. The church tower clocks were installed when the church structure was completed. Unfortunately, the wooden clock works that existed in the Terryville Congregational Church were lost in 1967 when the church was entirely destroyed by fire. The Plymouth Congregational Church clockworks are still in the church tower. (Both images courtesy of Plymouth Historical Society.)

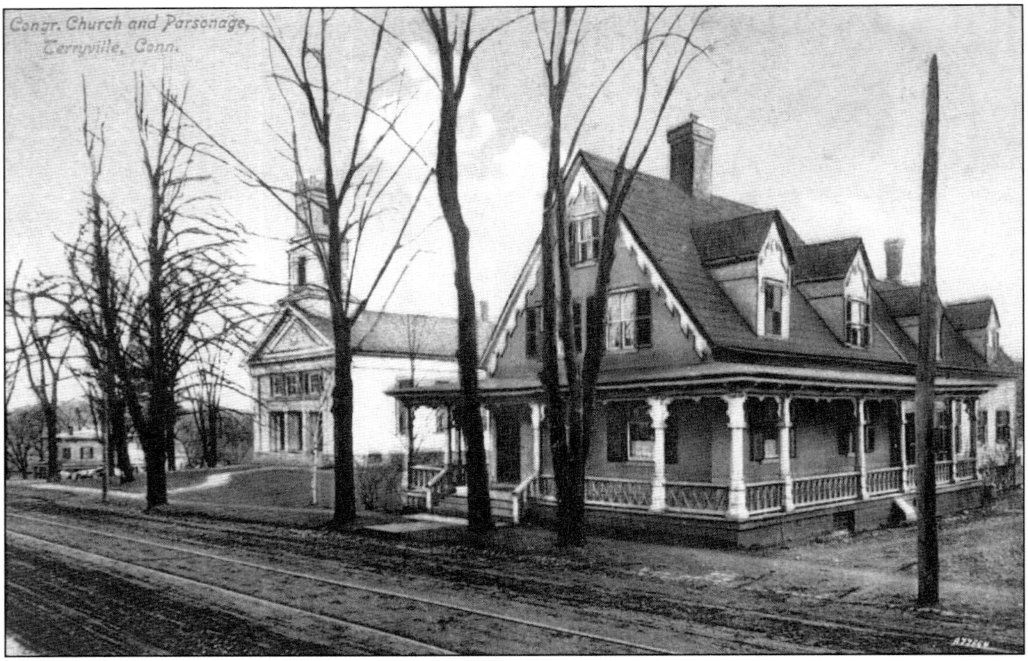

The Terry Parsonage building, another generous donation by Eli Terry, was next to the Terryville Congregational Church. The Terry Parsonage was torn down to make way for expansion of the church when it was rebuilt after the 1967 devastating fire. (Courtesy of Plymouth Historical Society.)

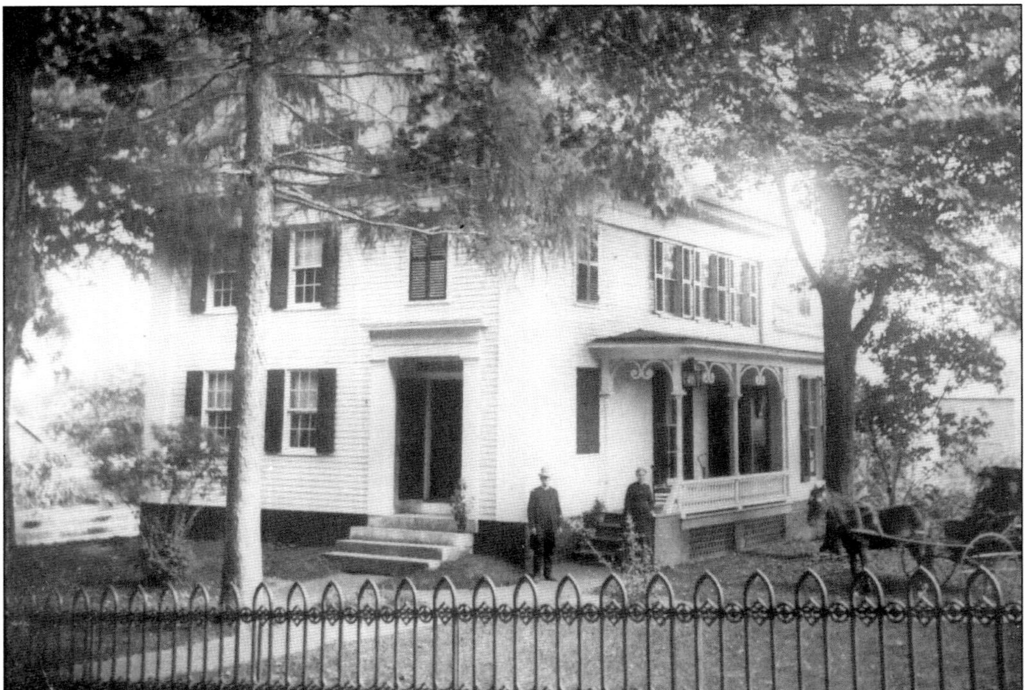

This is a 1902 view of the Terry building, formerly located on Main Street, across from Baldwin Park. The building is of very similar construction to the Terry Parsonage. It was demolished to make way for new businesses in that section of the street. (Courtesy of Plymouth Historical Society.)

Three

The Eagle Lock Company

Stephen G. Bucknall came to the United States in 1832. He is the first of cabinet lock makers in the United States and began to manufacture locks in Watertown. He sold his business to Eli Terry Jr., working for Mr. Terry for a number of years. The company was sold several times, and the early locks were crude and not able to compete with higher-quality, cheaper locks from England. In 1854, the company became the Eagle Lock Company. It was successful in making frames for the very popular carpet bags, mail bag locks, padlocks, trunk locks and later diversifying into wood screw manufacture.

The Eagle Lock held at least 11 patents for various locks. In 1900, almost 1,000 people worked for the Eagle Lock as it continued to expand and add to its facilities. In the 1920s, the Eagle Lock is credited with 1,800 employees and sufficient funding to purchase several competitors. The company built 30 homes called Hillside Park for its employees. The homes were of the Aladdin type and were constructed by the Westingham, Church & Curr Company of New York.

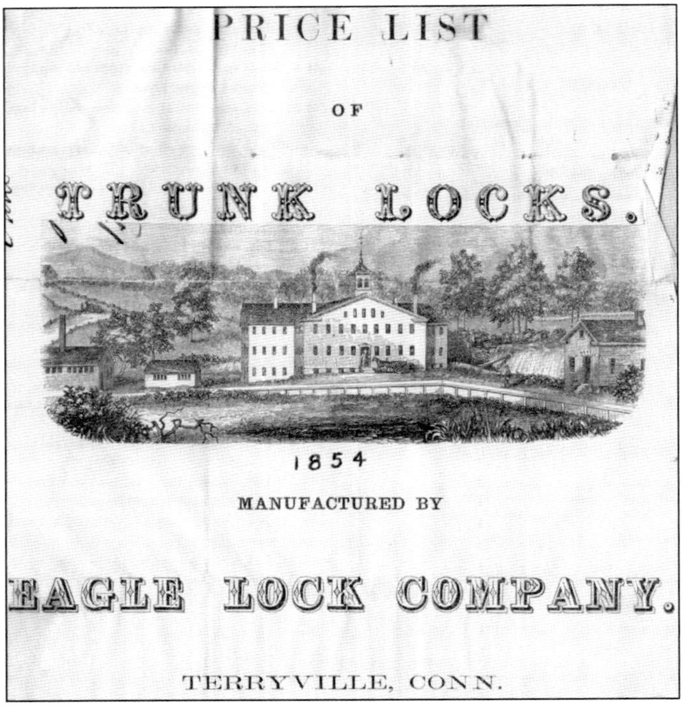

PRICE LIST

OF

TRUNK LOCKS.

1854

MANUFACTURED BY

EAGLE LOCK COMPANY.

TERRYVILLE, CONN.

This is the cover of an Eagle Lock Price List catalog dating from 1854. Other examples of price lists and products of the Eagle Lock Company are on display at the Lock Museum of America, located on the site of the former Eagle Lock office building on Main Street in Terryville. (Courtesy of Plymouth Historical Society.)

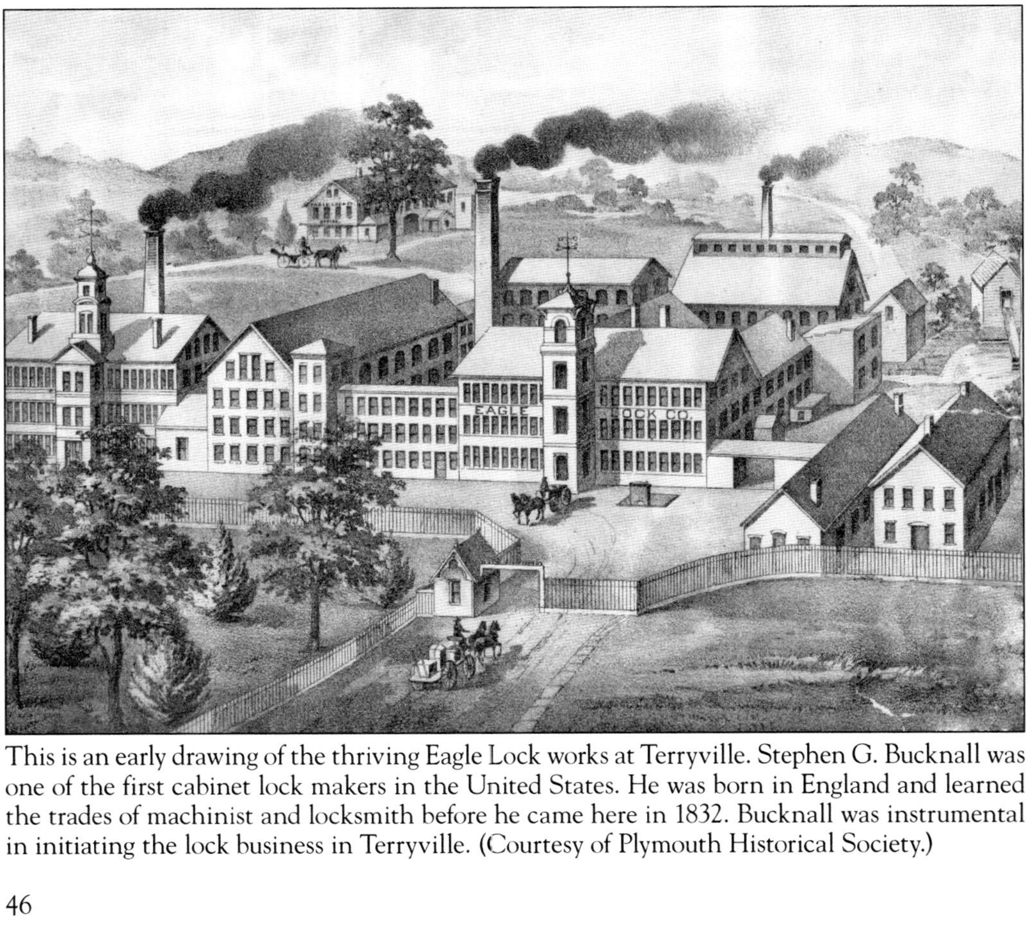

This is an early drawing of the thriving Eagle Lock works at Terryville. Stephen G. Bucknall was one of the first cabinet lock makers in the United States. He was born in England and learned the trades of machinist and locksmith before he came here in 1832. Bucknall was instrumental in initiating the lock business in Terryville. (Courtesy of Plymouth Historical Society.)

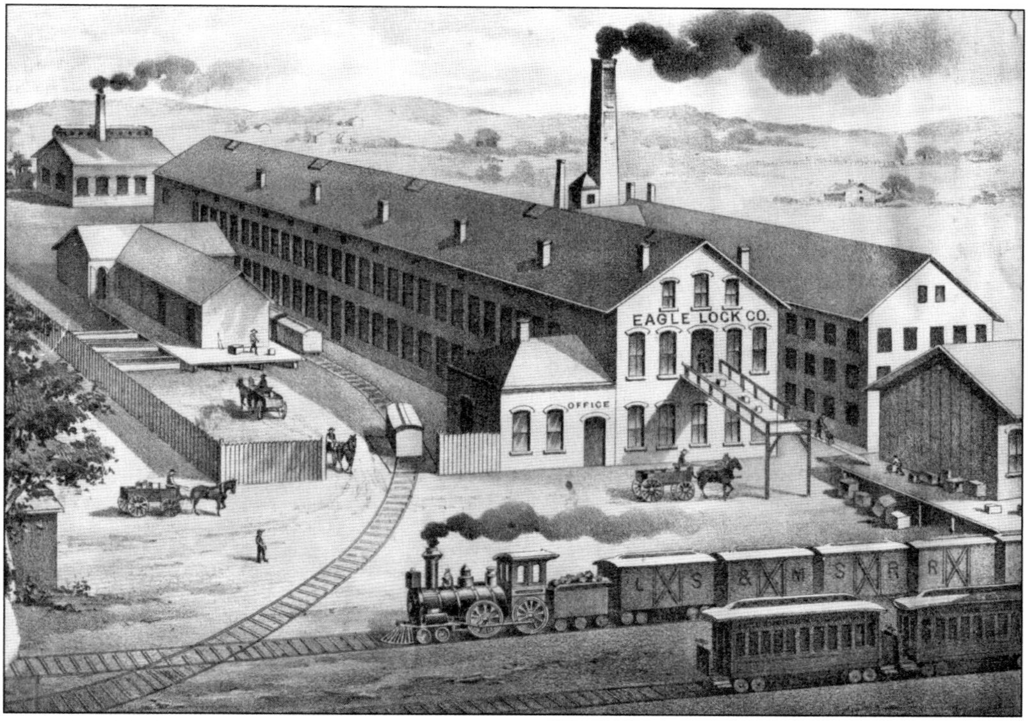

Eagle Lock Works at Geneva, Ohio, formerly the Western Lock Company and competitor to the Eagle Lock, is pictured here. The Western Lock Company was formed by E.L. Perkins after he sold the Bridgeport Lock Company. Western Lock Company was established in 1878 and was purchased by the successful Eagle Lock Company in 1882. It was renamed the Eagle Lock Company of Geneva, Ohio. (Courtesy of Plymouth Historical Society.)

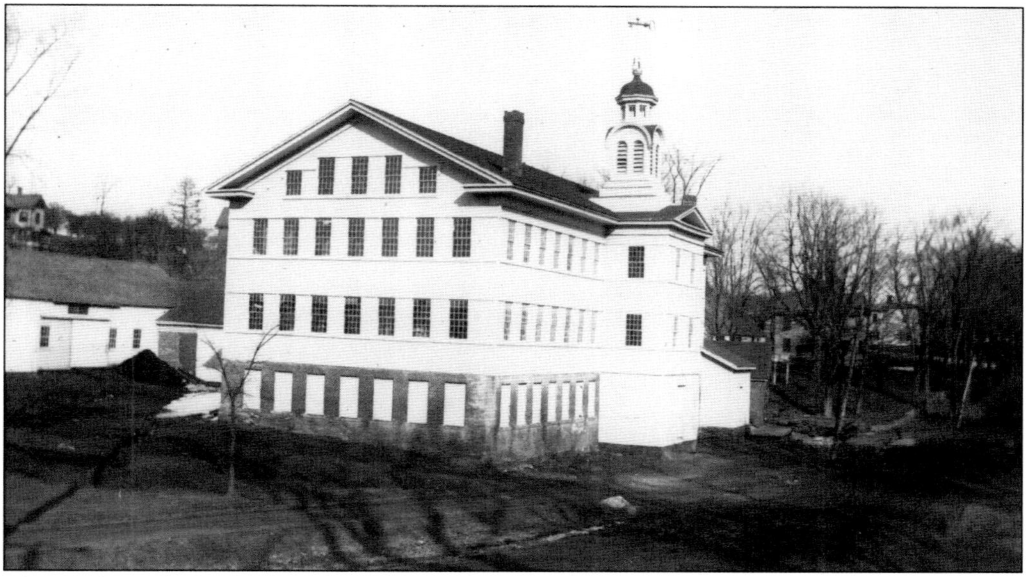

The Eagle Lock Company building was known as the upper lock shop and was the original location of the historic waterwheel. The sons of Eli Terry, Samuel, and Eli Jr. established their own clock factory in 1824, using the techniques developed by their father—in particular, water-powered machinery. (Courtesy of Plymouth Historical Society.)

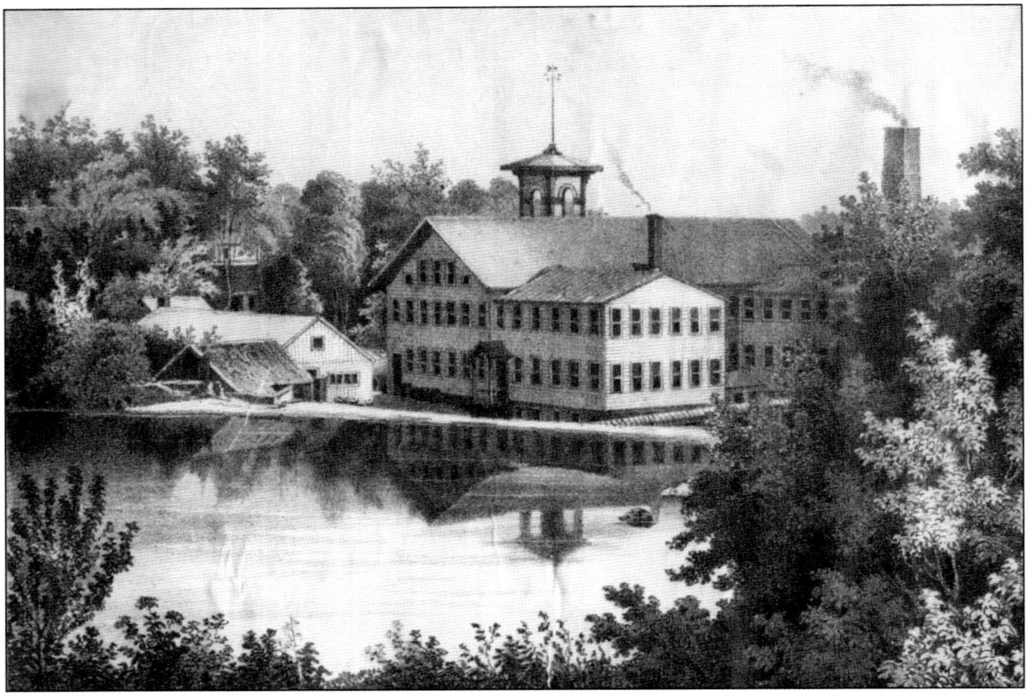

This picture denotes the Eagle Lock, Upper Lock Shop and holding pond for use with waterpower. The waterwheel was mounted in the wheel pit on the site of the now-demolished factory. The site is in the process of being reclaimed for use as a museum for the waterwheel and industries of Terryville. (Courtesy of Plymouth Historical Society.)

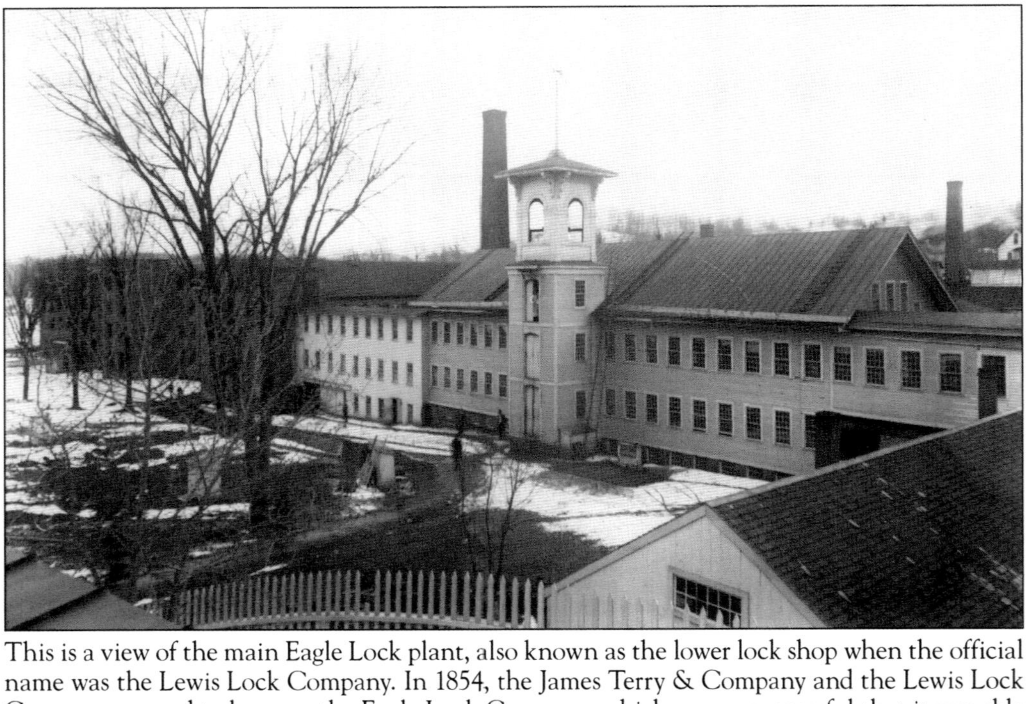

This is a view of the main Eagle Lock plant, also known as the lower lock shop when the official name was the Lewis Lock Company. In 1854, the James Terry & Company and the Lewis Lock Company merged to become the Eagle Lock Company, which was so successful that it was able to purchase six of its major competitors. (Courtesy of Plymouth Historical Society.)

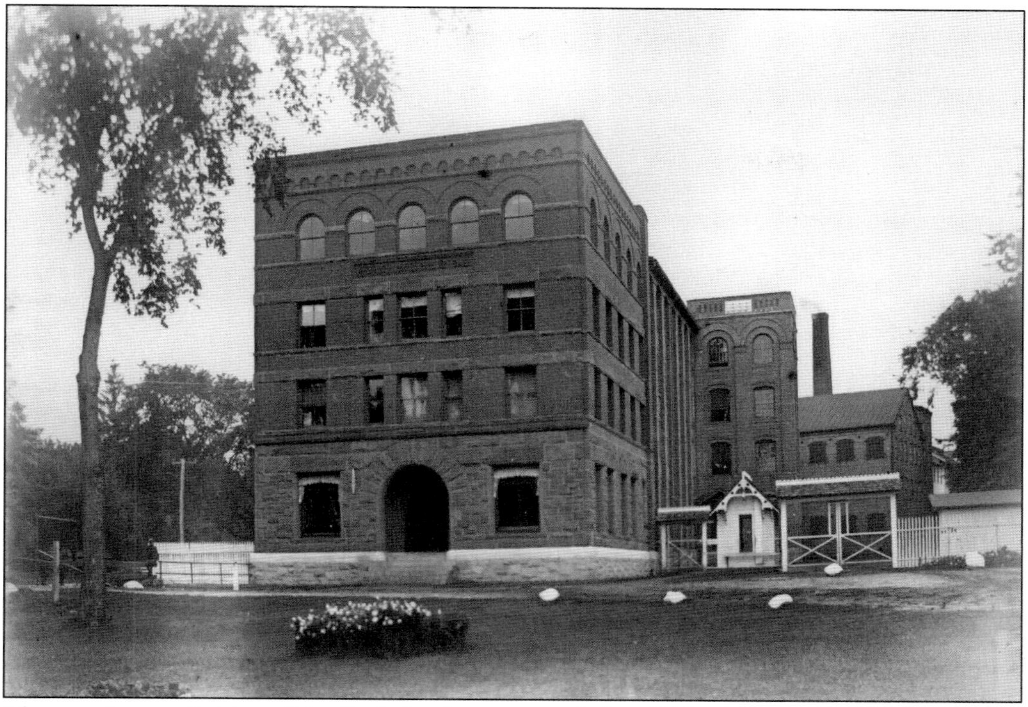

The wood screw division of the Eagle Lock was expanded in 1916, and a new building was added to house this phase of the business. The Eagle Lock Company grew into a major manufacturing complex that eventually dominated South Main, Eagle, and South Eagle Streets. (Courtesy of Plymouth Historical Society.)

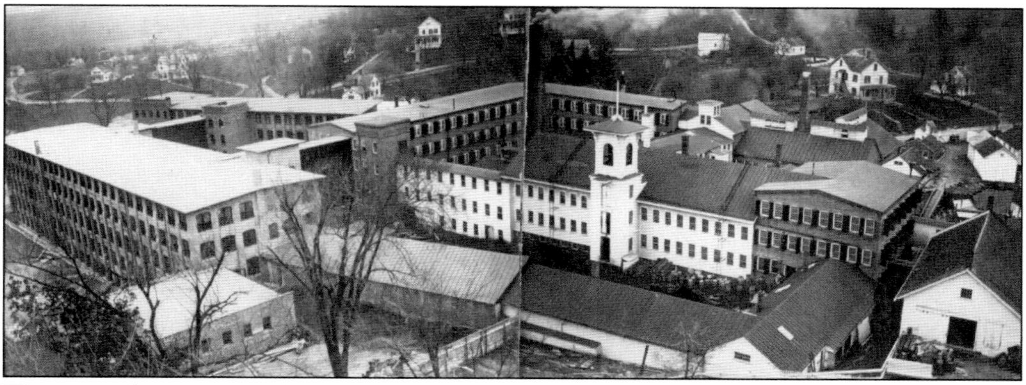

This is an alternate view from the parking lot of the Terryville Congregational Church, which is situated on the ground above the Eagle Lock main plant. The image demonstrates the size of the plant and the large area encompassed by it. Several additions were made to enlarge the factory. By 1900, the Eagle Lock employed nearly 1,000 workers. (Courtesy of Plymouth Historical Society.)

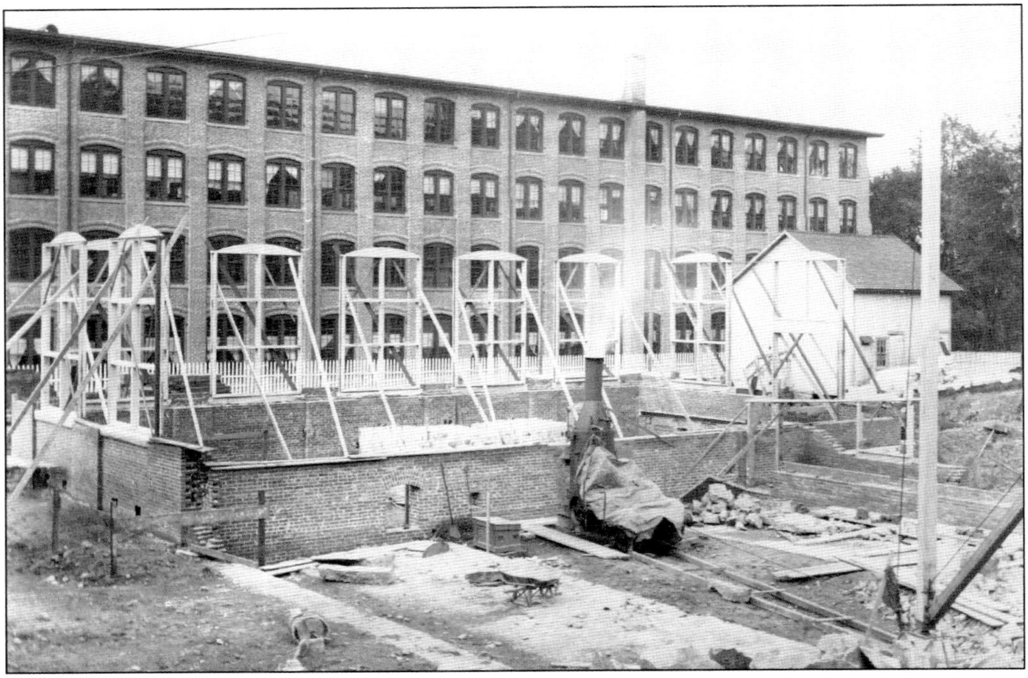

Additional office space was added in 1889 and again in 1905 with two large five-story factory buildings located on either side of the main office and again in 1907 construction continued for another addition to Eagle Lock main plant. The company built a boardinghouse containing 66 rooms on Prospect Street in 1902 for some of its male employees. (Courtesy of Plymouth Historical Society.)

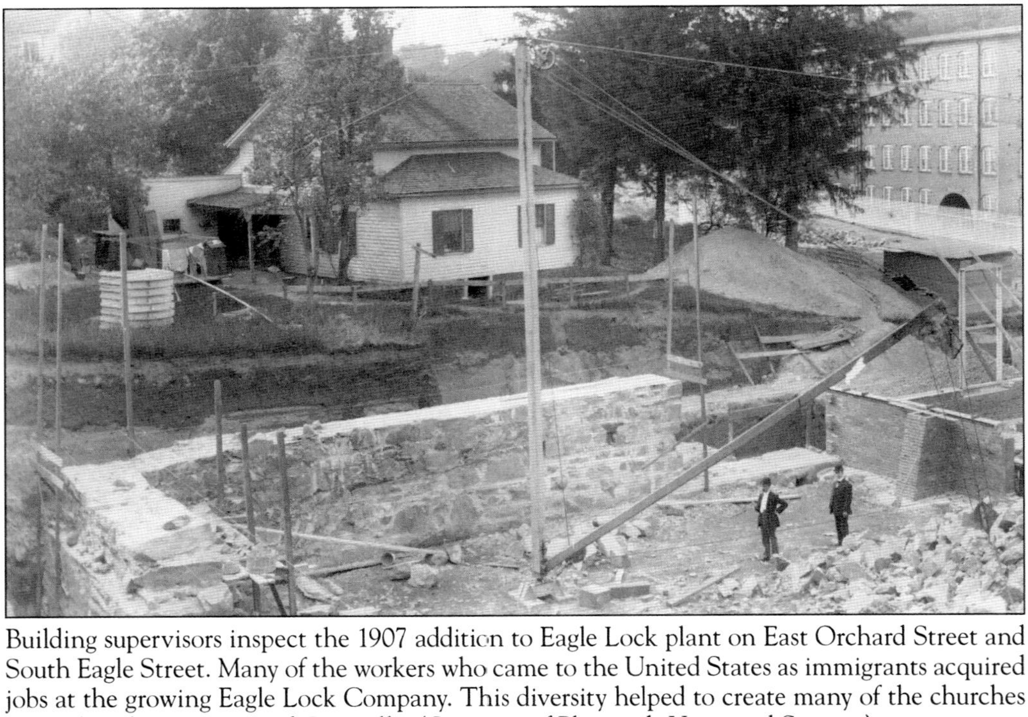

Building supervisors inspect the 1907 addition to Eagle Lock plant on East Orchard Street and South Eagle Street. Many of the workers who came to the United States as immigrants acquired jobs at the growing Eagle Lock Company. This diversity helped to create many of the churches and cultural institutions of Terryville. (Courtesy of Plymouth Historical Society.)

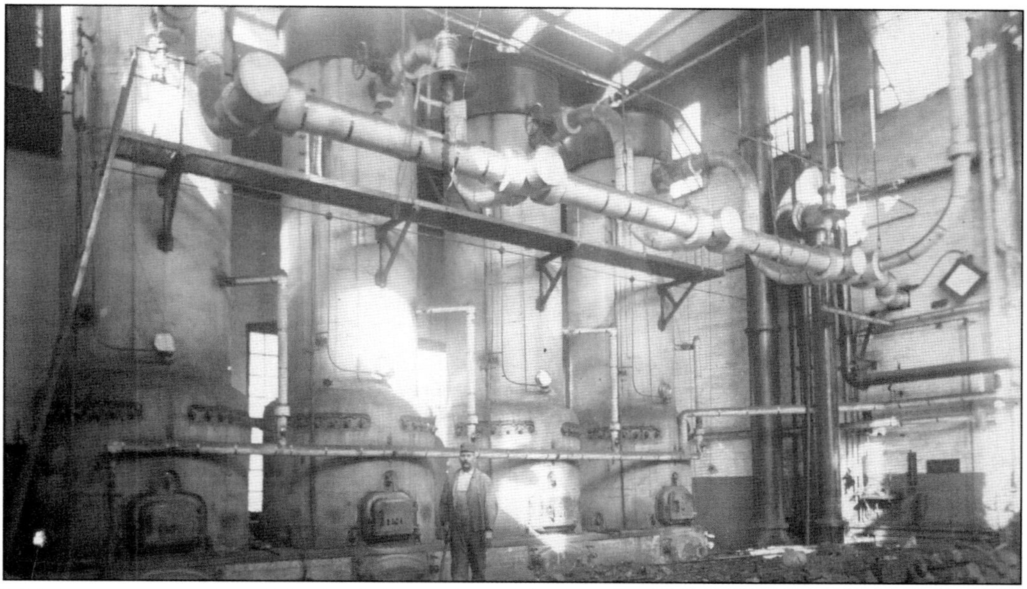

This is an interior view of the Eagle Lock plant. The factory was formerly run by waterpower and later by a 65-horsepower engine. Buildings included a brass foundry, japanning and tempering shops, and storehouse for brass and iron in the rough. A large vault adjoins the factory for storing dies that are used to cut out the lock plates. (Courtesy of Plymouth Historical Society.)

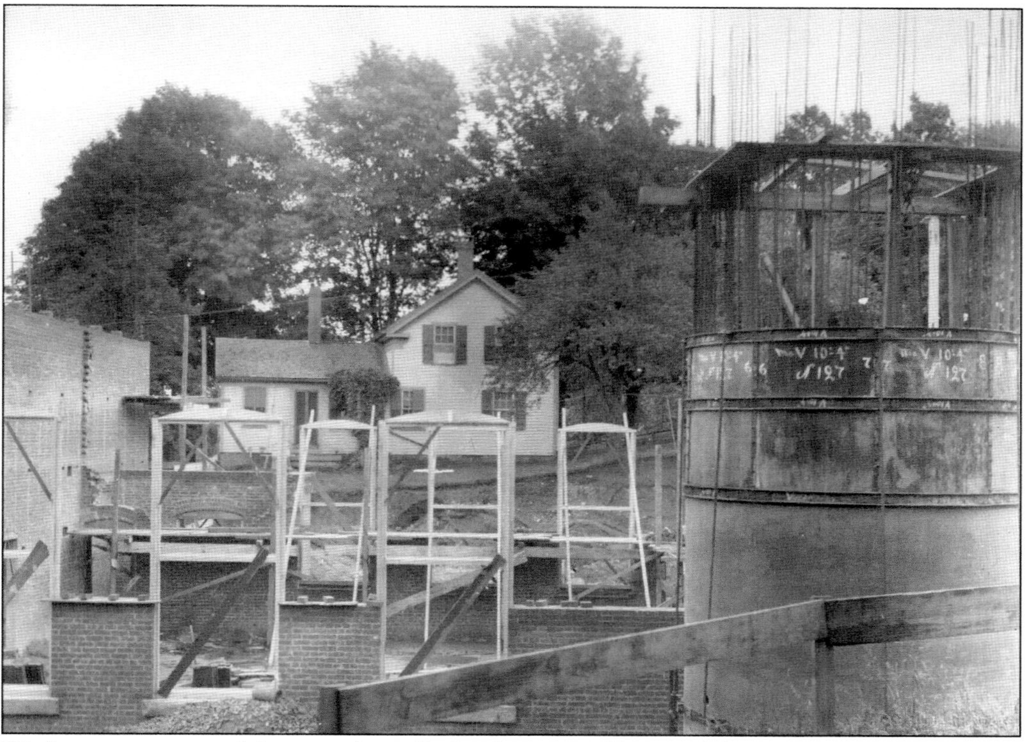

Workmen are pictured framing the walls for the 1907 addition of this growing enterprise. The success of this company was due to the quality of workmanship learned though research and innovation. Large teams of horses were used to transport products to the railway spur in Pequabuck for shipment. (Courtesy of Plymouth Historical Society.)

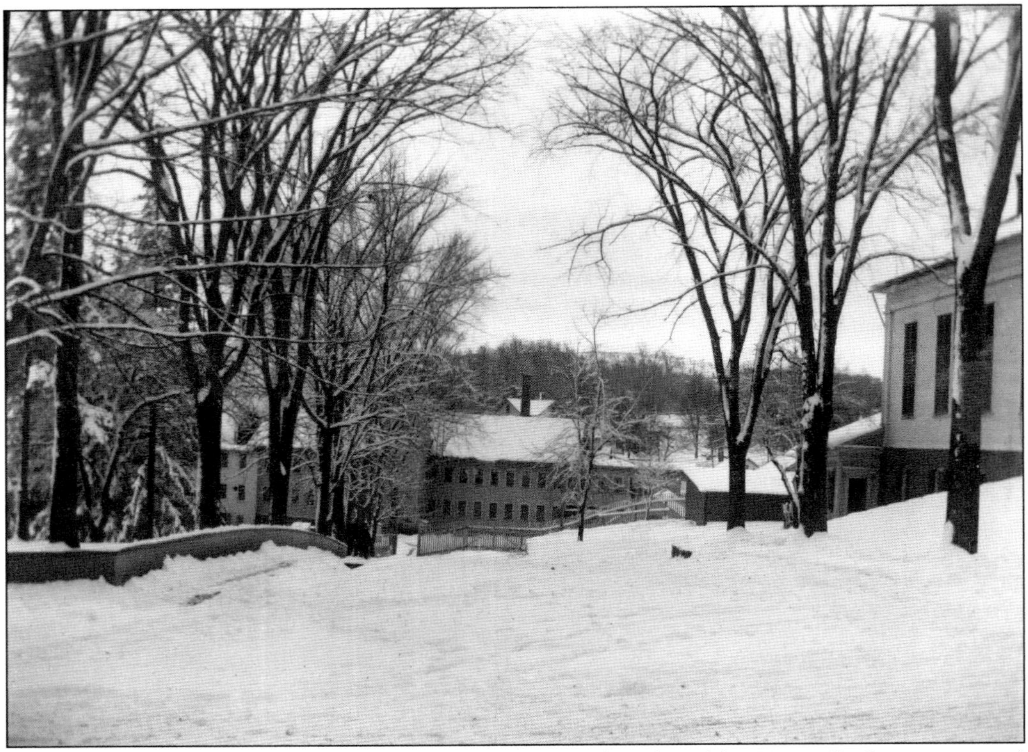

This view of the Eagle Lock works was taken from the parking lot of the Terryville Congregational Church and demonstrates the vast size of the Eagle Lock campus. During the peak era, employment surged to 1,800 workers. It was not until the Great Depression that the number of workers declined. (Courtesy of Plymouth Historical Society.)

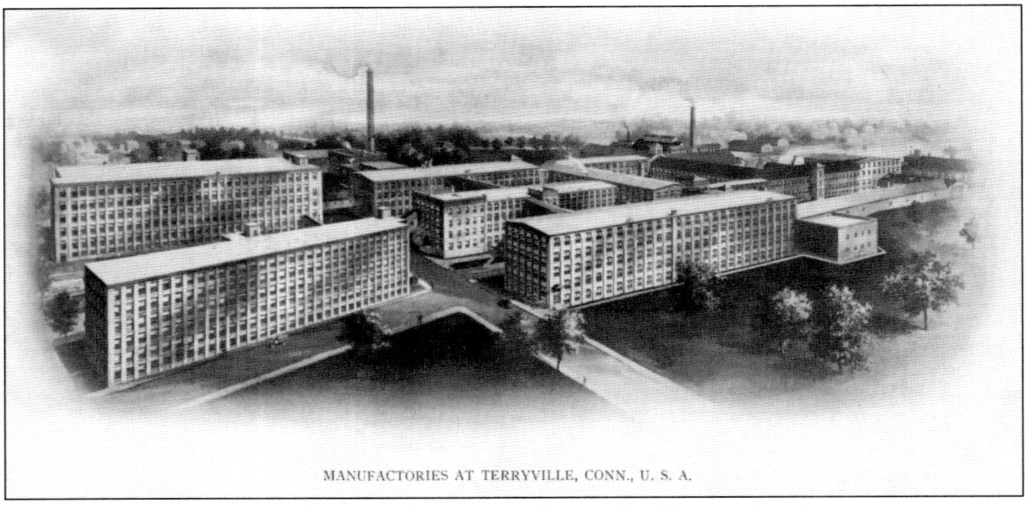

This advertisement shows the manufacturers at Terryville. The product line comprises more than 2,000 varieties of locks. A sales room was located on Chambers Street in New York City. The Eagle Lock catalog consisted of over 700 pages with over 6,000 different locks and hardware manufactured by Eagle and sold throughout the United States and overseas. (Courtesy of Plymouth Historical Society.)

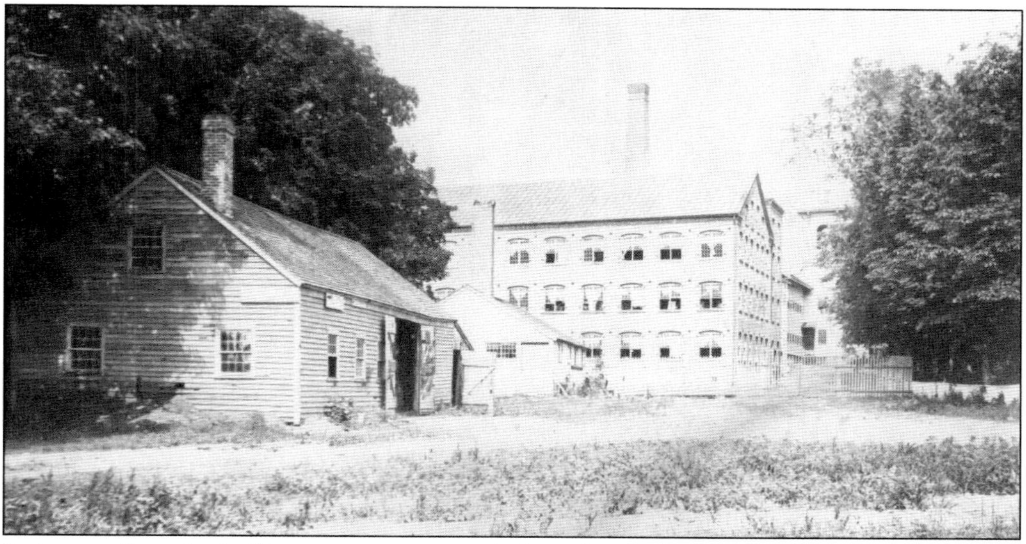

Early manufacturing buildings were constructed of wood, including the early Eagle Lock buildings. These buildings adjoined the main manufacturing plant. Wood buildings were in constant danger of fire from heat, lightning, or sparks. In 1859, the buildings of the lower lock shop burned and were replaced by larger buildings. Many of the replacement buildings were constructed with locally made bricks. (Courtesy of Plymouth Historical Society.)

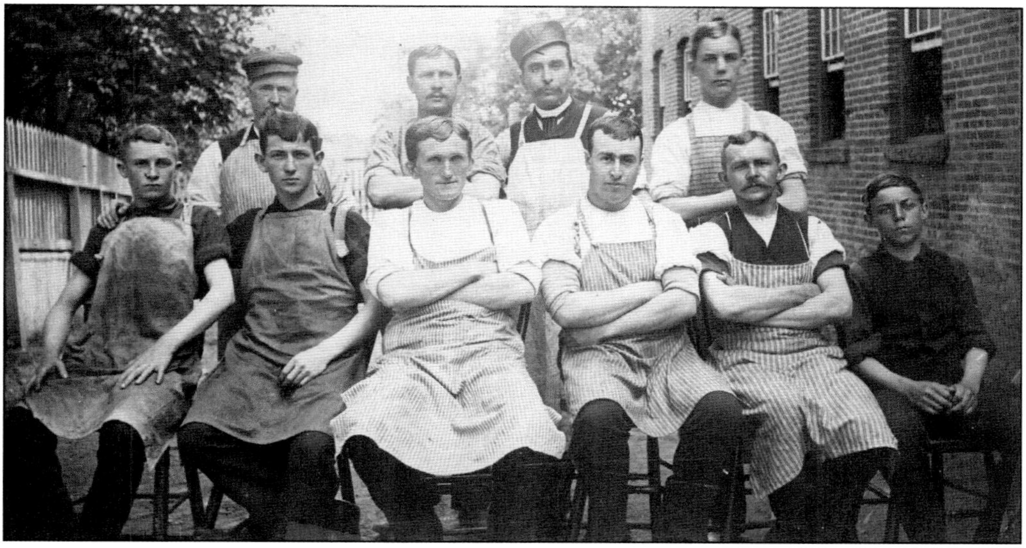

A group of workmen from Eagle Lock are pictured here. Some of the workers were quite young, as child labor laws did not go into effect until 1938 after numerous attempts to abolish child labor. Aggressive attempts to restrict child labor began as early as 1904. A 1916 federal law prohibited movement of goods across state lines if minimum age laws were violated, but the law was declared unconstitutional. (Courtesy of Plymouth Historical Society.)

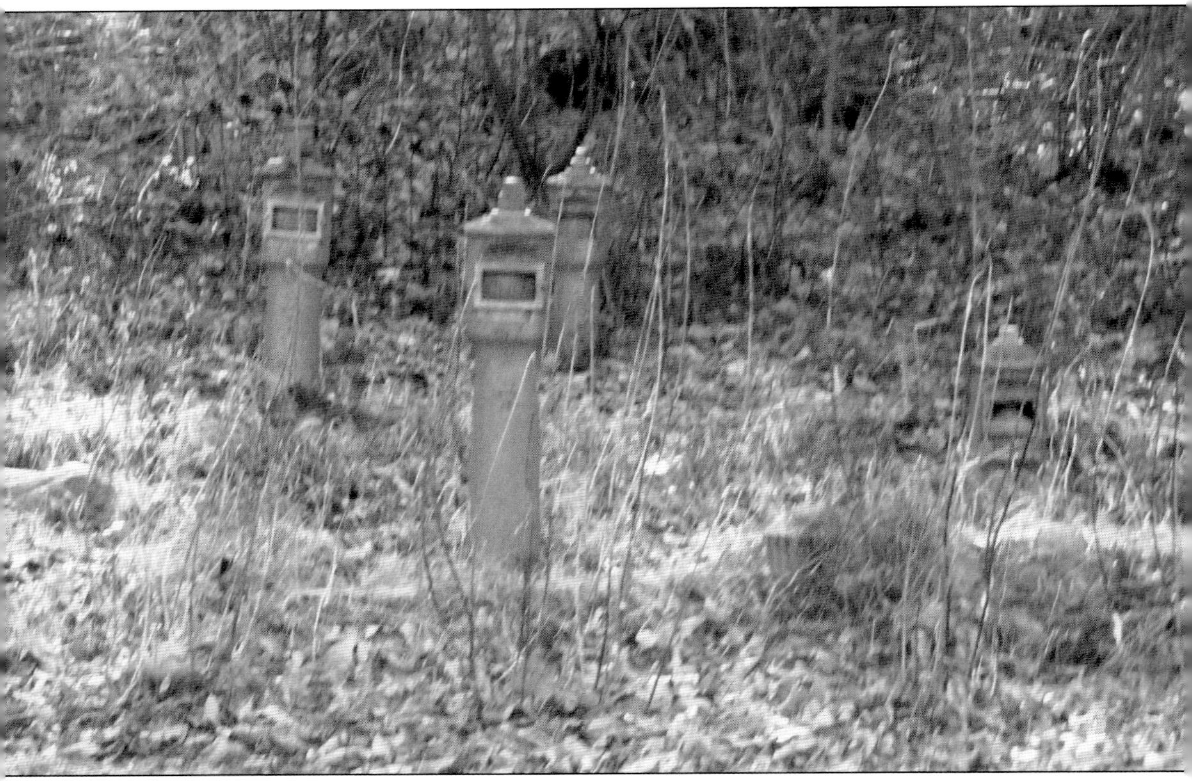

The water valves for the Eagle Lock factory still stand near the now defunct building. Previous to World War II, a group of financiers from Boston gained control of a majority of stock. Their goal was efficiency, placing the tool room on piece work and the mail boy was required to use roller skates on this rounds. They tried to diversify the product line by making soapbox derby car kits, which were also unsuccessful. After World War II, the company was sold to the S.F. Bowser Company, later known as Bowser, Inc. The buildings were sold and leased back to the Eagle Lock Company. Attempts were made to diversify the product line but were unsuccessful. The company, at this time had about 750 workers. Yearly annual sales averaged $4.8 million. In 1959 the company changed again and became the Eagle Lock & Screw Company to reflect additions to the product line. In 1960 the company was sold to Penn-Akron Corporation and by 1964 had only 250 workers. Annual yearly sales declined to $4.5 million. The company continued to decline and closed in 1975. (Photograph by Judy Giguere.)

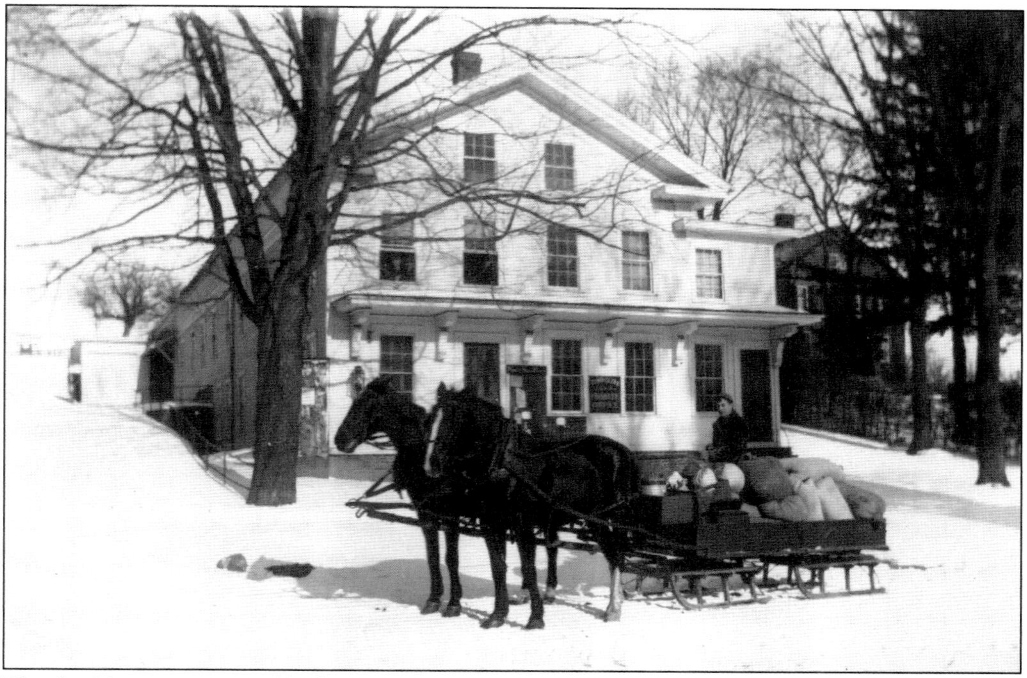

This building was originally the Eagle Lock office, which later became the Plymouth town hall building and firehouse. It was in use until it was replaced in 1974 and then demolished. A new building was built that is now the home of the Lock Museum of America. (Courtesy of Plymouth Historical Society.)

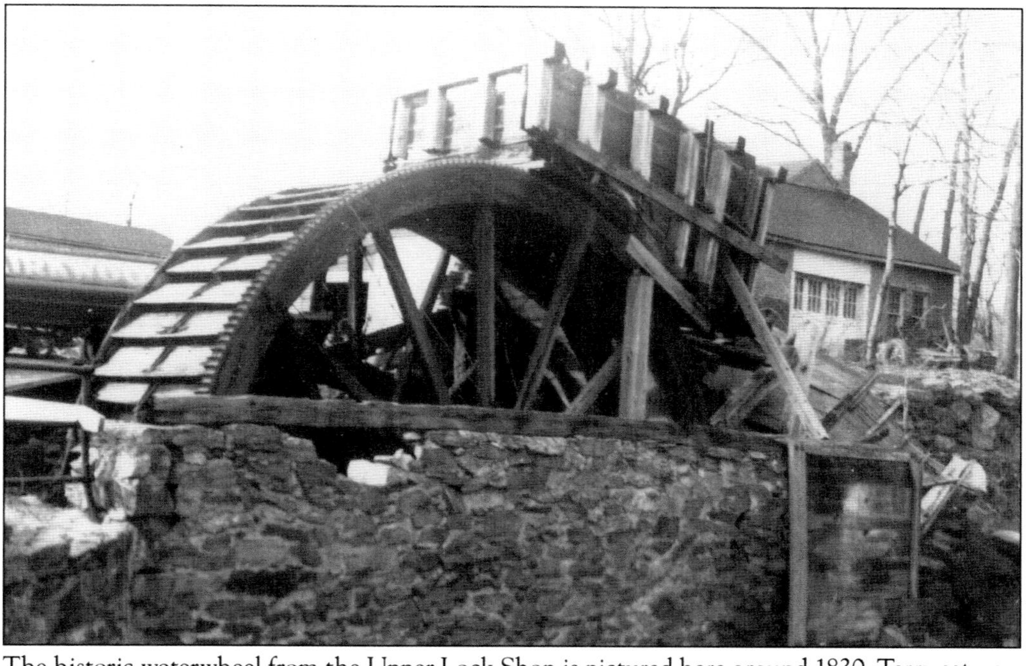

The historic waterwheel from the Upper Lock Shop is pictured here around 1830. Terry set up a clock shop on this site in 1824, using the Pequabuck River for waterpower. The same site was later used in 1851 by the Lewis Lock Company, the precursor to the Eagle Lock Company. (Courtesy of Plymouth Historical Society.)

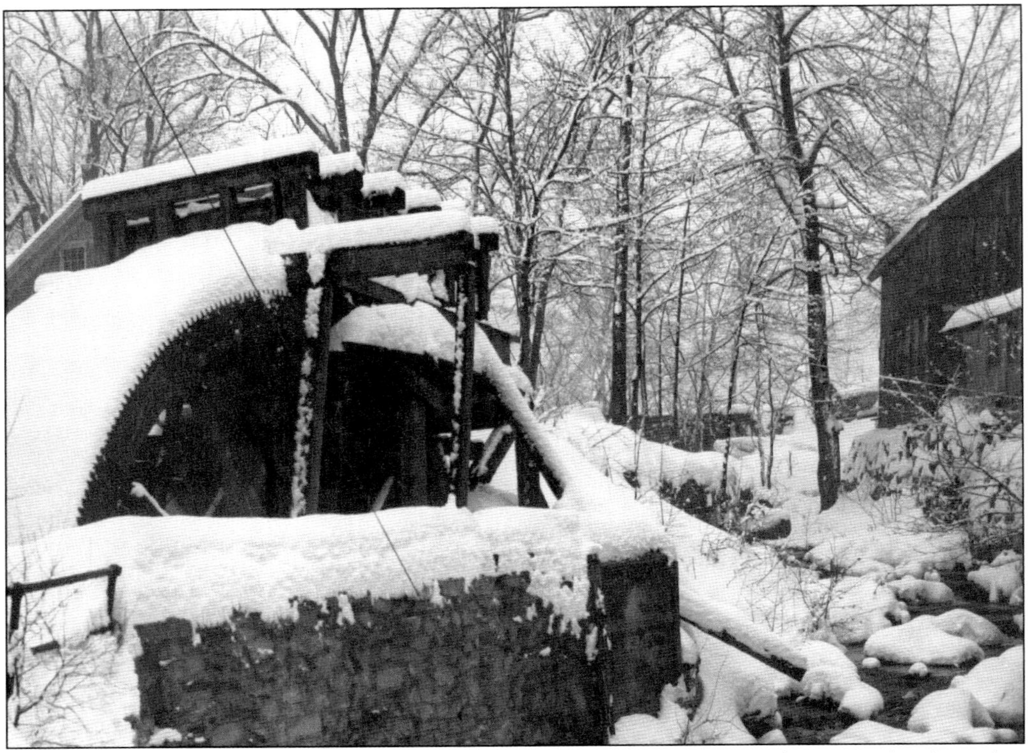

The historic waterwheel is pictured here, covered in snow. It represents the pinnacle of wooden waterwheel technology with a combination of iron and wood workings. The waterwheel has scoop-shaped buckets that quickly fill with water and provide venting so that air is not trapped. (Courtesy of Plymouth Historical Society.)

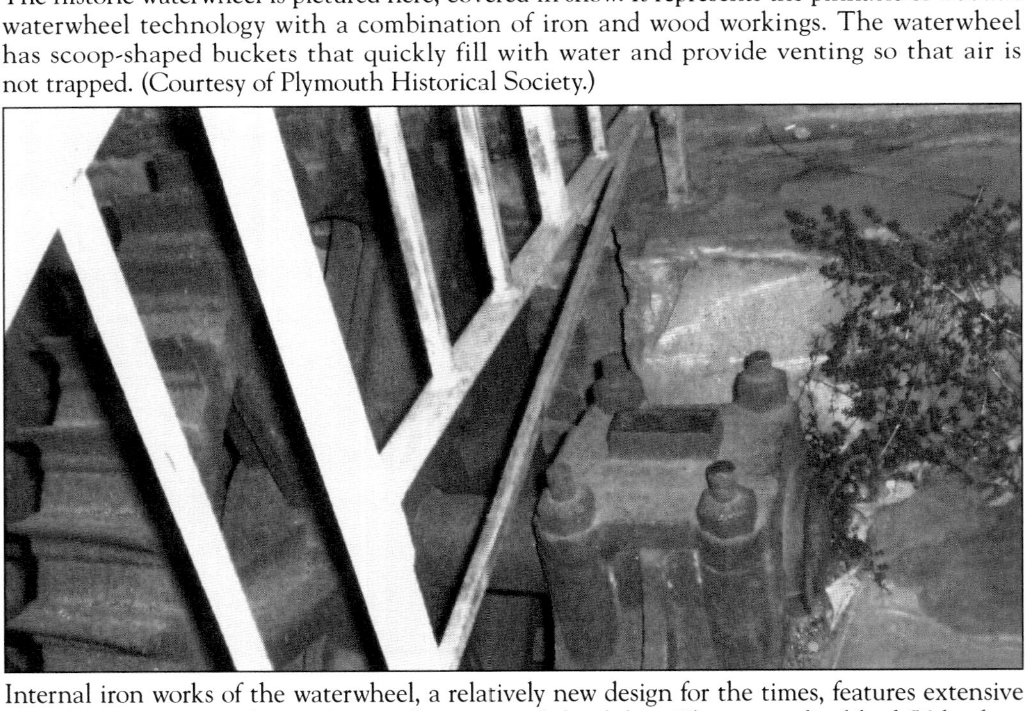

Internal iron works of the waterwheel, a relatively new design for the times, features extensive use of iron. Iron was chosen for its efficiency and durability. The waterwheel had 56 buckets and was capable of generating about eight horsepower from the waters of the Pequabuck River. (Photograph by Judy Giguere.)

The waterwheel is about 20 feet in diameter and 7 feet wide. The spokes, felloes, soling, and flat buckets are made of wood. The wheel was rehabilitated in the early 1990s in order to restore the wooden parts. The wooden flume that brought the water from the dam upstream has been lost to history. (Courtesy of Plymouth Historical Society.)

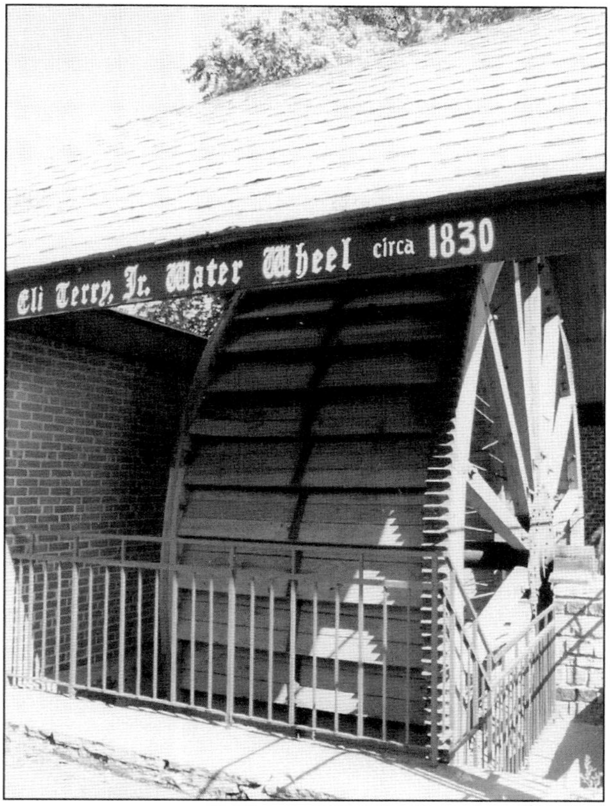

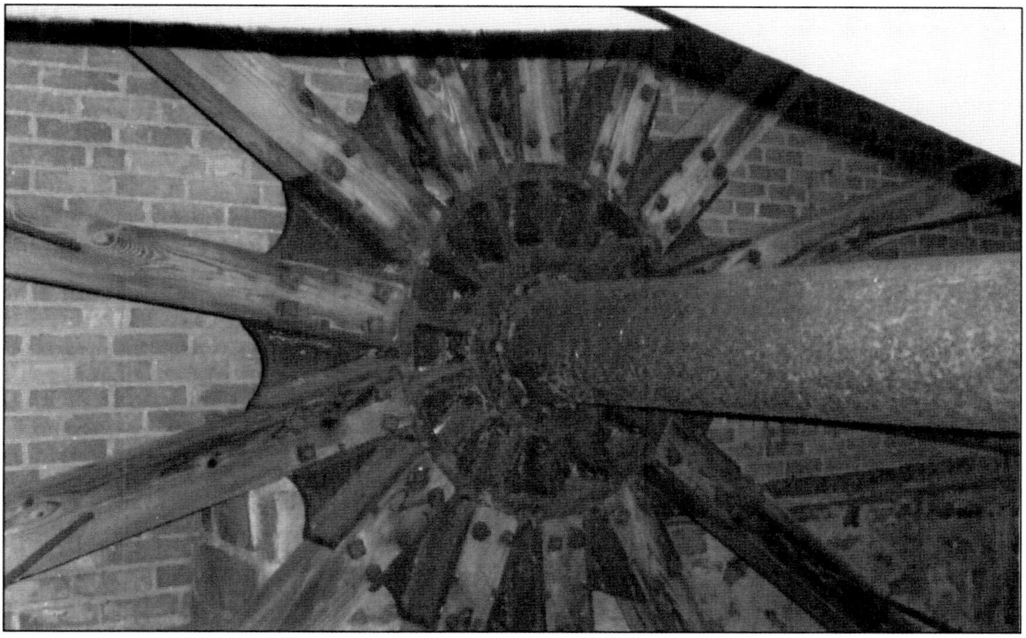

This is the iron gear mechanism of the waterwheel. The ring gear was cast in segments of 20 teeth. It engaged a six-spoked gear with 1.5-by-2-inch teeth called a pinion. The pinion was mounted onto a four-inch shaft supported on cast-iron split bearings with bronze sleeves. (Photograph by Judy Giguere.)

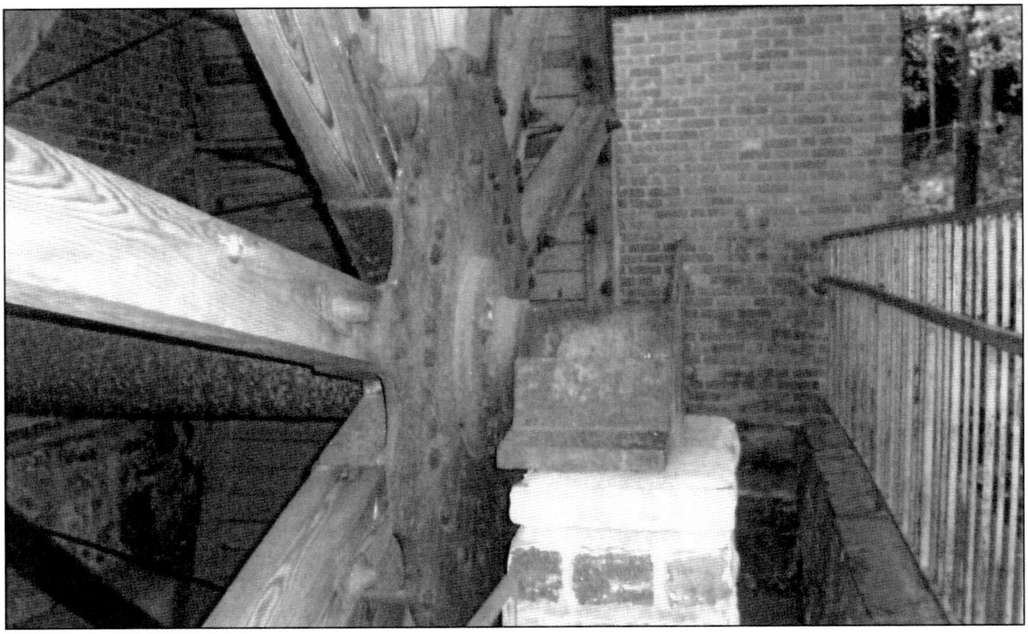

The restoration of the wheel's main bearings for historical purposes required that they be placed on short piers in order to raise the wheel above the water level. The elevation allows the internal iron gear mechanism of the waterwheel to be visible from the front of the site. (Photograph by Judy Giguere.)

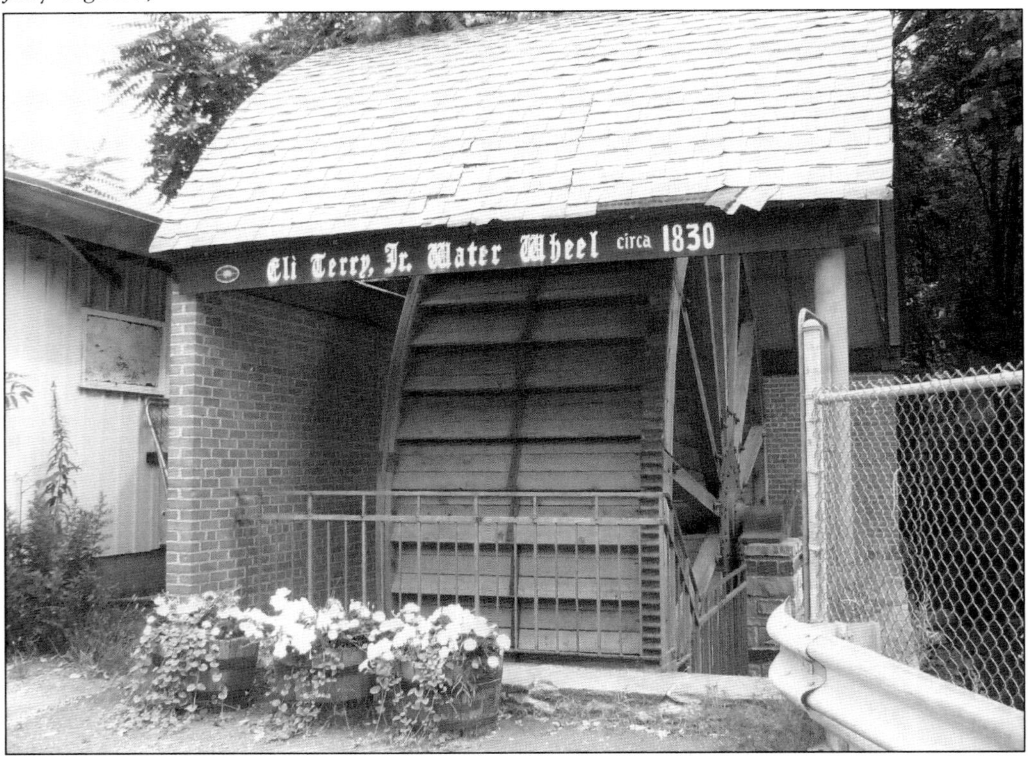

This is a present-day view of the waterwheel that is believed to date from the construction of Eli Terry Jr.'s clock factory that was on this site in 1824. The factory was destroyed by fire in 1851, and it is assumed that the waterwheel was rebuilt. (Courtesy of Plymouth Historical Society.)

Four

A. Terry & Company

The company was formed by Andrew Terry, son of Eli Terry Jr. and grandson of Eli Terry. It was incorporated on February 2, 1860, with Andrew Terry as its first president. Terry, a lieutenant colonel in the 8th Regiment, Connecticut Volunteers in the Civil War, first realized the potential for the malleable iron industry in the United States in 1847.

Ground was broken on November 24, 1847, for the pioneering A. Terry & Company's foundry. Originally, the shop was 40 feet square with one furnace and three small annealing kilns. It grew into a plant covering 1.5 acres, employing 108 men, and producing an output of superior-quality malleable iron casing of nearly two tons daily. It was a new industry to the United States with great demand, and the resourceful Eli Terry gathered the best around him. Often, representatives of the company traveled to Ellis Island to find immigrants with exceptional knowledge of malleable iron production to employ in the factory.

A. Terry & Company grew to melting six tons of iron daily. The furnaces were operated by steam power with water privileges from the Pequabuck River. Horseshoe Falls was built to create a retaining pond as a water source. The stone work is excellent and still remains today.

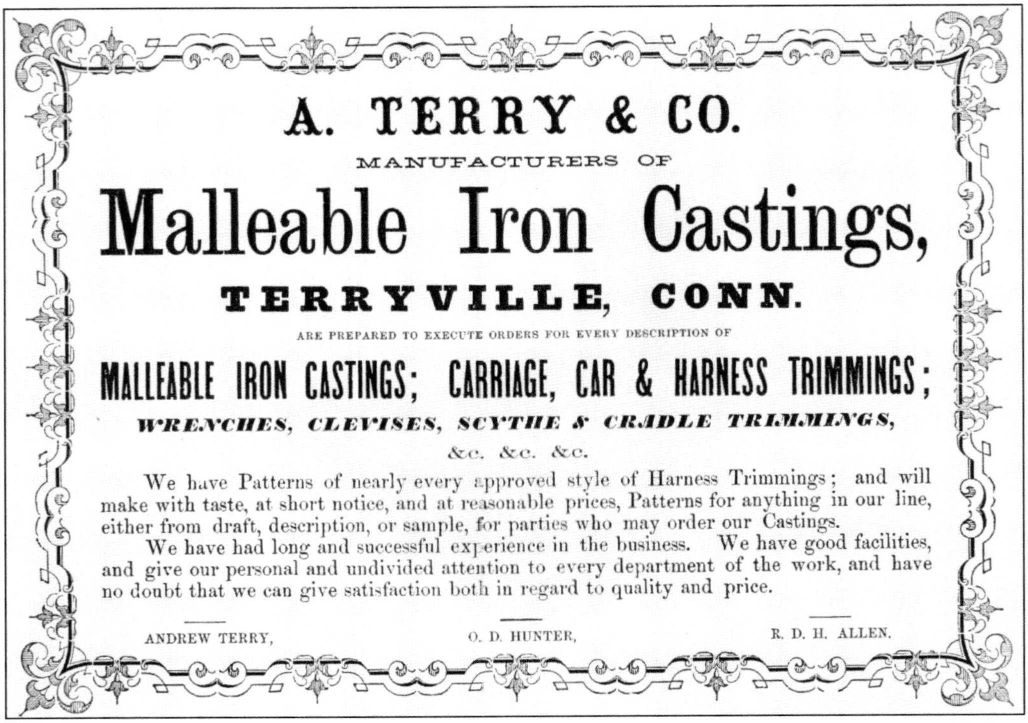
A. TERRY & CO.

MANUFACTURERS OF

Malleable Iron Castings,

TERRYVILLE, CONN.

ARE PREPARED TO EXECUTE ORDERS FOR EVERY DESCRIPTION OF

MALLEABLE IRON CASTINGS; CARRIAGE, CAR & HARNESS TRIMMINGS;

WRENCHES, CLEVISES, SCYTHE & CRADLE TRIMMINGS,

&c. &c. &c.

We have Patterns of nearly every approved style of Harness Trimmings; and will make with taste, at short notice, and at reasonable prices, Patterns for anything in our line, either from draft, description, or sample, for parties who may order our Castings.

We have had long and successful experience in the business. We have good facilities, and give our personal and undivided attention to every department of the work, and have no doubt that we can give satisfaction both in regard to quality and price.

ANDREW TERRY, O. D. HUNTER, R. D. H. ALLEN.

This is an early advertisement for the A. Terry & Company's malleable iron factory. Listed below are three primary individuals in this joint-stock company: Andrew Terry, O.D. Hunter, and R.D.H. Allen. (Courtesy of Plymouth Historical Society.)

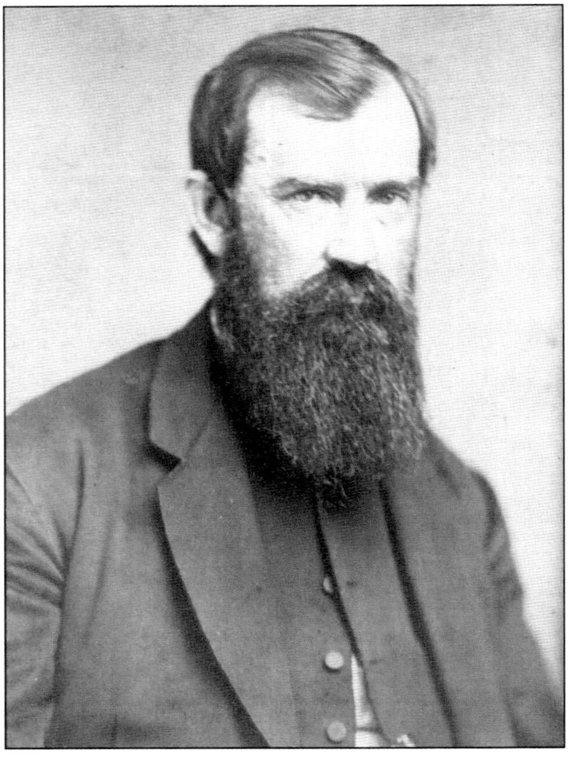

Andrew Terry was born December 29, 1824, the second son of Eli Terry Jr. and Samantha McKee. He attended Deacon Hart's school in Farmington. He married Susan Orr on October 16, 1844. He and Susan had two daughters, Gertrude who died on April 10, 1856, of diphtheria and Margaret who married C.S. Treadway of Bristol. Margaret died in 1880. (Courtesy of Plymouth Historical Society.)

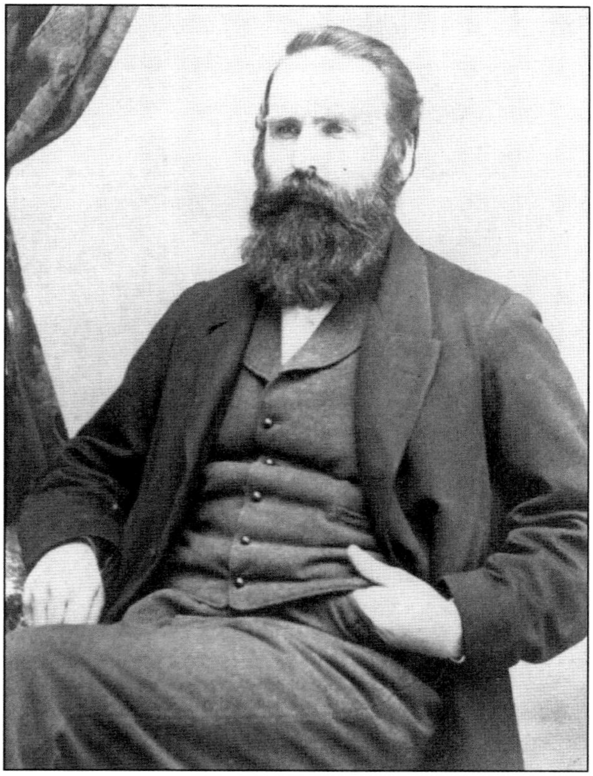

O.D. Hunter (right) was born in Wendall, Massachusetts, and came to Terryville in 1850. He worked for Andrew Terry as a carpenter and joiner, later as an executive in the A. Terry & Company foundry. Hunter constructed many buildings and took an active part in the reconstruction and modernization of the foundry after the devastating 1893 fire. He became president after Andrew Terry left the company in 1871. Mrs. O.D. Hunter was the former Harriet E. Trask of Deerfield, Massachusetts. The couple was married on October 17, 1852, and had one son, Dr. Dwight W. Hunter of New York. (Both images courtesy of Plymouth Historical Society.)

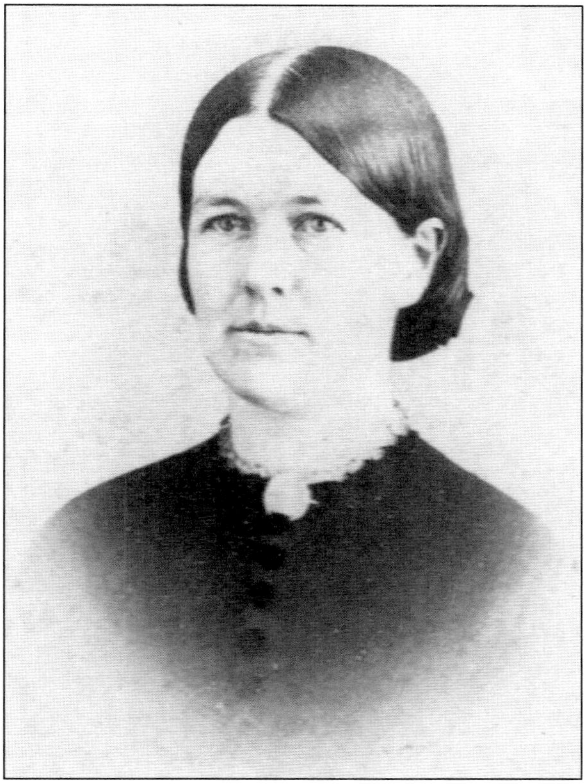

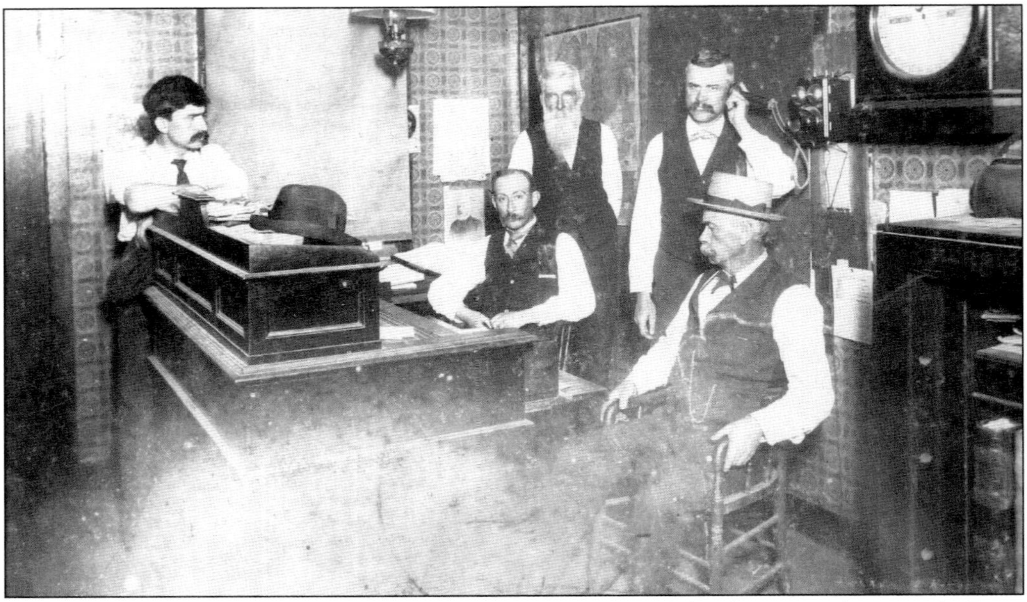

Executive staff in the main office of A. Terry & Co gathered for this 1896 photograph. From left to right are George Clark, Jonathan Starr, George E. Bushnell, Edgar Pond, and Charles Livingston. The molding shop was under the charge of Edgar L. Pond, and Mr. Starr was the assistant secretary and bookkeeper. (Courtesy of Plymouth Historical Society.)

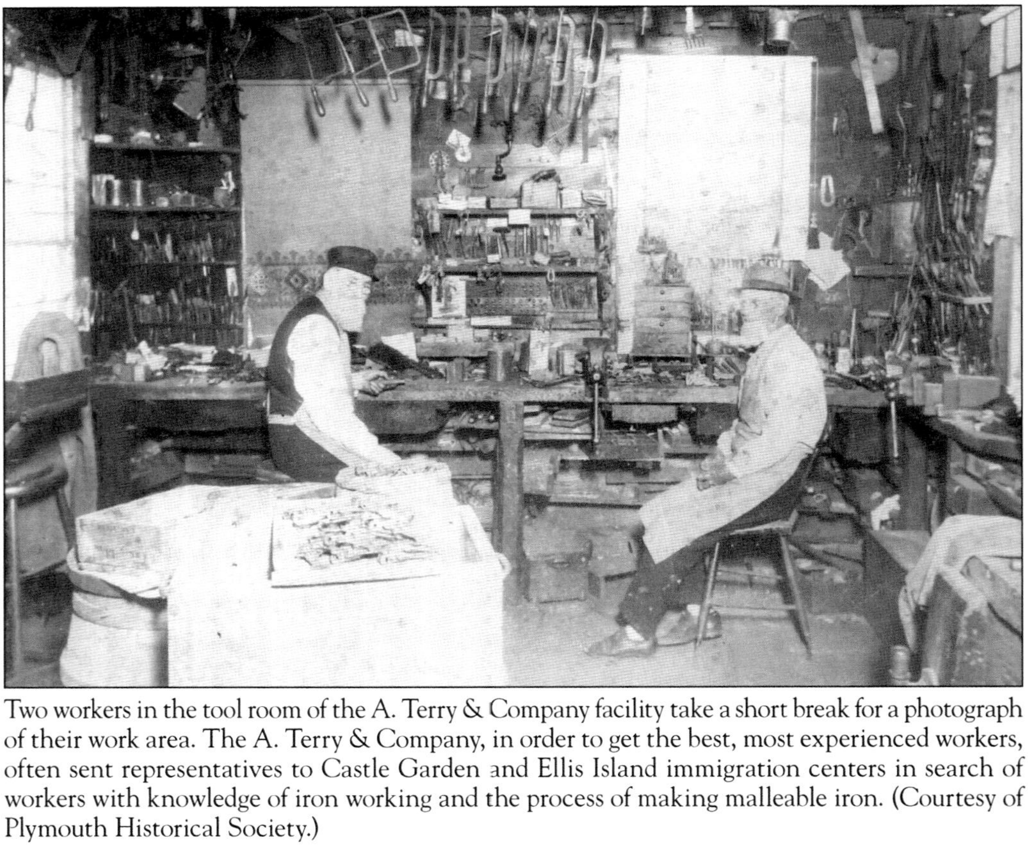

Two workers in the tool room of the A. Terry & Company facility take a short break for a photograph of their work area. The A. Terry & Company, in order to get the best, most experienced workers, often sent representatives to Castle Garden and Ellis Island immigration centers in search of workers with knowledge of iron working and the process of making malleable iron. (Courtesy of Plymouth Historical Society.)

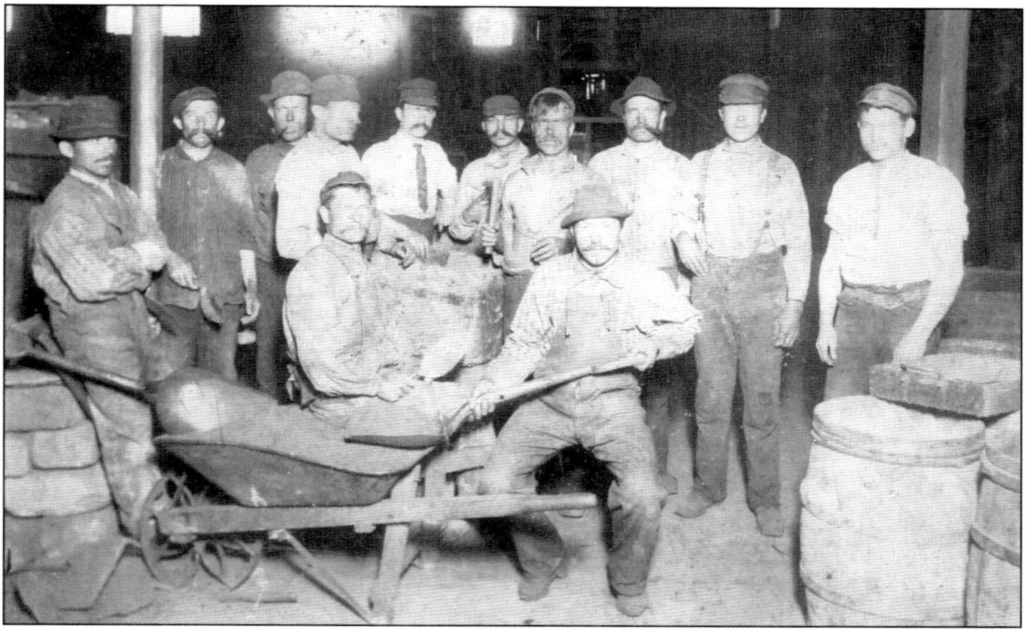

This is a group of workers from the A. Terry & Company. The annealing department was under the supervision of Charles Purrington for more than 25 years. Annealing is the most important function of the process of making malleable iron. Dwight W. Pond, graduate of Sheffield Scientific School at Yale University and son of Edgar Pond, joined the company in 1909 as a trained metallurgist. (Courtesy of Plymouth Historical Society.)

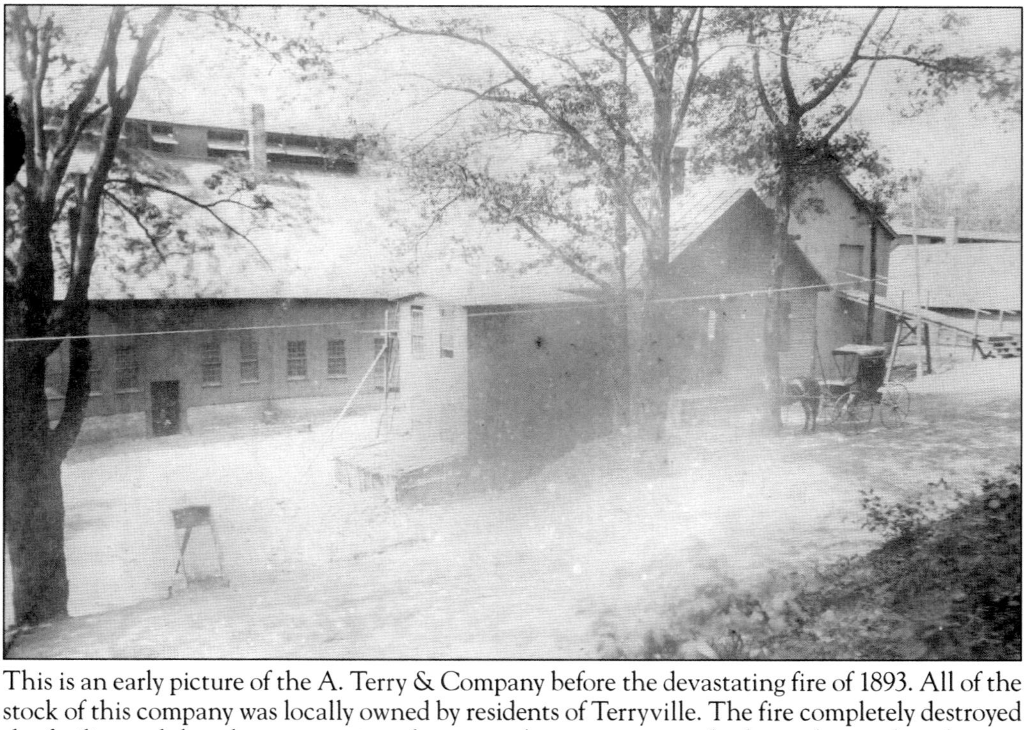

This is an early picture of the A. Terry & Company before the devastating fire of 1893. All of the stock of this company was locally owned by residents of Terryville. The fire completely destroyed the facility and shut down operations for a time, but it was soon rebuilt, modernized, and active again. (Courtesy of Plymouth Historical Society.)

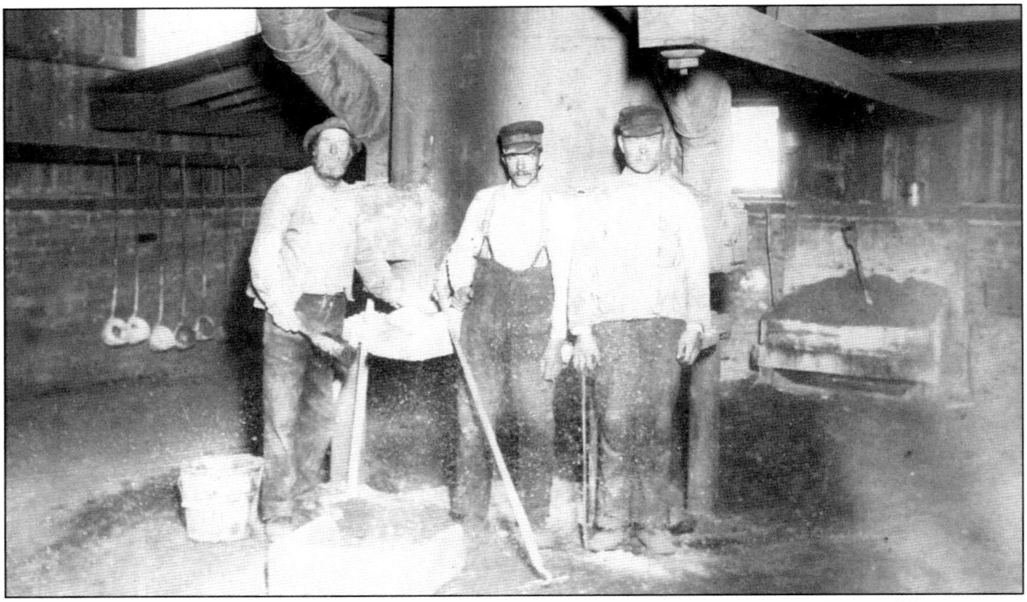

A small group of workers in the A. Terry & Company stand beside the long ladles used for pouring hot molten iron into molds. Six tons of iron was melted daily. Two cupolas were exclusively dedicated to casting annealing pots specifically for use in the factory. (Courtesy of Plymouth Historical Society.)

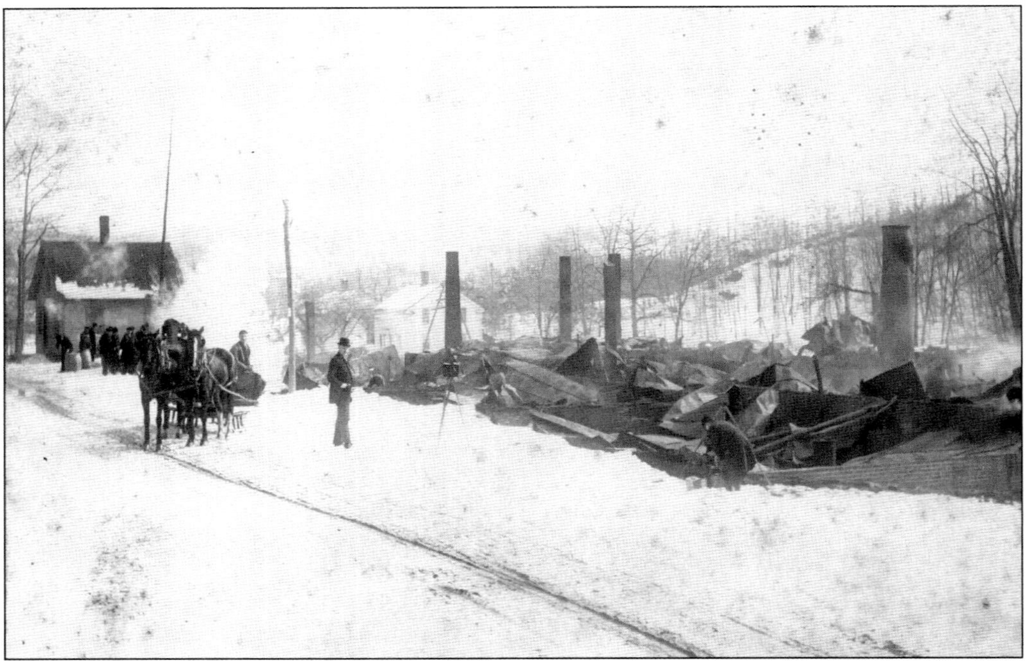

This image shows the extensive damage of the 1893 fire that destroyed the wood structures of the A. Terry & Company. The total devastation of the fire is apparent from the expanse of crumpled, decimated wooden buildings. Several chimneys are all that remain of many structures. Tiny figures clustered on the middle left demonstrate the vastness of the destruction. Very little was left intact. Terryville did not yet have a fire department and was totally unprepared for such a massive fire. (Courtesy of Plymouth Historical Society.)

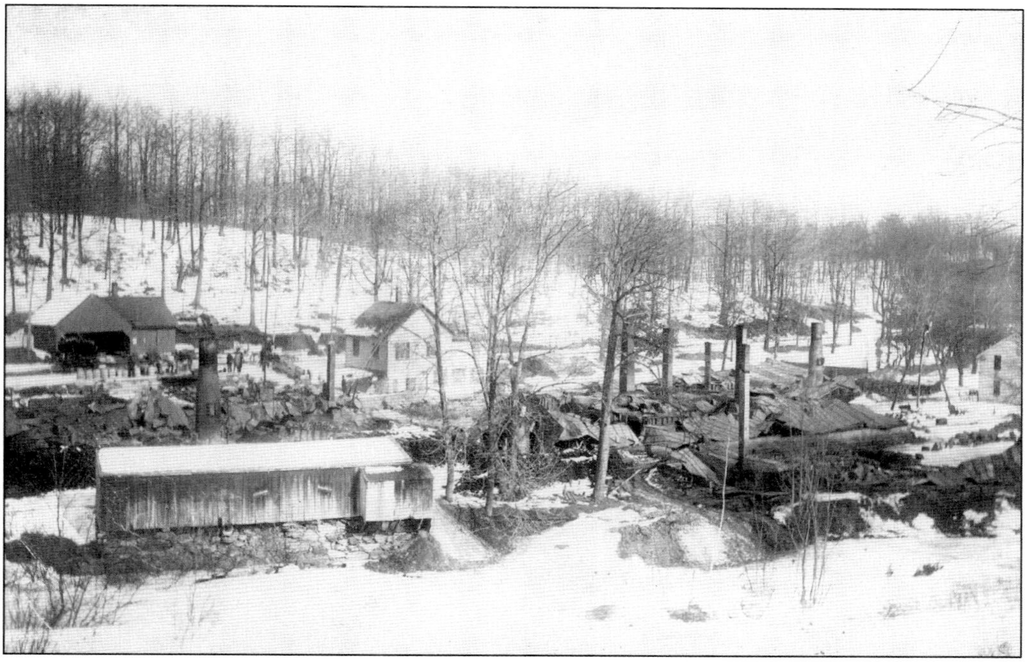

The Pequabuck River flows through the site, and the retaining pond is behind the factory. Without an equipped fire department, however, there was little to stop the conflagration. It was not until 1911 that the Terryville Fire Department was formed and staffed by volunteers. (Courtesy of Plymouth Historical Society.)

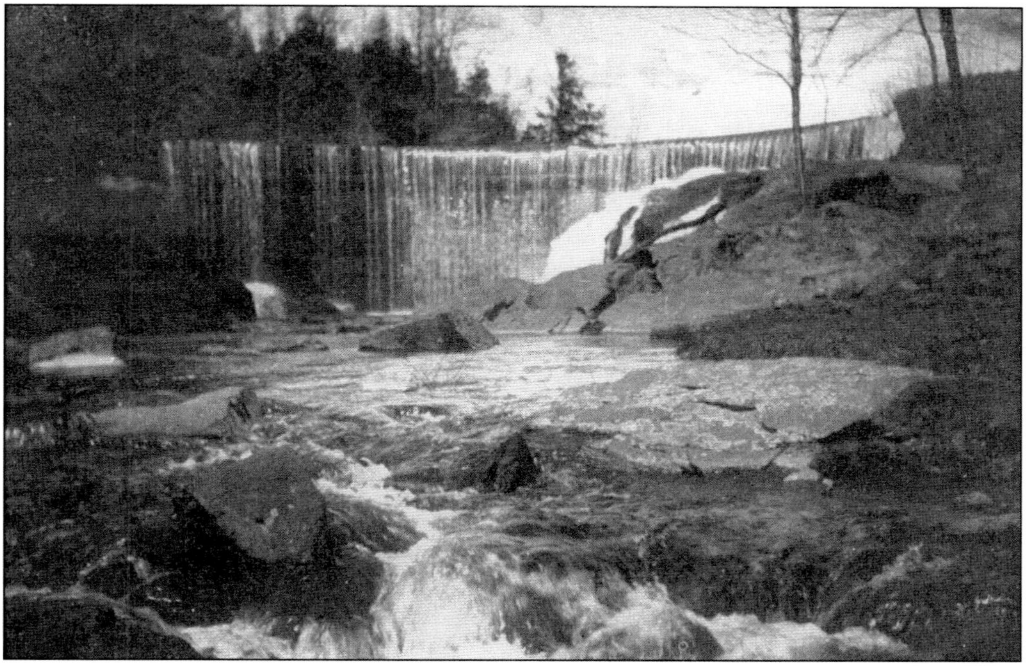

Horseshoe Falls, a fantastic 19th-century, man-made waterfall behind the A. Terry & Company, was built to create a retaining pond for waterpower. The water was needed to generate steam for the furnaces. The newly rebuilt bridge on Canal Street offers a charming view of the pond and waterfall. (Courtesy of Plymouth Historical Society.)

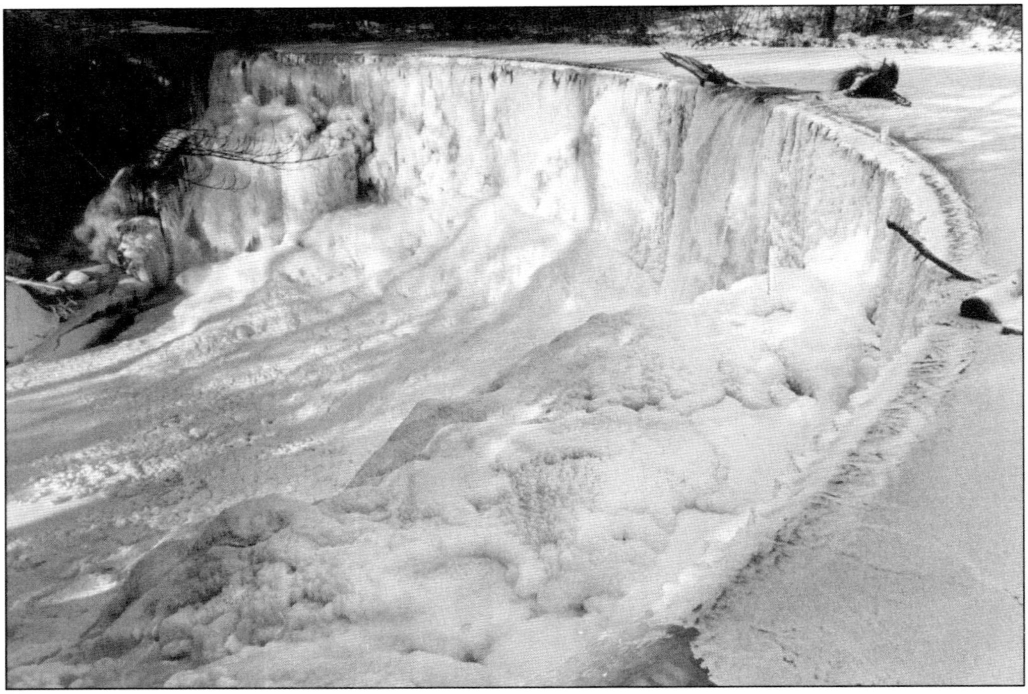

Horseshoe Falls, the man-made waterfall for the A. Terry & Company retaining pond, remains a popular view from Canal Street, even in the worst of winters, with significant ice covering the falls; it still retains its picturesque beauty. The curvature of the falls is evident in this view of the falls. (Courtesy of Plymouth Historical Society.)

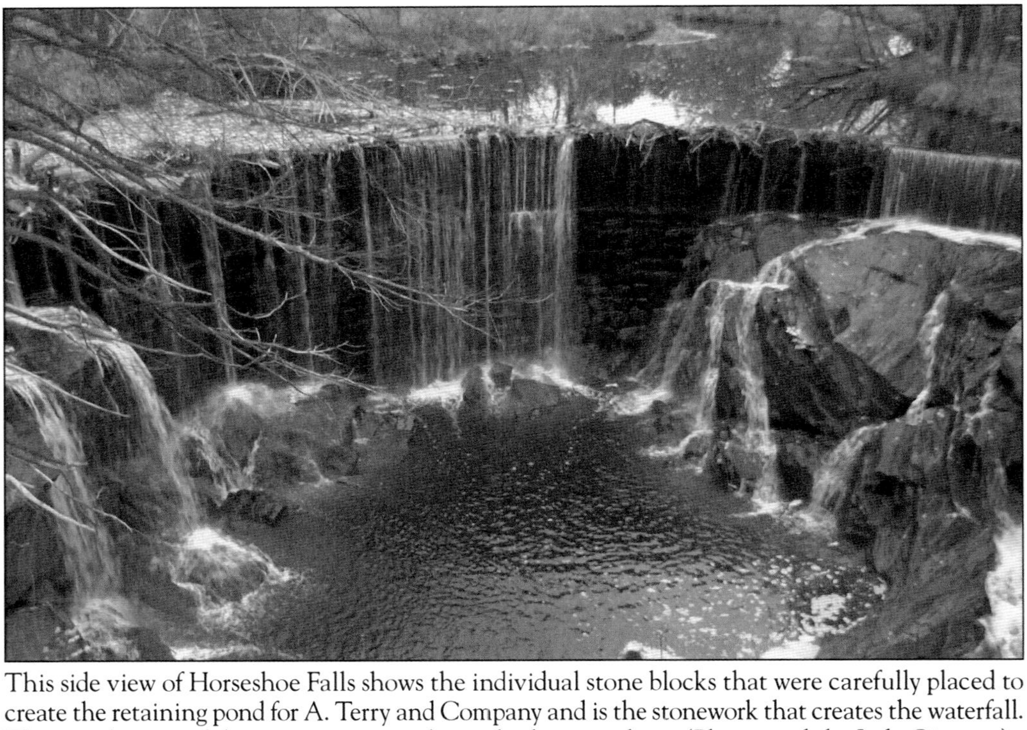

This side view of Horseshoe Falls shows the individual stone blocks that were carefully placed to create the retaining pond for A. Terry and Company and is the stonework that creates the waterfall. The very beauty of the site is very popular with photographers. (Photograph by Judy Giguere.)

Five

Cooper Oven Thermometer Company

In the spring of 1886, David G. Cooper came to Pequabuck to initiate production of the very first oven thermometer. After hearing many complaints about baking difficulties due to the guesswork involved to determine the heat of an oven, the former New Hampshire resident and inventor decided he could make an instrument that would solve the problem. Prior to Cooper's invention, oven thermometers did not exist. He experimented for several months and finally designed the very first bimetal oven thermometer in the United States.

David G. Cooper, born in Exeter, New Hampshire, was a machinist by trade. He worked as an engineer on a sugar plantation in Cuba on the processes of grinding cane into sugar. After nine years in Cuba, he became interested in Chile. The voyage took the vessel around the Cape of Good Hope, stopping to visit the Sandwich Islands. Cooper arrived in Chile with $20 in his wallet. He found work in the silver mines as an assayist, engineer, and superintendent in the smelting works. He spent some time in the South Seas as a pearl fisherman. Using his experience with the properties of metals, Cooper experimented with various conceptual thermometers and often visited neighbors to ask them to test his new inventions. As he got off the train in Pequabuck, he was impressed with the shop of Gleason & Allen, which manufactured hardware specialties and decided to stay here.

Bimetal thermometers measure temperature by the expansion and contraction of two different metal alloys that move the needle on the dial. Cooper gave his first order of 200 oven thermometers to the G.M. Allen Company of Pequabuck. Ingeniously, he rented space alongside the railroad tracks within the G.M. Allen Company. This was the start of D.G. Enterprises, which later became Cooper Thermometer Company. Cooper Oven Thermometers were sold and well liked by consumers, and it was not long before the product became world famous. The design improved, and many large companies bought Cooper's thermometers.

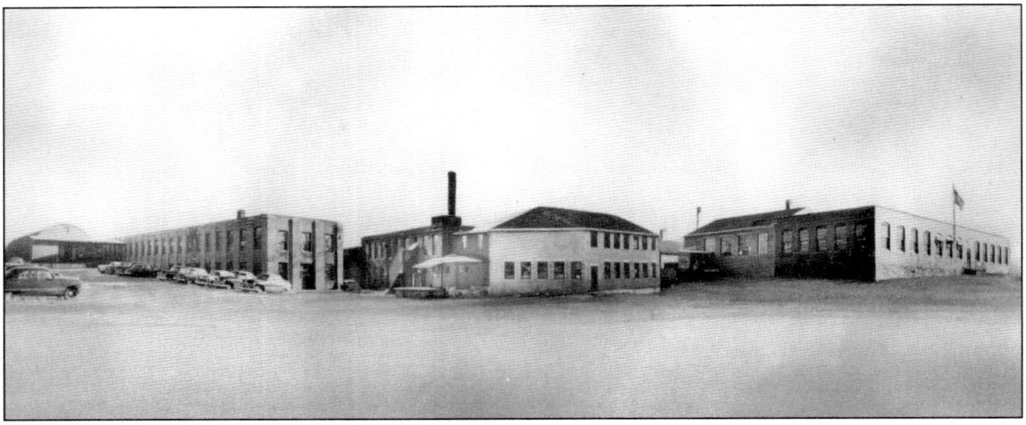

The Cooper Thermometer Company, located on Route 72 in the Pequabuck section of the Plymouth, is pictured here. The picture was taken after World War II, approximately in the late 1940s. The highly successful company evolved into a major manufacturing concern. (Author's collection.)

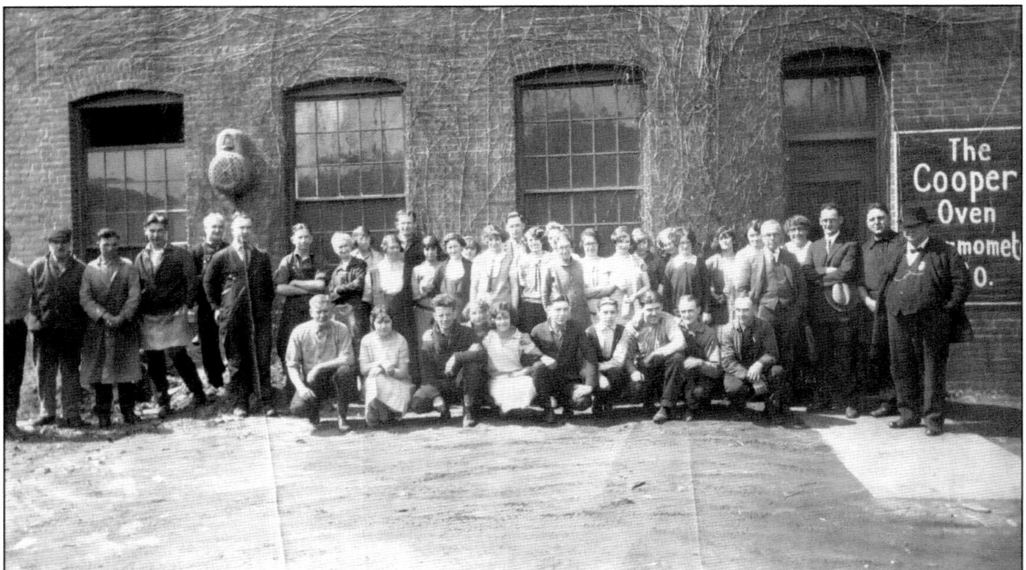

Employees of the Cooper Oven plant pose for a group photograph outside the factory in front of the Cooper Oven Thermometer Co. sign. In 1907, when Cooper died, Albert E. Whittier, superintendent of production, became president. He expanded the thermometer line and purchased additional machinery. (Author's collection.)

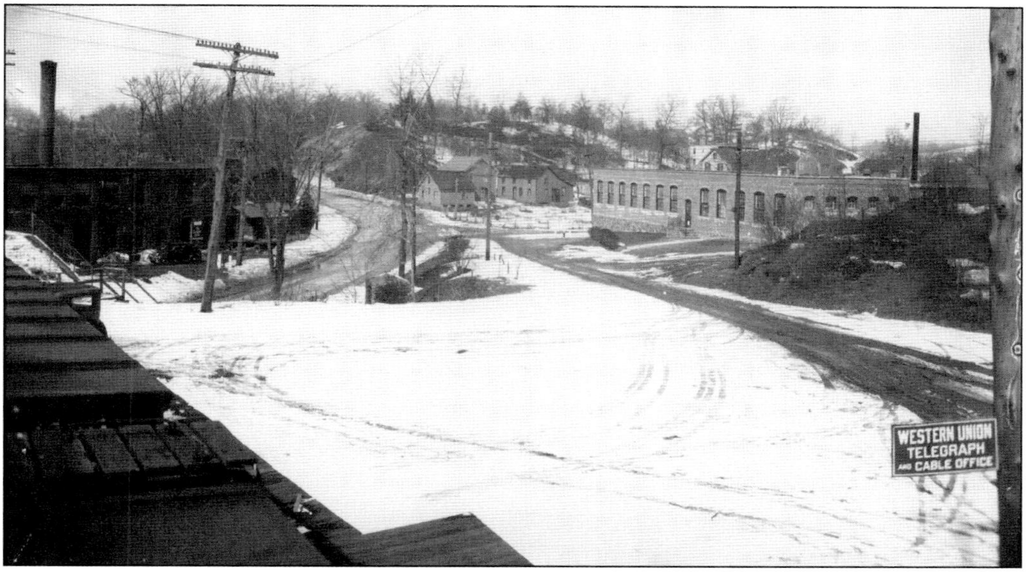

Pictured is a westerly view of the Cooper Oven works from the Pequabuck Train Station with a Western Union Cablegram station sign. This is the intersection of School Street and Route 72 showing Cooper Oven Thermometer on the left and the Western Union Telegraph and Cable Office on the right. (Author's collection.)

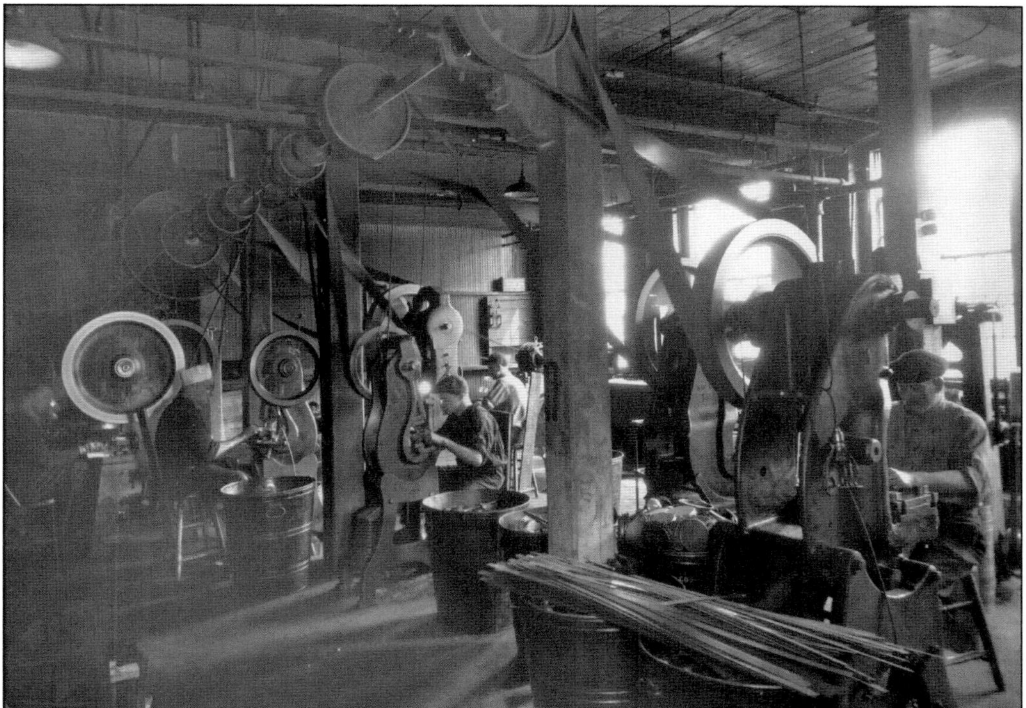

Albert E. Whittier, president of Cooper Thermometer Company, after Mr. Cooper died, increased the quality and variety of machinery used in the production of thermometers. He is also credited with expansion of the thermometer products made by Cooper Thermometer Company. Whittier's son Horace joined the company in 1912 and later also became president. (Author's collection.)

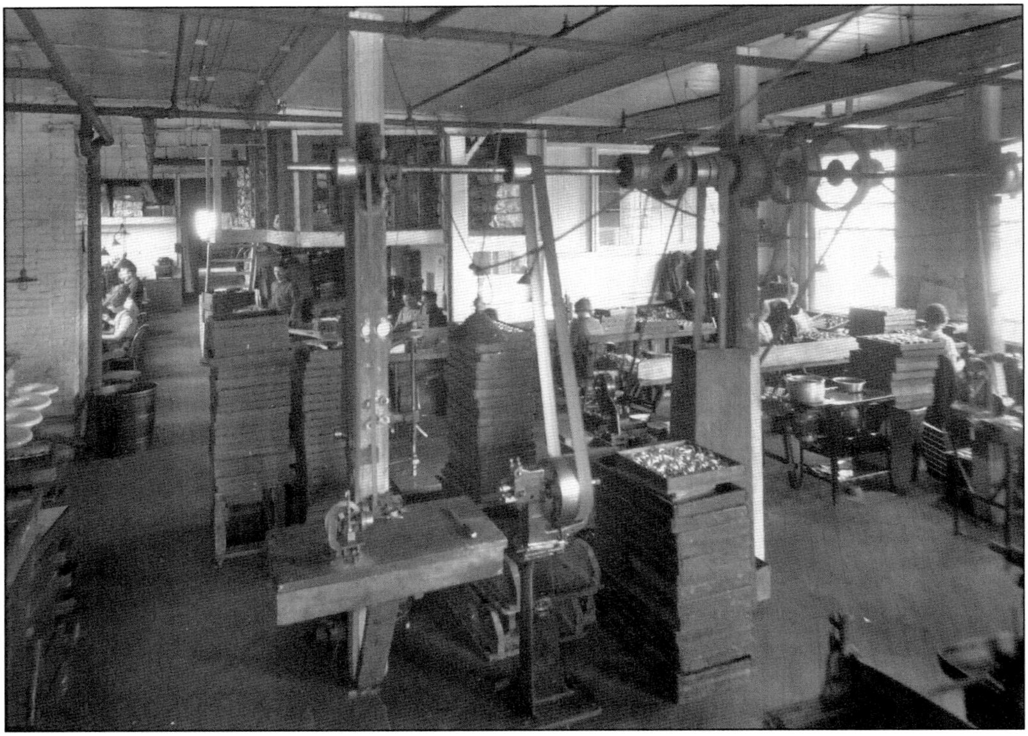

This is an alternate view of the Cooper Thermometer Company interior factory at the intersection of School Street and Route 72. The Pequabuck train station and loading platform served various manufacturing concerns in the town of Plymouth. (Author's collection.)

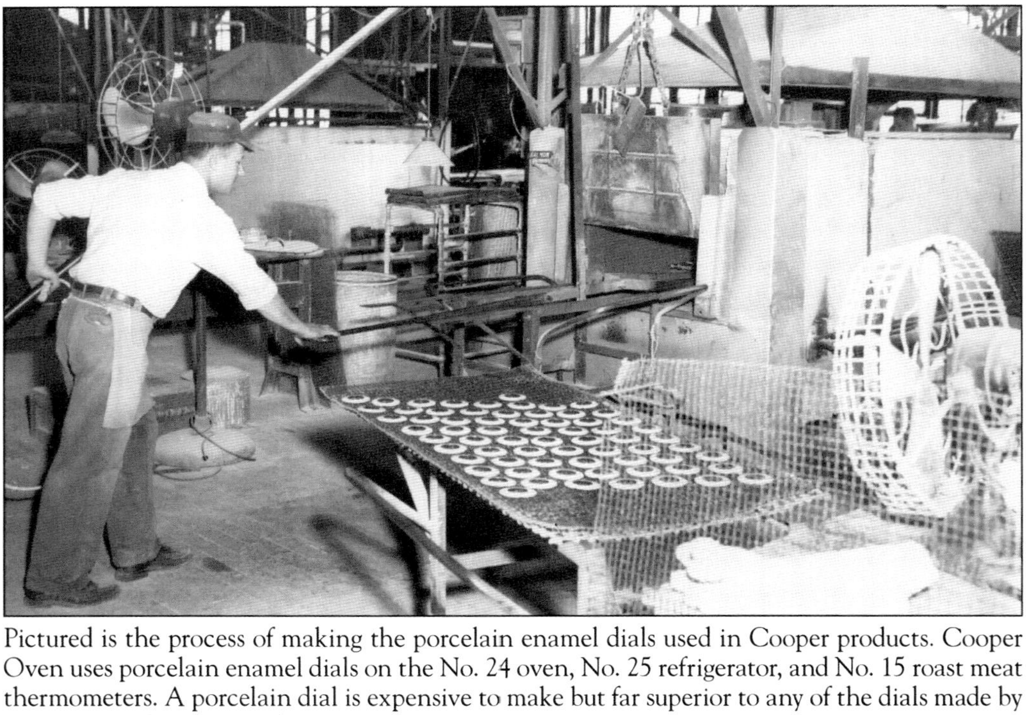

Pictured is the process of making the porcelain enamel dials used in Cooper products. Cooper Oven uses porcelain enamel dials on the No. 24 oven, No. 25 refrigerator, and No. 15 roast meat thermometers. A porcelain dial is expensive to make but far superior to any of the dials made by competitors. (Author's collection.)

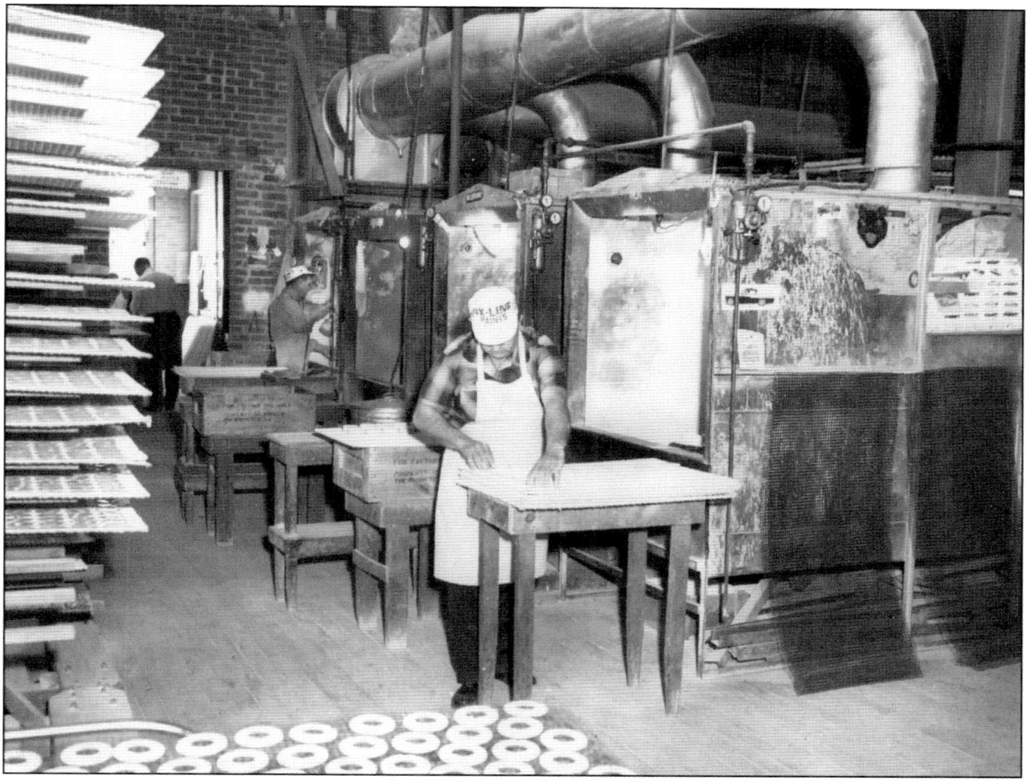

This image shows the operator opening the furnace by a counterbalance level operating a balanced fork to introduce a flange of dials into the furnace. The same arrangement is applied to the other side of the furnace to remove the dials. This is part of the process of making the porcelain enamel dials for oven, refrigerator, and meat thermometers. (Author's collection.)

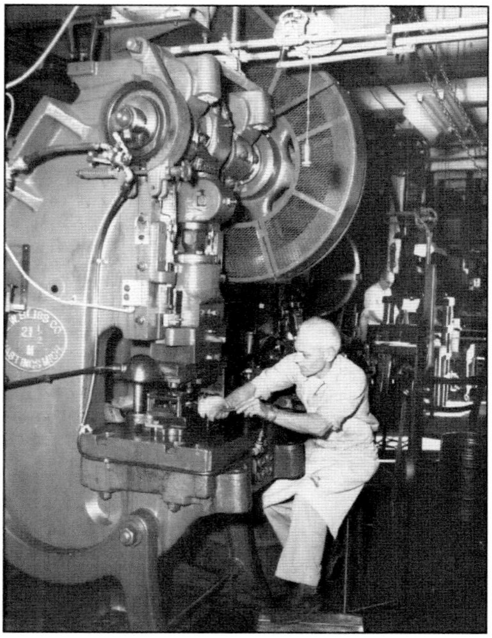

This is a detailed picture of a 21½ Bliss press that is two years old. It is used by Cooper Oven. The company owns several of these presses which can be set up to be interchangeable for use with a variety of tools. (Author's collection.)

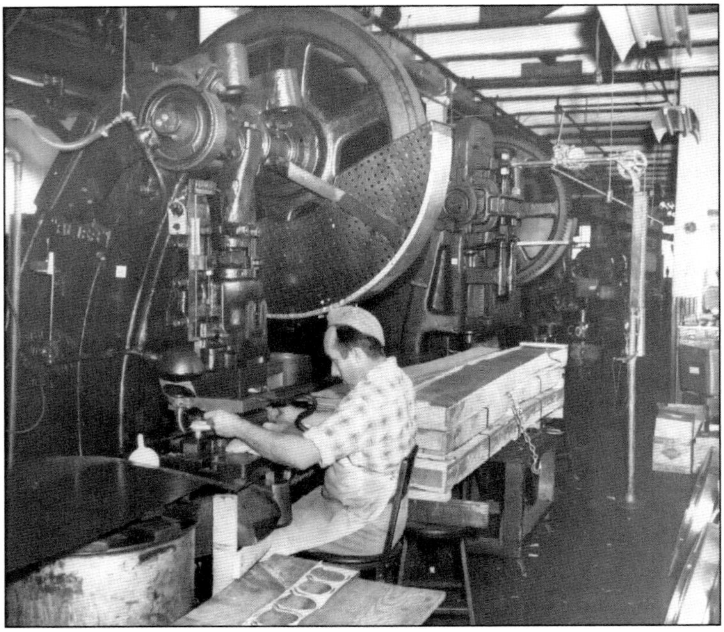

This operator is blanking skillet thermometers on a press of substantial size, which is essential for high-speed production. Both flat and coiled stock is fed into the machine. It is necessary to use heavy equipment for handling these heavy boxes, as the coils weigh hundreds of pounds each and are placed on the automatic electrically operated un-coilers. (Author's collection)

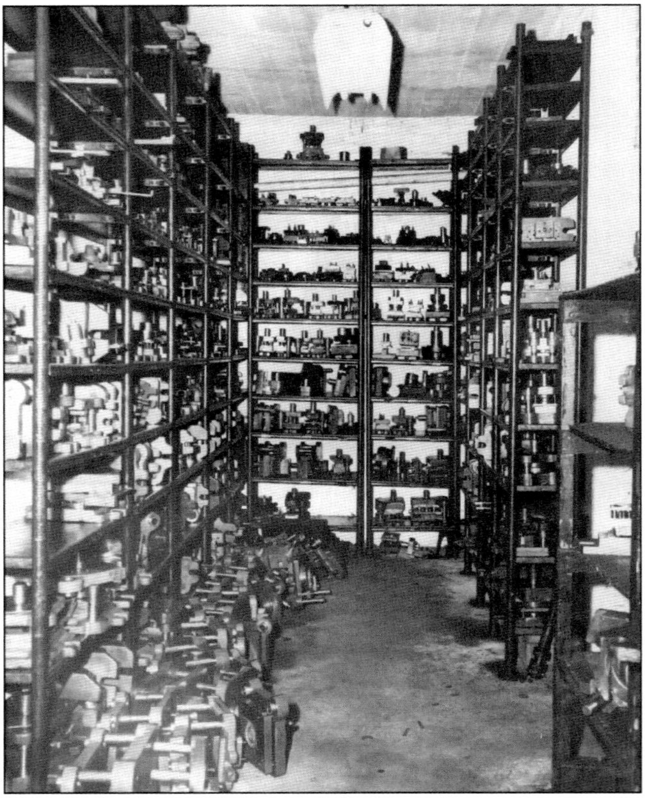

Early in the history of Cooper Thermometer Company, a fire destroyed many tools and dies. The factory rebuilt on the same site and installed a fireproof vault designed to protect tools and dies against such a fire. Many thousands of dollars are tied up in the tools made in this factory. (Author's collection.)

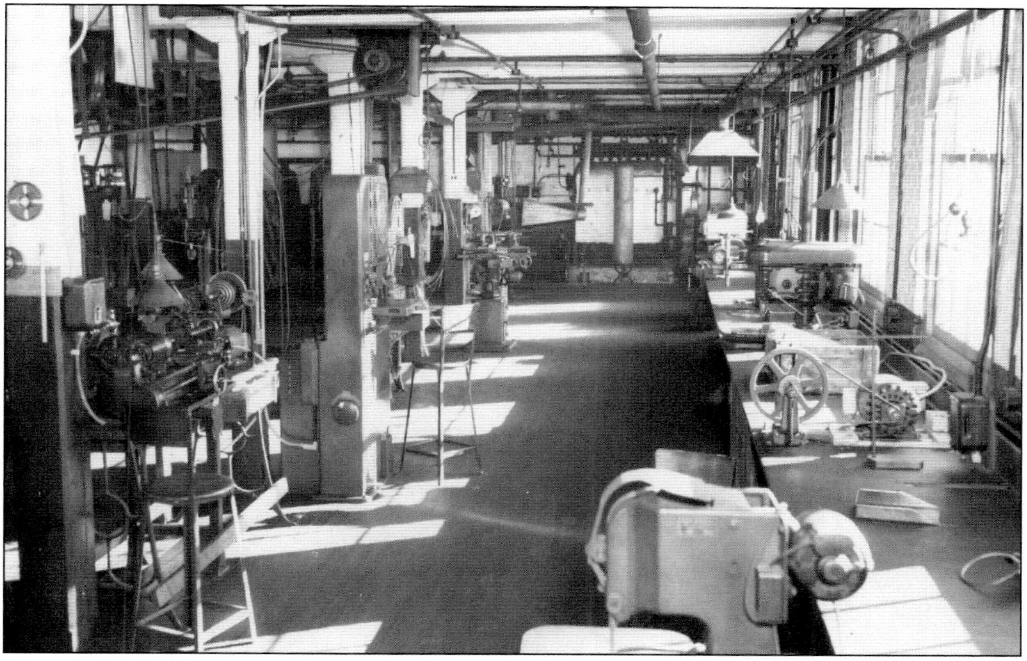

This photograph shows the Tool & Die Department, where all the tools used are custom-made to Cooper's specifications. Tool Room has various machines such as lathes, die machines, drills and filing machines. (Author's collection.)

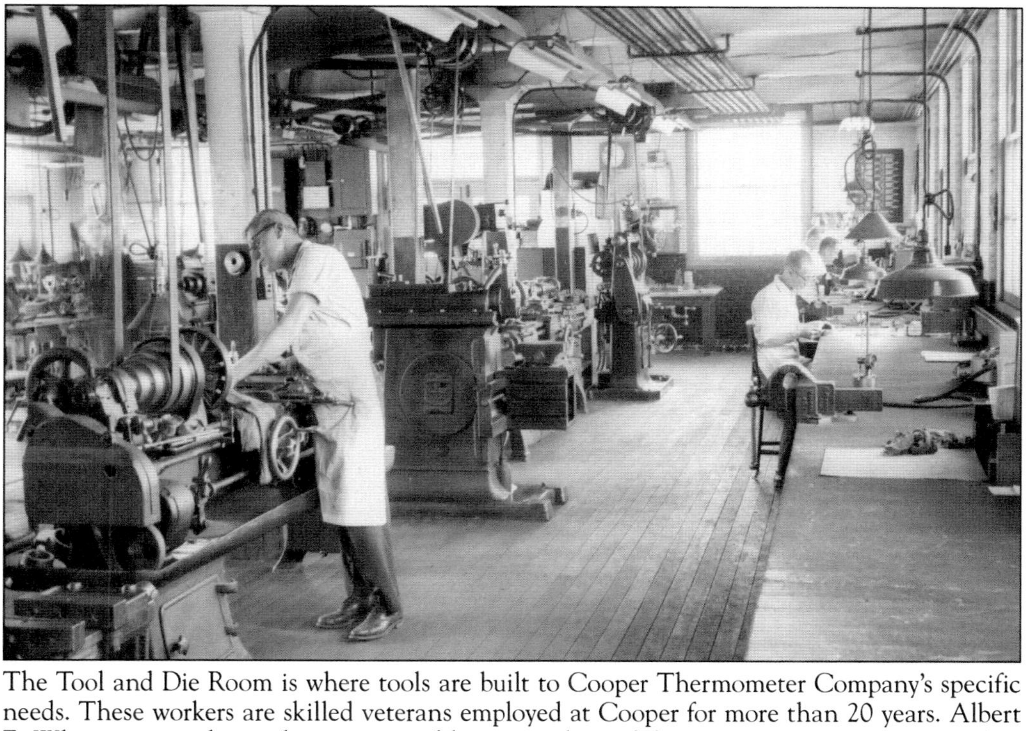

The Tool and Die Room is where tools are built to Cooper Thermometer Company's specific needs. These workers are skilled veterans employed at Cooper for more than 20 years. Albert E. Whittier, a mechanical engineer and later president of the company, was instrumental in making improvements to the factory and encouraging design and research advancements. (Author's collection.)

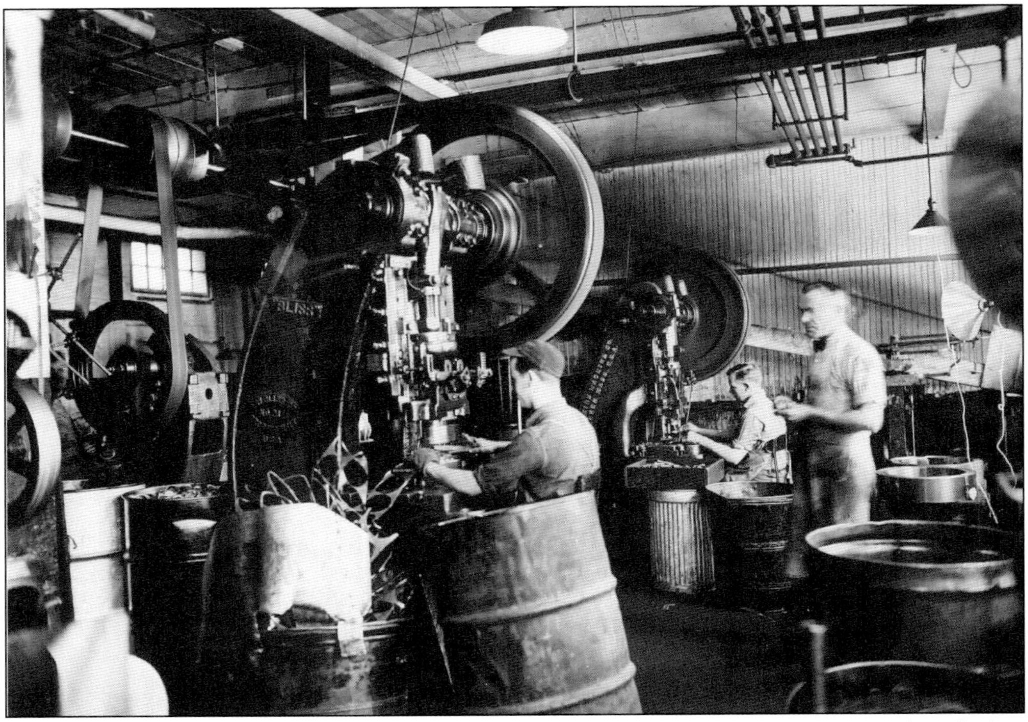

Early designs of oven thermometers were imperfect in looks and function. It was not long before many of the larger stove companies adopted Cooper Thermometers into their best ranges. Later, products designed and fabricated at the Cooper factory evolved into attractive and excellently functioning thermometers. (Author's collection.)

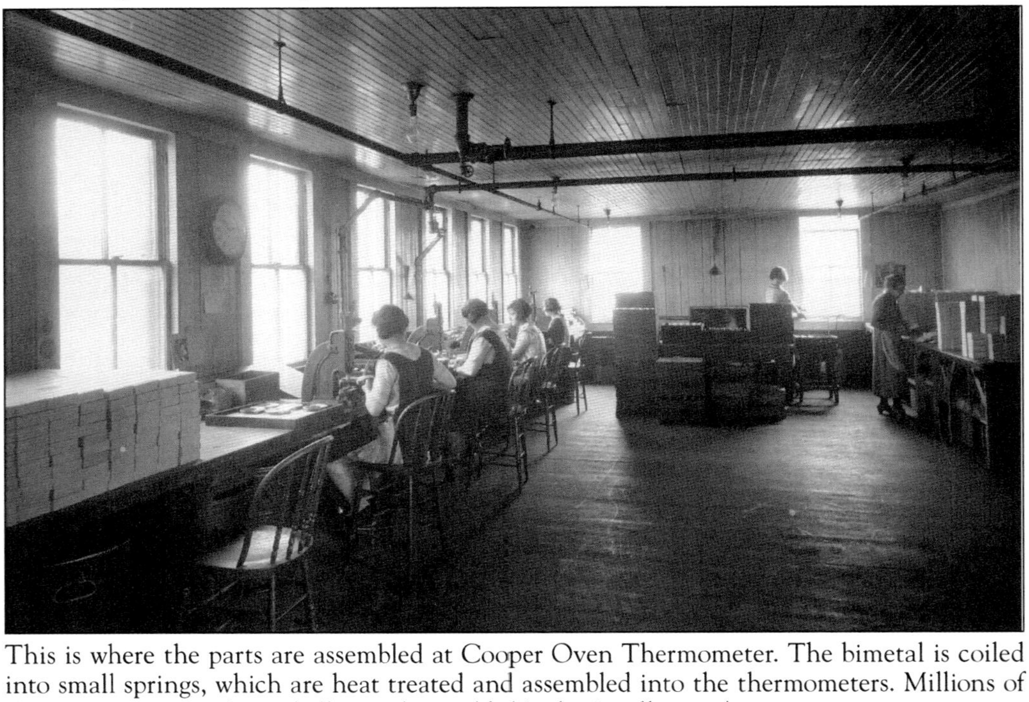

This is where the parts are assembled at Cooper Oven Thermometer. The bimetal is coiled into small springs, which are heat treated and assembled into the thermometers. Millions of thermometers were shipped all over the world. (Author's collection.)

Six

Ives Manufacturing Company

E.R. Ives & Company originated in Plymouth and, by the 1880s, became one of the largest and most important toy manufacturers in the United States, with significant exports to Europe and South America. From 1868 to 1932, the E.R Ives & Company toy makers were the largest manufacturer of toy trains in the United States until 1924, when Lionel Trains took over the market.

At the same time that Eli Terry was initiating his experiments in mass production, Truman and Eunice Ives, Terry's neighbors, often let their sons investigate the fascinating interior of Terry's shop. Riley, the fifth child of Truman and Eunice, was entranced by the factory workings.

Several manufacturing endeavors are credited to the industrious Ives family. William Ives, Riley's brother, operated a successful manufacturing firm. Riley established a production shop in about 1850. The metal stamping unit of the Ives factory produced buttons for Union soldier uniforms. The factory was on North Street at Mattoon Pool, which served as the mill pond.

Manufacturing was the destiny of the Ives family, and several manufacturing concerns were to the family's credit. Products produced were augers, pewter mugs, steel springs, and revolutionary toys. The company produced paper dolls whose limbs moved in response to hot air, but soon began producing a wide range of toys, including a toy cannon that shot using real gunpowder, and clockwork-powered dolls and animals that could move. By the 1880s, Ives was a leading producer of toys.

Ives' trains were made of tin or cast iron and were initially powered by clockwork mechanisms; but, like later electric trains, some models could whistle and smoke. On December 22, 1900, a fire destroyed Ives' main factory and its tooling, prompting a redesign for 1901 that resulted in Ives' first toy train that ran on track. Ives opted to retain clockwork mechanisms, because so many United States homes still lacked electricity.

Financial troubles caused Ives to file for bankruptcy in 1928, and the company was eventually purchased by Lionel and American Flyer Trains.

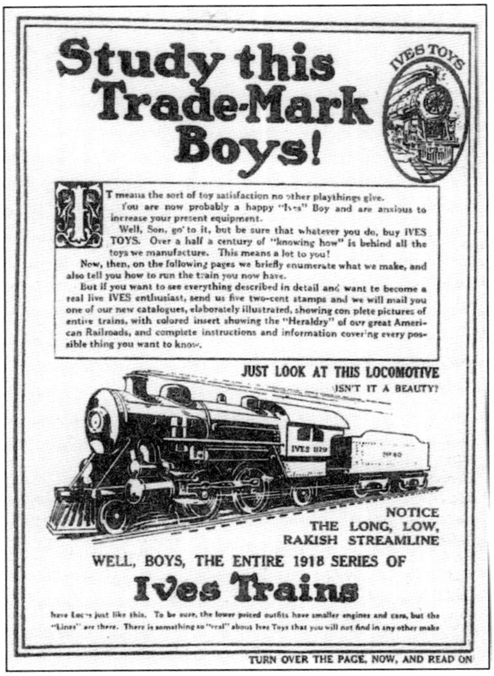

This is a 1918 advertisement for Ives Toys. Ives targeted this market to 12-year-old boys, emphasizing the look of reality in their trains. Advertising addressed the boys as business partners, and the success of the fictional Ives Railway Lines depended on their shrewd business management. (Courtesy of Plymouth Historical Society.)

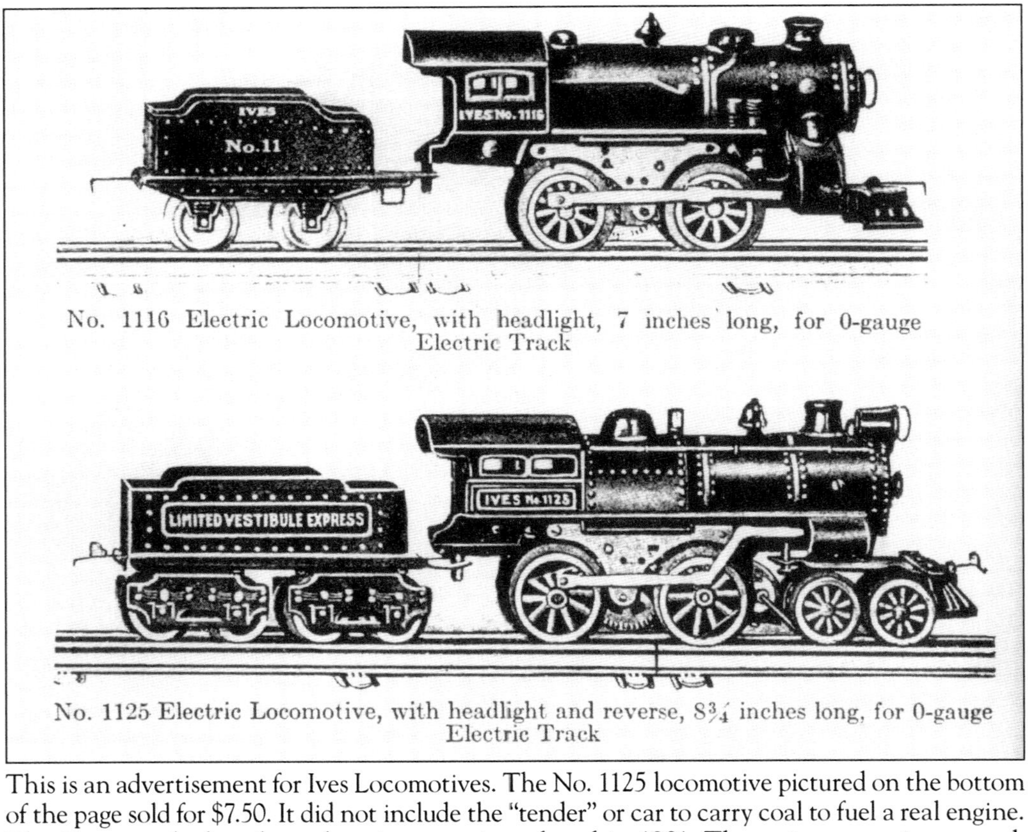

This is an advertisement for Ives Locomotives. The No. 1125 locomotive pictured on the bottom of the page sold for $7.50. It did not include the "tender" or car to carry coal to fuel a real engine. The O-gauge clockwork track trains were introduced in 1901. The train was spring-wound. (Courtesy of Plymouth Historical Society.)

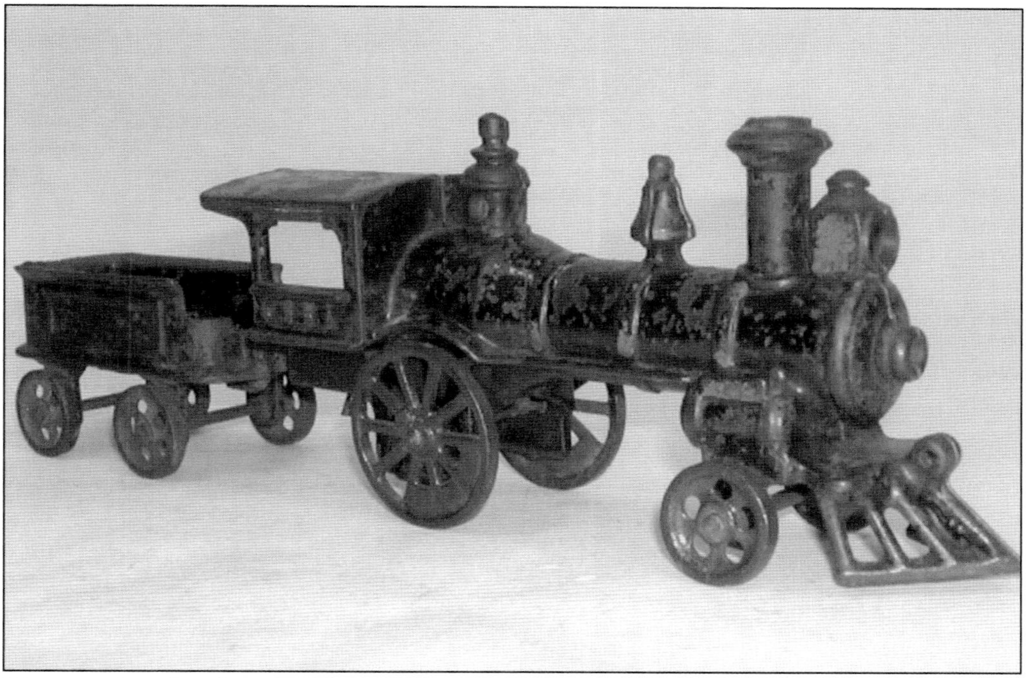

This is an Ives Cast Iron trackless pull locomotive of the 1880s and 1890s. It was very similar in appearance to the tin models. Some models were supplied with a removable brakeman in the gondola car. Ives Company advertised that their railroad system was unhampered by the Interstate Commerce Commission and was immune to freight rate regulation. (Courtesy of Dave McEntarfer, historian, Ives Train Society.)

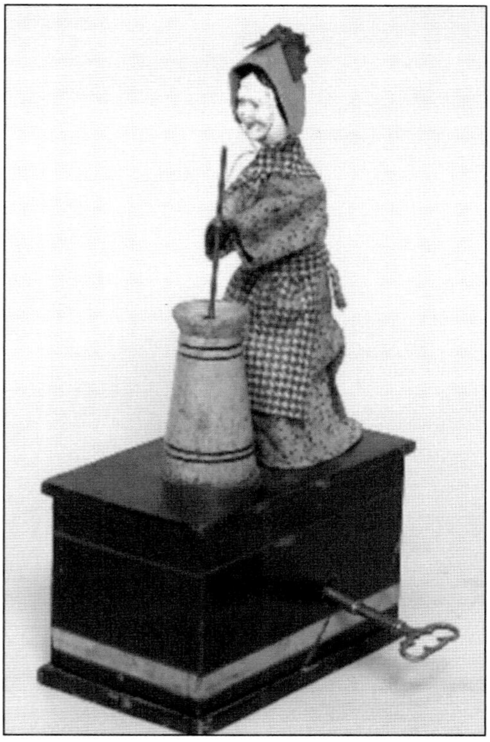

The Ives Butter Churner toy works by a key to wind a movement similar to the one used by clock makers to turn the hands of clocks. The clockwork movement is contained in the base and animated the figure by a series of rods or wires. The tiny clothing for figures was handmade at an Ives facility in Bridgeport. (Courtesy of Dave McEntarfer, historian, Ives Train Society.)

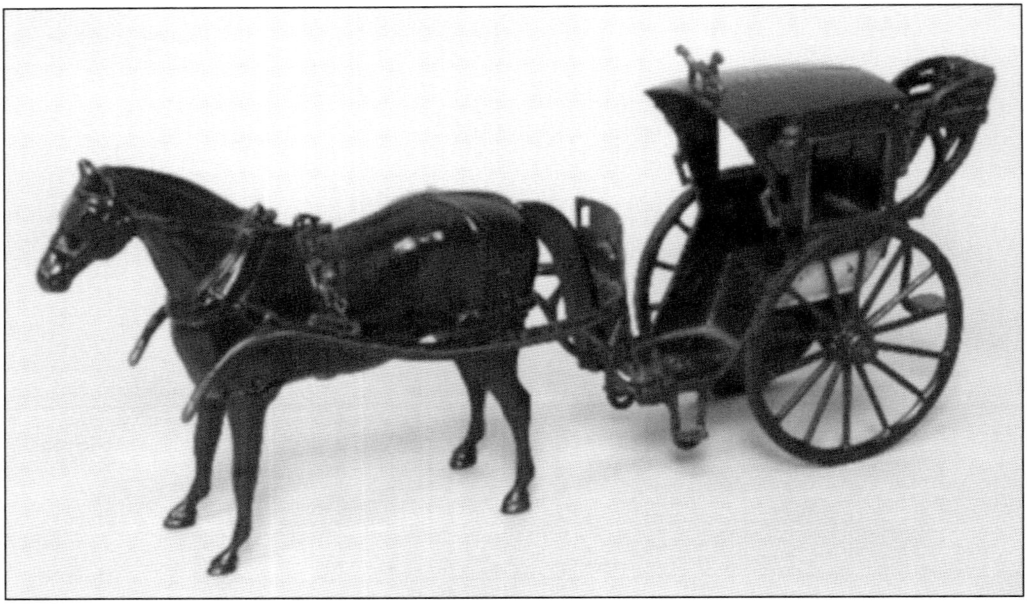

This is a picture of a stunningly detailed cast-iron hansom carriage toy made by Ives Toys. It is complete with footholds, hand grips at the sides to facilitate entry, a realistic harness for the horse, and lanterns. (Courtesy of Dave McEntarfer, historian, Ives Train Society.)

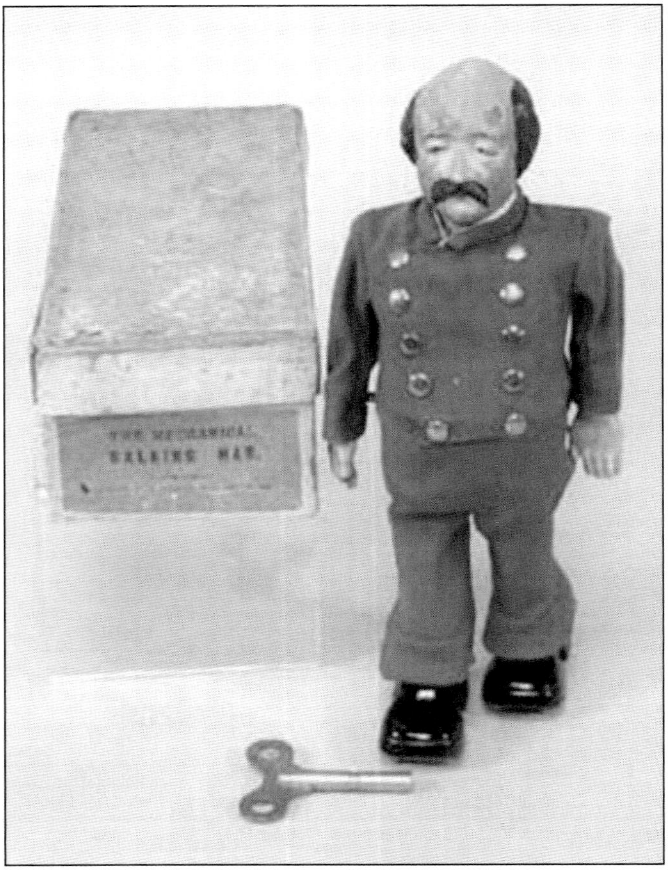

Using a series of wires and rods, a clockwork winding mechanism allows this well-dressed figure to walk. (Courtesy of Dave McEntarfer, historian, Ives Train Society.)

Seven

The Pequabuck Railway Tunnel

The Pequabuck railway tunnel was a monumental project in the history of Plymouth. It was needed for transport of the raw materials and products of manufacturers in Plymouth. Construction of the Pequabuck tunnel began on February 21, 1907, for a long cement railway tunnel of 3,850 feet, with a width of 32 feet and height of 26 feet in Pequabuck. It took three years to complete. The financial panic of 1908 temporarily halted work after only 300 feet of construction had been completed. Water leakages created soft areas that endangered workers as they dug the tunnel by hand. Leakages of water delayed construction as well as in the midst of hard mica, laborers hit a large drift of soft sand. Approximately 700 men worked day and night to tunnel under Sylvan Hill off Allen Street. The tunnel passes under pastureland, woods, and a pond.

The tunnel allowed for a double track for two trains to pass. Several treacherous curves were corrected, and a steep grade was modified. Previously, the grade and the curves so complicated travel that frequently two engines were required to pull the load through this section of Pequabuck.

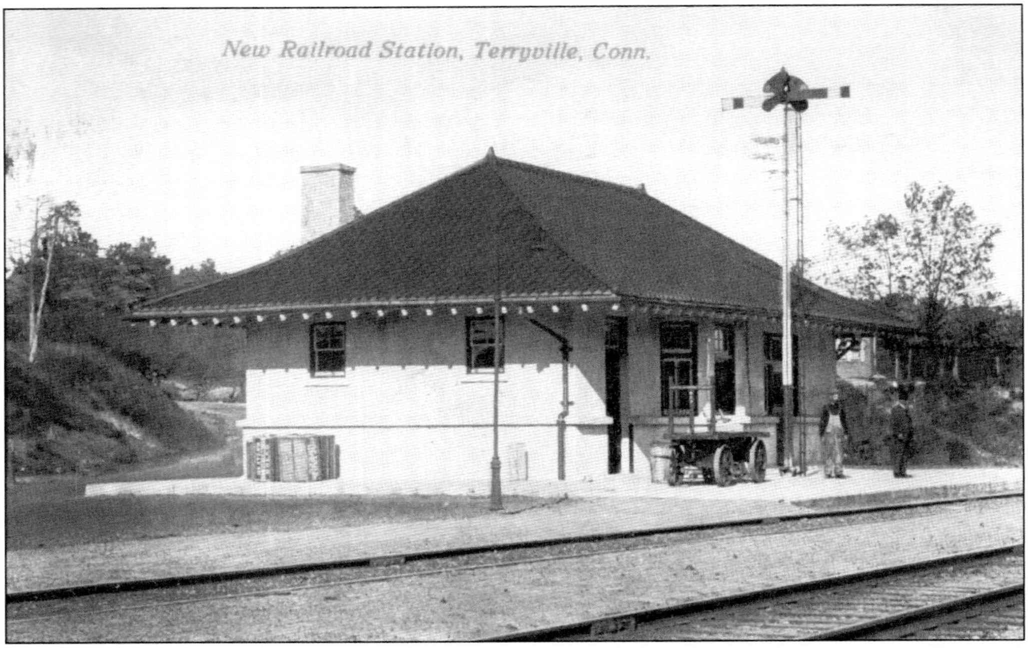

The new Terryville Train station, pictured here, replaced the former station in its new location above the Route 72 train trestle. Upon completion of the Pequabuck Tunnel, this new train station opened. It provided for the increased freight and passenger traffic using the train system. (Courtesy of Plymouth Historical Society.)

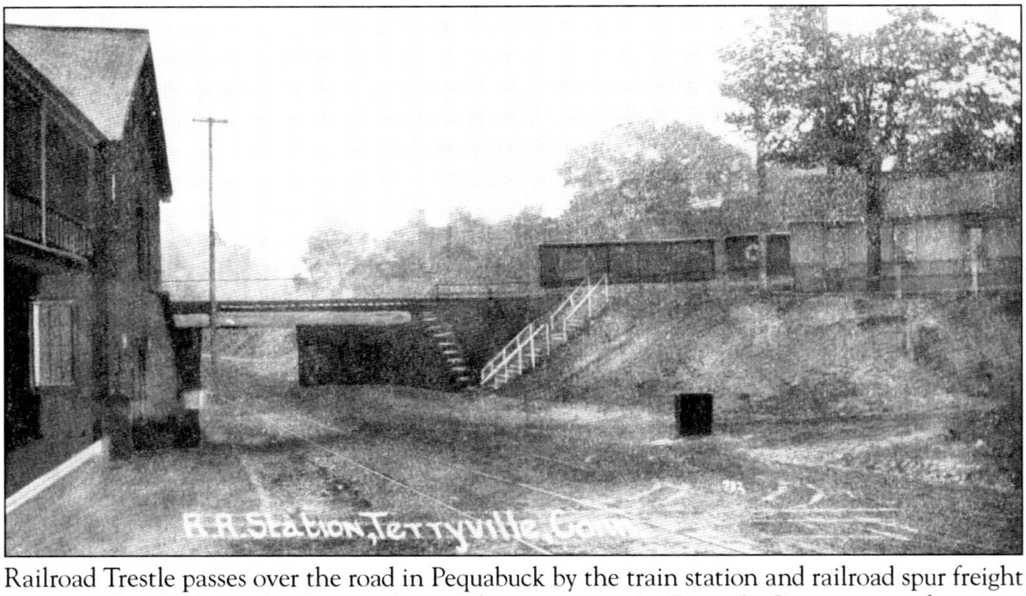

Railroad Trestle passes over the road in Pequabuck by the train station and railroad spur freight station. The Eagle Lock, Cooper Oven Thermometer, A. Terry & Company, and various manufacturers delivered products to the staging area via the trestle. It was the place products were shipped from and materials received for the various industries in Pequabuck and Terryville. (Courtesy of Plymouth Historical Society.)

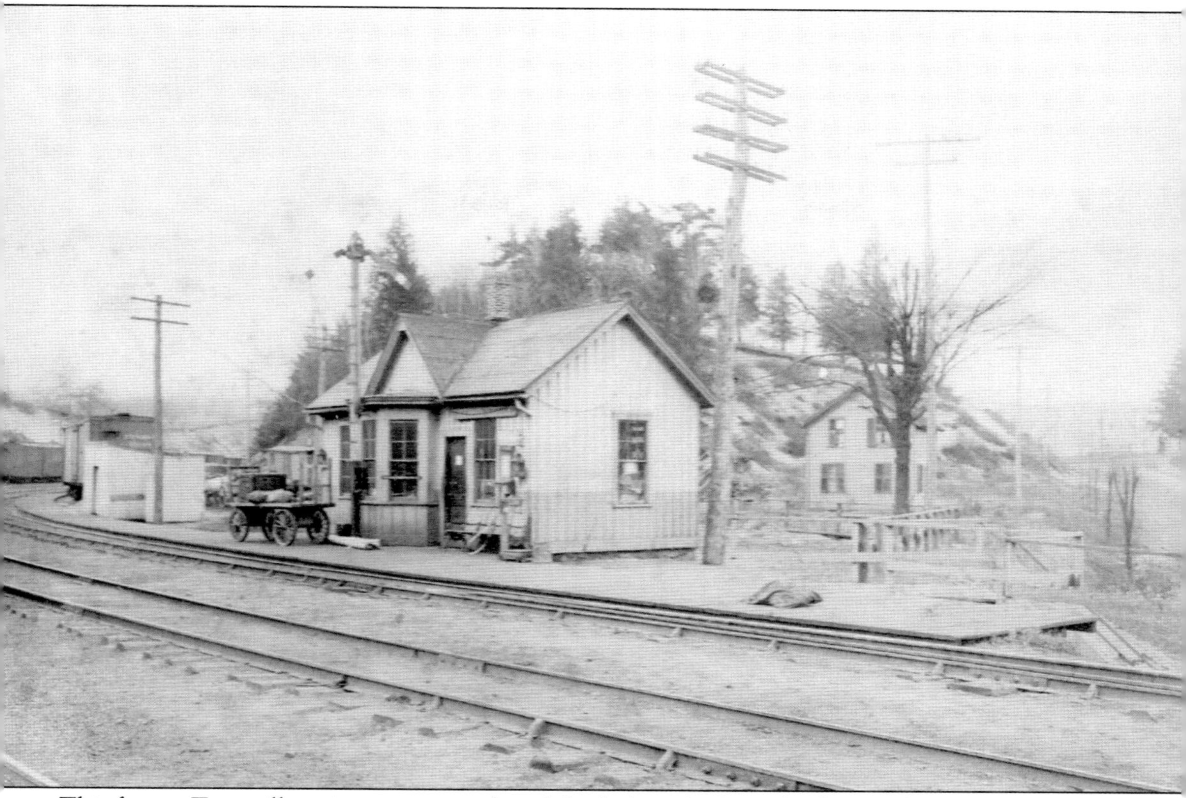

This former Terryville train station was demolished when the Pequabuck tunnel was completed. It was replaced by a larger, more passenger-friendly station. Railroad authorities did not consider this station sufficient for anticipated increase in train traffic and decided it needed to be replaced. (Courtesy of Plymouth Historical Society.)

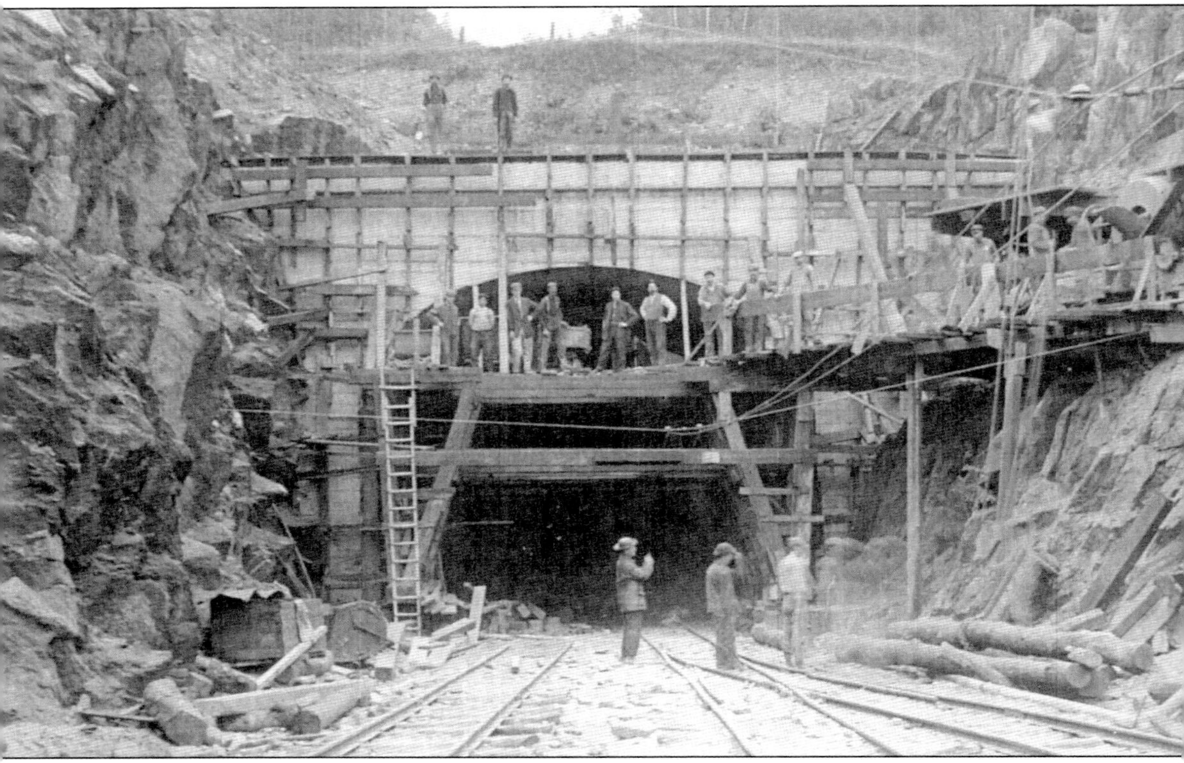

Wooden timbers were used to support the tunnel structure during digging and blasting. A camp was set up on Allen Street for the Italian workers sent here to work on the tunnel. The project took more than three years to complete. The three-quarter-mile-long tunnel went directly under the Allen farm property. (Courtesy of Plymouth Historical Society.)

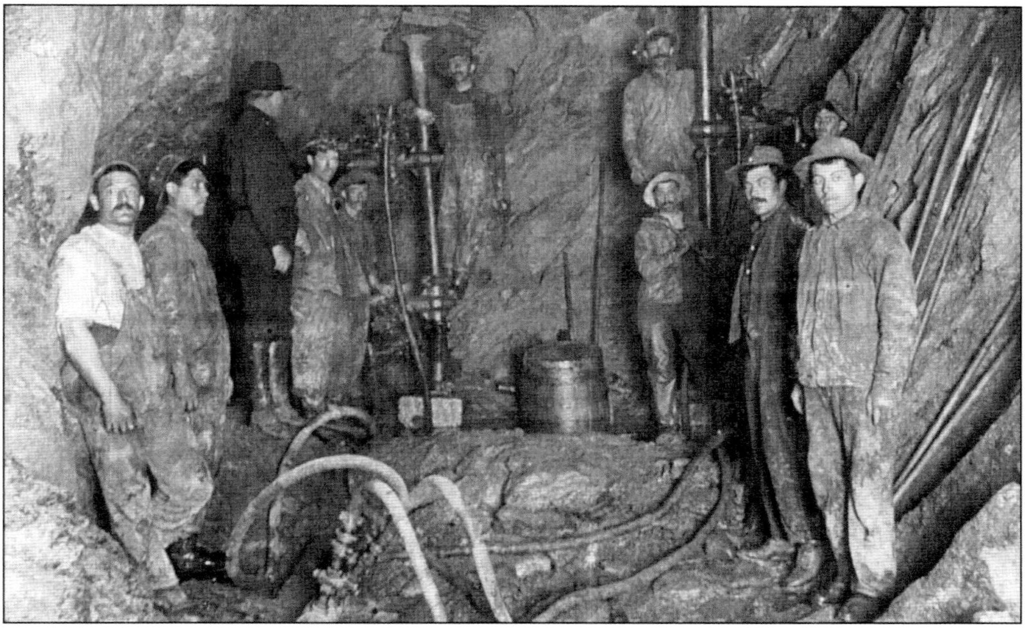

Workmen take a break to pose for pictures of work on this historic tunnel construction. The railroad rented pasture land off Allen Street near the ice pond to set up a camp for the workers. The majority of the labor was done by hand. The superintendent and engineers had rooms at Bessie Scott's in Pequabuck. On Sunday afternoons, neighbors recall listing to the workmen singing on their day off. (Courtesy of Plymouth Historical Society.)

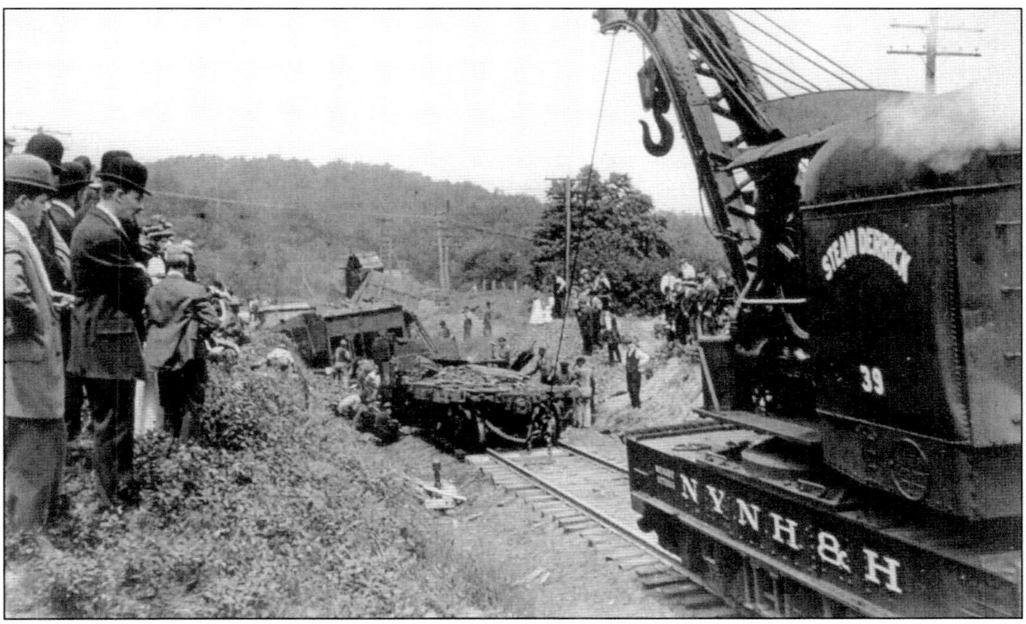

Spectators gather as workmen load rock on to a railway car for disposal. The concrete abutment for the bridge over the road is at the section of the Pequabuck River known as Devil's Backbone. The rocks had to be broken by pick and shovel in order to modify the course of the river. (Courtesy of Plymouth Historical Society.)

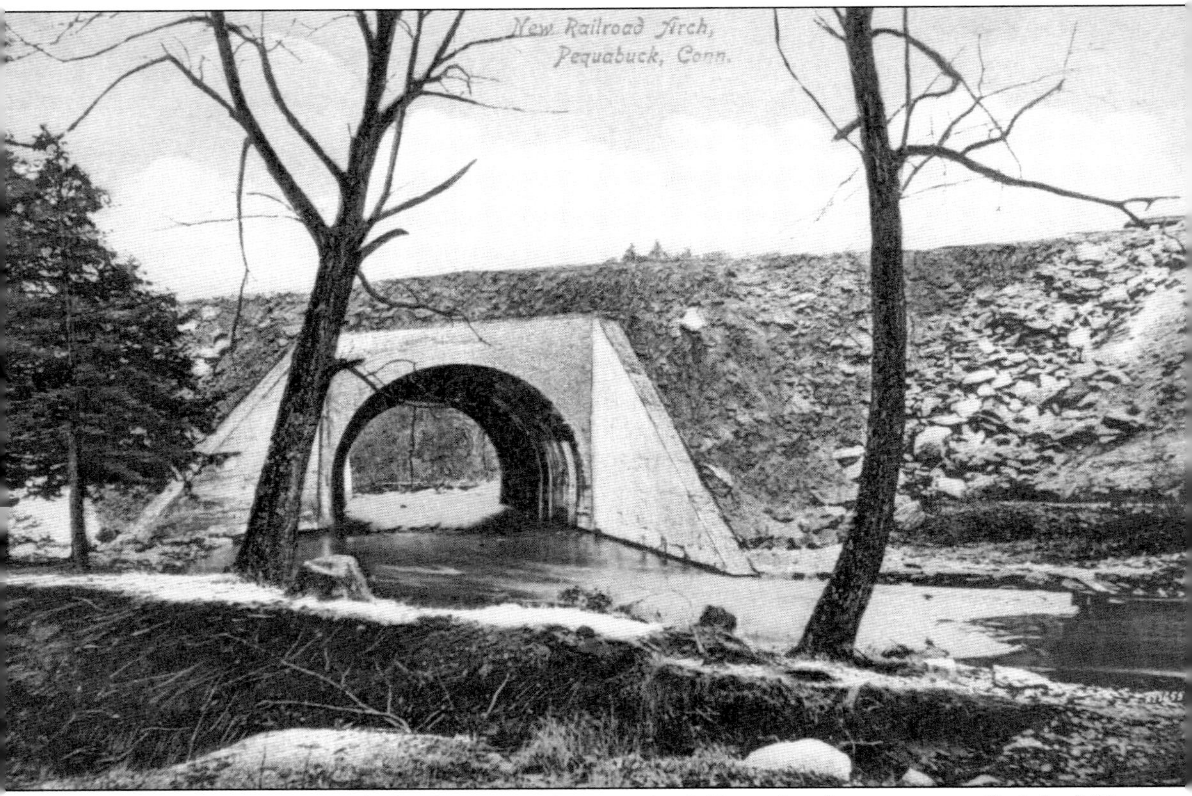

The Sylvan Hill Tunnel, also known as the Pequabuck Tunnel and sometimes called the Mile Long Tunnel, was completed primarily by hand digging. The railroad did not buy the land for the tunnel, but it did pay for a right-of-way to go under the Allen Farm. Construction began in 1907 and was completed in 1910. (Courtesy of Plymouth Historical Society.)

Eight

People and Places

Plymouth was founded on exercising the right to worship as one chooses. Plymouth Green was given to Northbury by the Town of Waterbury in order to create a place for a burying ground and a meeting place for worship. Deacon Moses Blakeslee of Town Hill was appointed to set the site. The land was swampy, but history records that it was easily drained. Plymouth Green became the home of the first churches of Plymouth and the beginning of the town of Plymouth.

Later, as people came into Plymouth to work in businesses and factories, they found a sense of community and created the various churches established here. Each one was founded by a small committee seeking their own religious freedom through togetherness, hard work, and sacrifice. These same generous souls contributed by building the area's schools, libraries, roads, houses, civic facilities, and businesses.

Plymouth, as it enters the 21st century, maintains small-town character while building for the future. Plymouth Industrial Park was initiated in 1973. Sites for Phase I and Phase II are sold, and Phase III has over 40 acres of developable land available for business. A volunteer ambulance service operates from the center of town out of a new facility. The Plymouth Volunteer Ambulance Corp began providing services in 1968, with the donation of the first ambulance by the Terryville Lyons Club. The Lock Museum of America is located on the Main Road. The Animal Rescue Foundation, churches, libraries, fire stations, restaurants and a new center for history is planned around the historic waterwheel. Plymouth is poised for the new millennium.

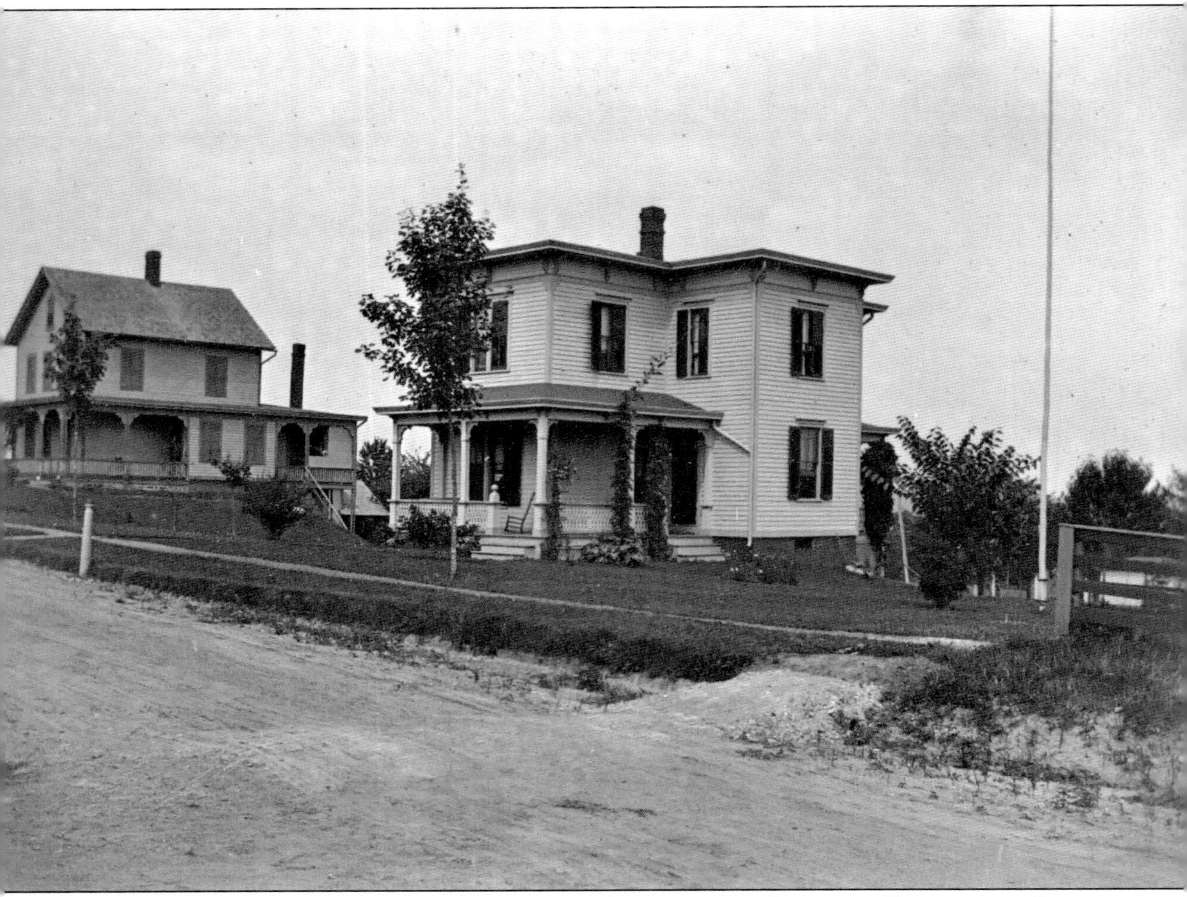

New homes were built on Prospect Street in early 1900. It was the time trolley men got a big raise in pay—new workers would now be paid 25¢ per hour, and existing workers would be raised to 27.5¢ per hour! The Plymouth grand list totaled $2,130,058, and the mill rate was set at 12 mills. The *Bristol Press* sold for 3¢! (Courtesy of Plymouth Historical Society.)

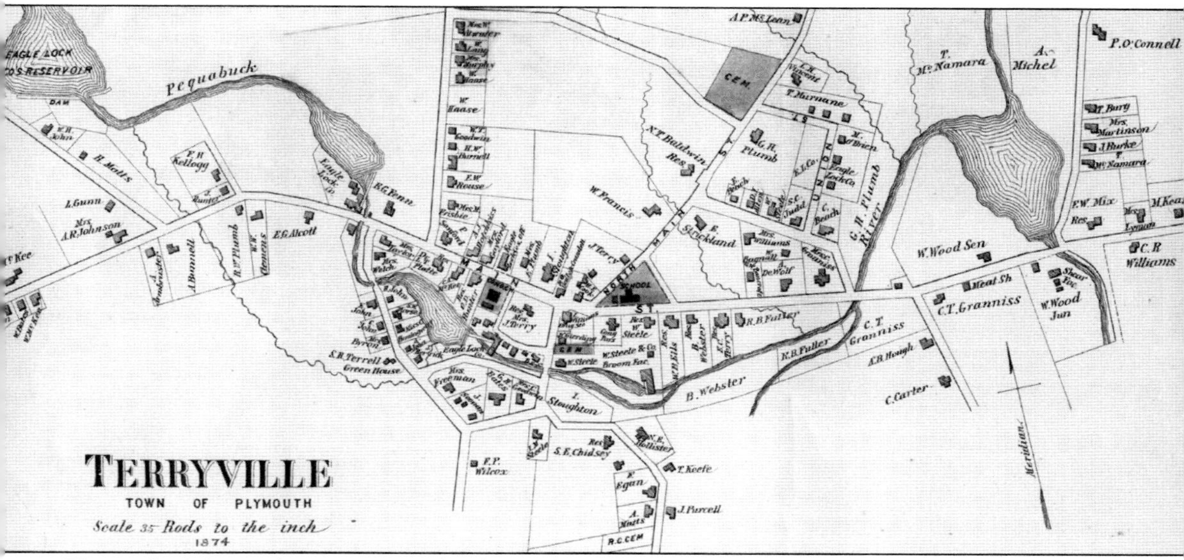

The end of the 19th century was bright as the United States moved toward the forefront in industrialization. The conversion from an agrarian world controlled by the cycles of nature into the mass exodus of Europe to the United States and the repetitiveness of industrialized jobs heralded a new "made-made" world. New growth in science, medicine, and manufacturing gave rise to new discoveries and new confidence for new and better times for the masses. In the years of 1890–1910, a total of 13 million people left their homes to enter the United States and the Industrial Revolution in search of a better life. Many settled in the growing industrial portion of Plymouth called "Terryville." (Courtesy of Plymouth Historical Society.)

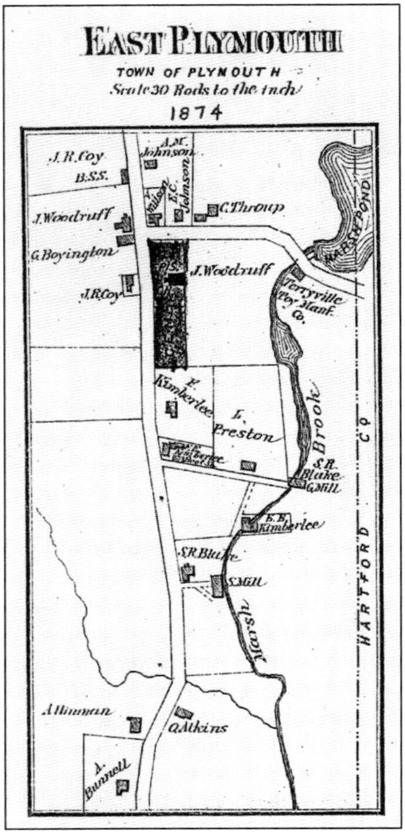

The story of East Plymouth, also known as East Church, is the story of conservatives, not revolutionaries. This community was formed of numerous farms and industrious farmers who were loyal to England. East Church is in the corner of Bristol, Plymouth, and Harwinton and separated itself because of an internal dispute within the congregation of the Church of England located in New Cambridge, later known as Bristol. The first group belonged to the Calvinistic doctrine called "New Lights." The second group, "Old Lights," rebelling against fundamental Calvinism, chose to remain with the Church of England. During the Revolutionary War, many East Church residents retained their allegiance to England. After the revolution, in 1790, upon petition to the General Assembly, the residents were granted the right to form a society that became the parish of St. Matthew. The church building was constructed and consecrated in 1795. Economic growth followed the small community and a variety of small, successful industries located within the East Church community. (Courtesy of Plymouth Historical Society.)

Noted for the Pequabuck River, which provided waterpower to many local industries, Pequabuck is a small suburb of Plymouth. Andrew Terry, son of Eli Terry Jr., formed one of the first malleable iron factories in the United States. The industrious David G. Cooper, inventor and owner of Cooper Thermometer Company, also located in Pequabuck. The Sylvan Hill Nurseries and Fruit Farm located along the Pequabuck edge of Terryville. The Highland Golf Club (later Pequabuck Golf Club), a woodturning concern, ice pond, and several industries are credited to Pequabuck. The W.H. Scott & Company operated a three-story warehouse for coal, hay grain, flour, feed, boots, shoes, lumber, dry goods, fertilizers, and patent medicines. Listing on their business card that they were "dealers in everything," they also located in Pequabuck, by the train yard. Many new residents who came to the United States to work in the factories settled in Pequabuck to be near their jobs. Pequabuck's first post office was established in 1857 in response to the growing community. (Courtesy of Plymouth Historical Society.)

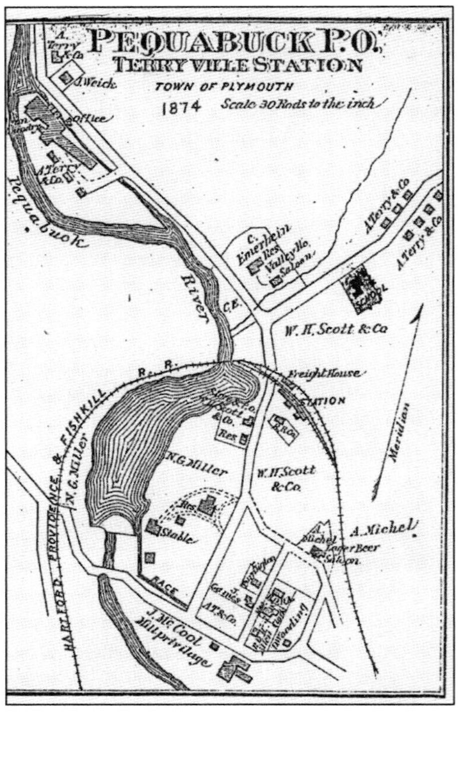

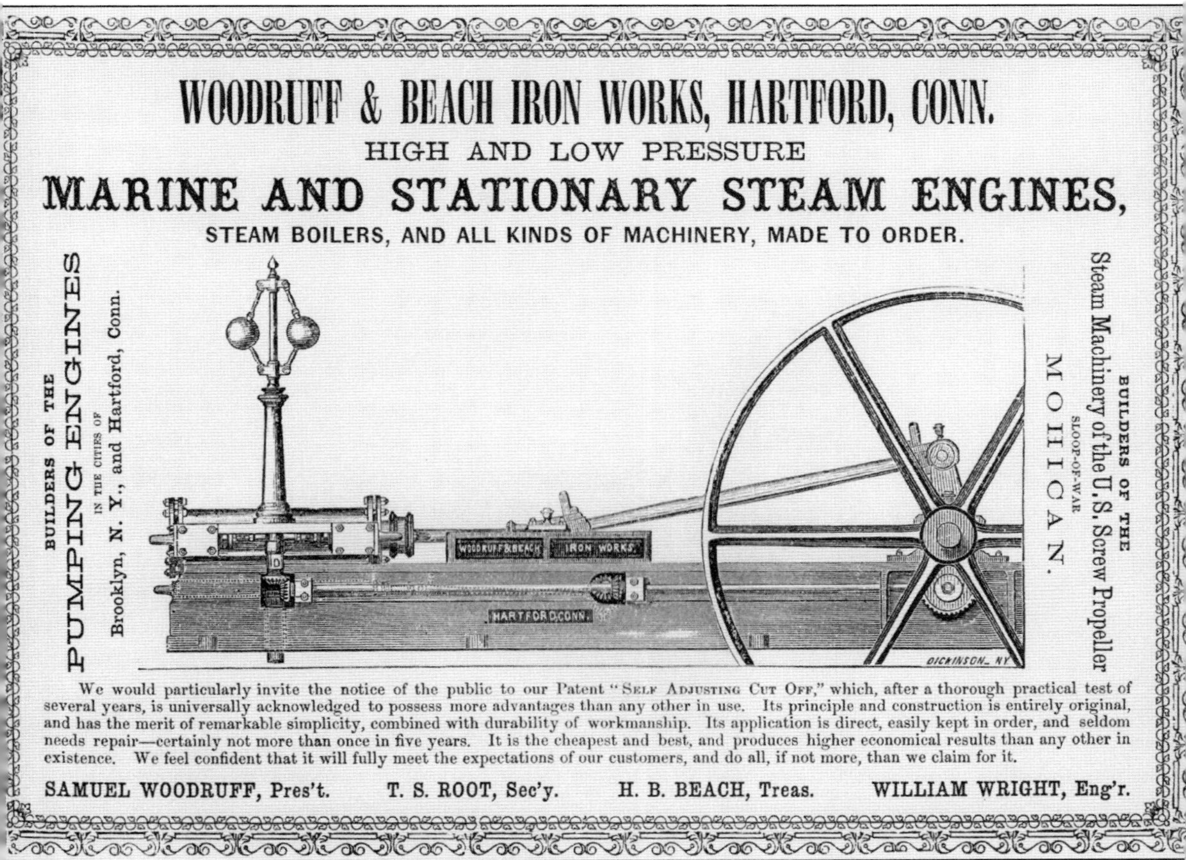

This is an advertisement for the Woodruff & Beach Steam Engine, which was purchased by the A.C. Shelton & Tuttle Carriage Company and then sold to Hiram Minor. It was used for Minor's sawmill and was later donated by the Minor family to the Plymouth Historical Society. It has been completely reconditioned and is displayed on special occasions by Plymouth Historical Society. Power produced by the engine would be transferred by use of belts to operate a small circular wood-cutting saw. The engine has an eight-inch cylinder bore, and the piston has a three-foot stroke. The engine bed is 13 feet long. (Courtesy of Plymouth Historical Society.)

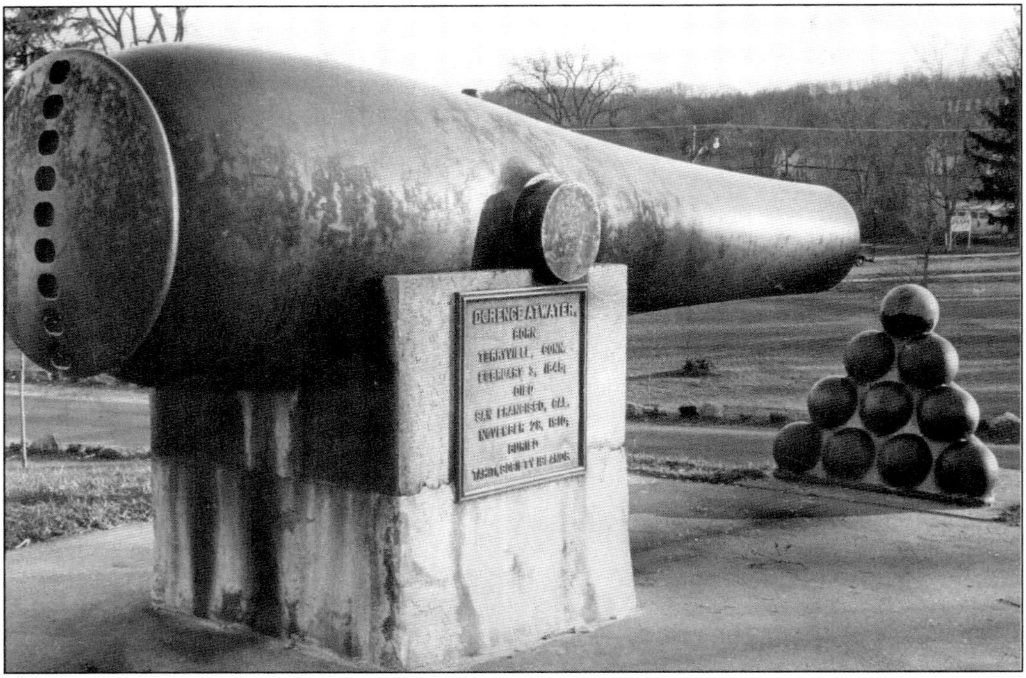

While at Andersonville Prison during the Civil War, Dorence Atwater determined that Southern methods of record keeping for the dead were woefully inadequate. He began to make detailed records of the dead. Dorence Atwater recorded the deaths of 13,000 and the locations of their graves. These records were used in the trial of the commander of the camp, Henry Wirz, toward his conviction for war crimes. When Dorence Atwater was released from Andersonville at the close of the war, he hid the documents in his coat, intending to publish them for the benefit of the families of the deceased, who without the lists might never have known what happened to their fathers, husbands, sons, and brothers. A Rodman cannon was donated by the federal government, taken from Boston Harbor. It was dedicated on Memorial Day 1907, with Clara Barton present. The cannon today, a memorial to local hero Dorence Atwater, stands on a small hillside overlooking Main Street. (Both images courtesy of Plymouth Historical Society.)

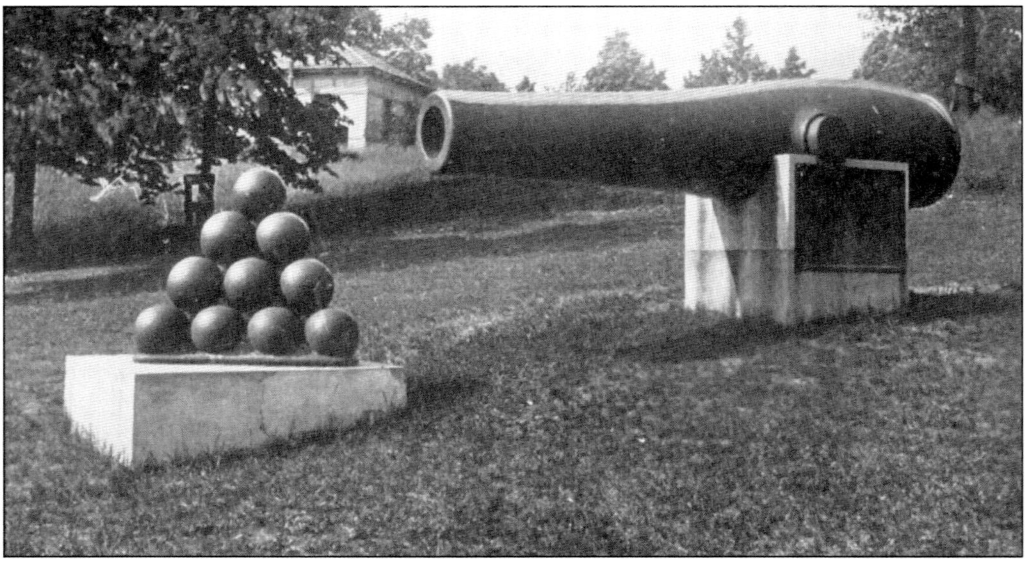

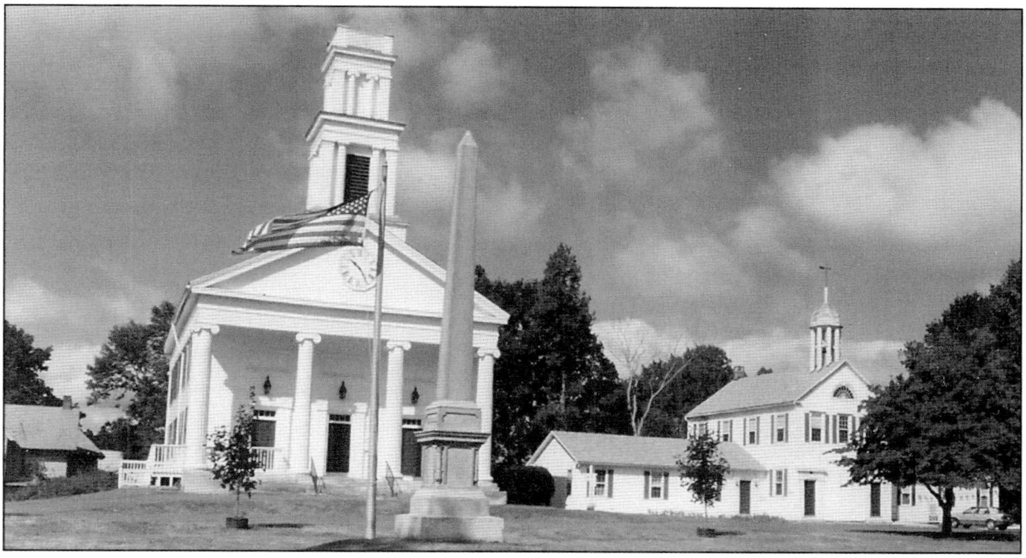

This later view of Plymouth Green shows the Civil War memorial. The Soldier's Monument located on the Green is nearly 20 feet high on a granite pedestal and obelisk. The actual date of origin is unknown but possibly as early as 1865 and refers to the Civil War as the "War of 1861" and includes President Lincoln's name. (Courtesy of Plymouth Historical Society.)

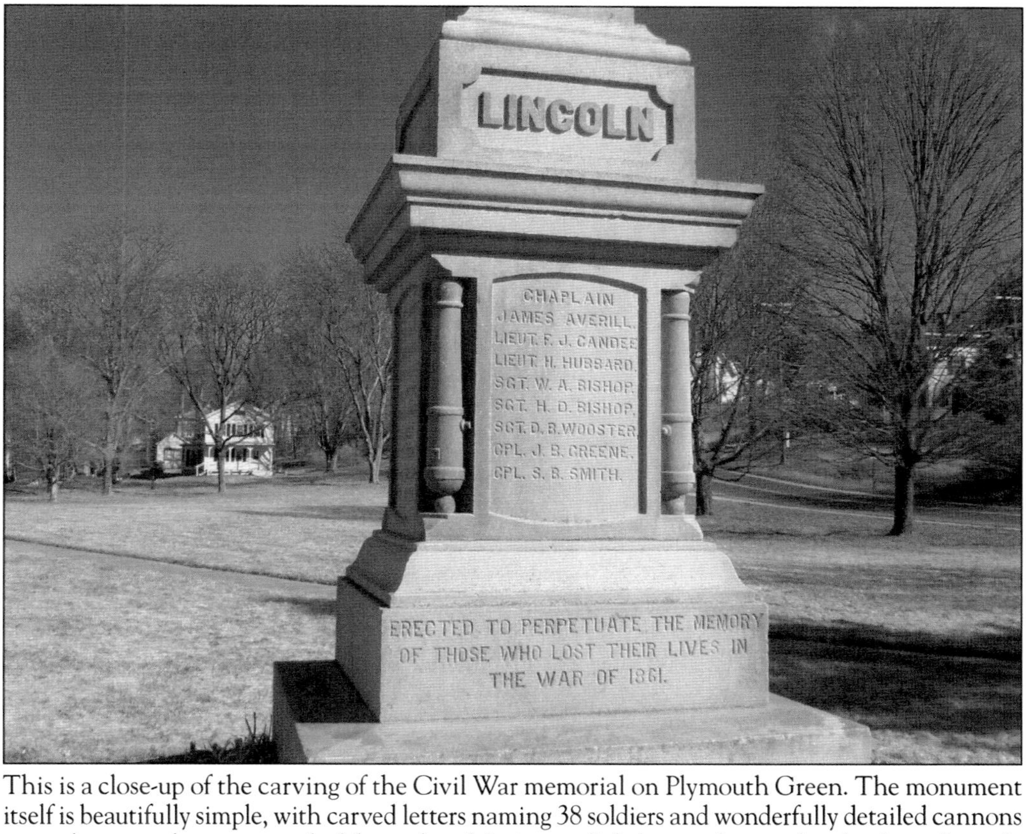

This is a close-up of the carving of the Civil War memorial on Plymouth Green. The monument itself is beautifully simple, with carved letters naming 38 soldiers and wonderfully detailed cannons on each recessed corner panel of the pedestal. It sits on slightly raised ground with a large flagpole to one side. (Photograph by Judy Giguere.)

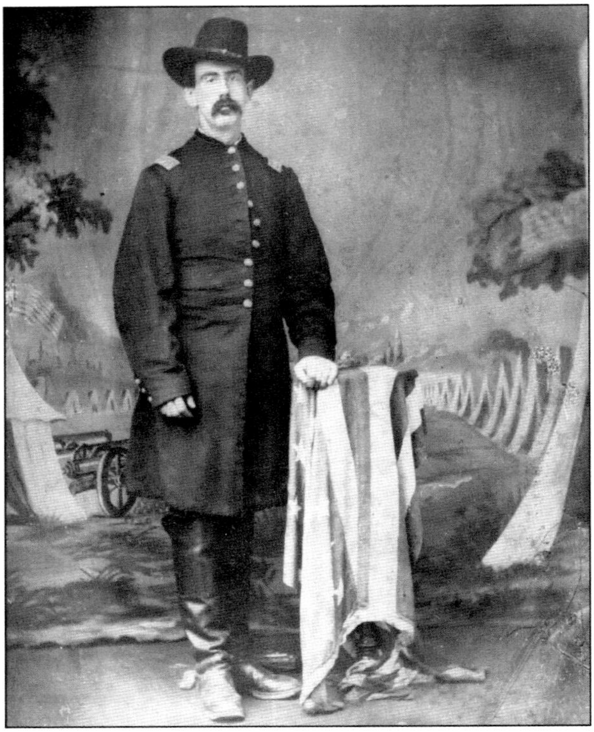

Civil War soldier Lt. Edward H. Mix, son of James and Lucy Mix, was born in Terryville on December 11, 1838. He worked in the lock making business with other members of his family until the Civil War. He enlisted May 23, 1861, in Company C, 1st Artillery and was promoted to the rank of captain, Company B, 16th Connecticut Volunteers. He died by drowning in Albemarle Sound, North Carolina, in 1864. (Courtesy of Plymouth Historical Society.)

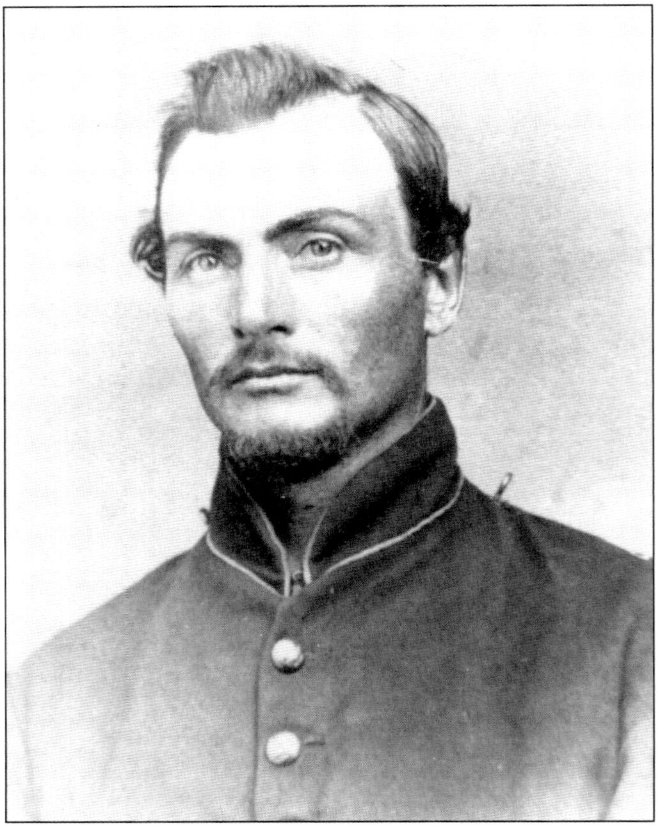

Plymouth Civil War soldier Sgt. Emory B. Taylor enlisted on August 12, 1862, Company D, and was wounded on September 19, 1864, at Winchester, Virginia. He was promoted to sergeant September 13, 1864, and was discharged May 18, 1865. More than 250 men from Plymouth enlisted in various branches of the military during the Civil War. (Courtesy of Plymouth Historical Society.)

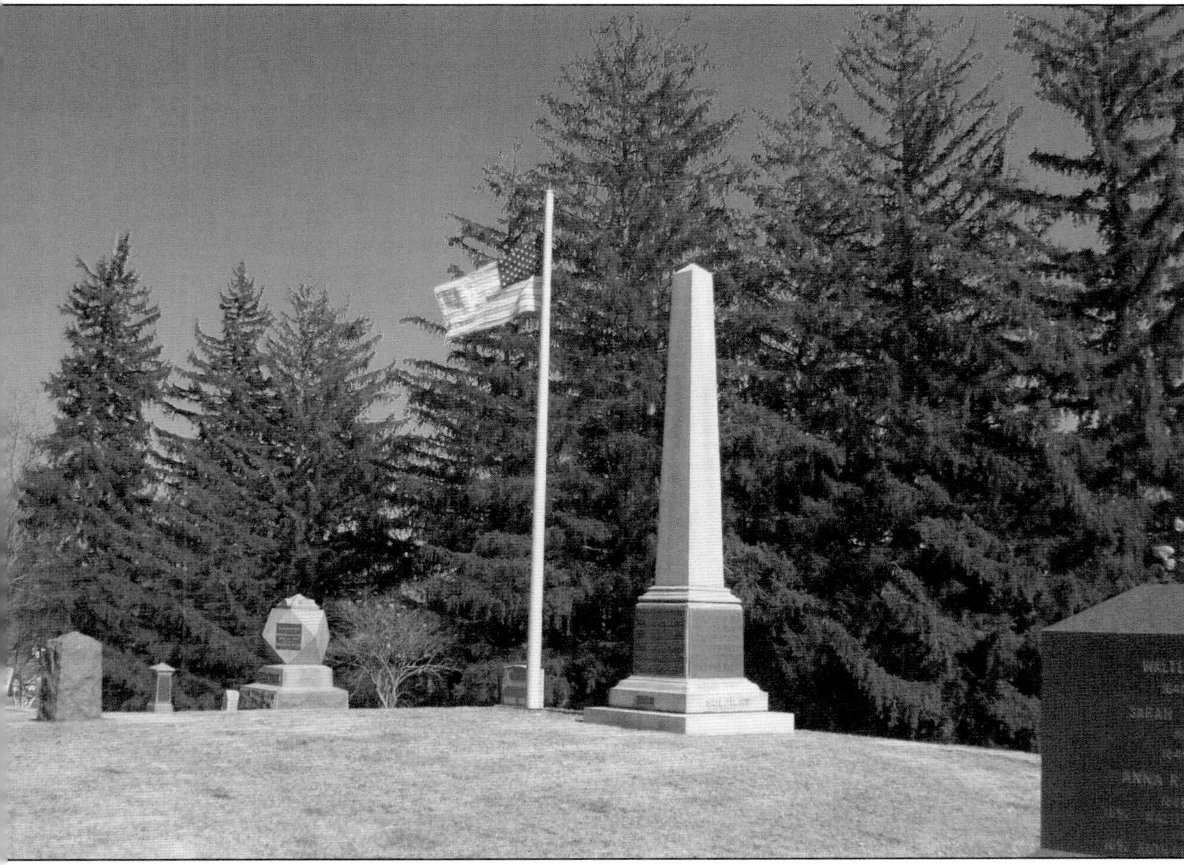

The 19-foot stone obelisk lists the names of some of the dead of the Civil War. It is possibly one of the earliest monuments in Connecticut. It stands tall on top of a hill with its companion flagpole as a memorial to men of Terryville who died in the Civil War. Related graves form a square around the monument, leaving a large, open, humble space around the monument. (Photograph by Judy Giguere.)

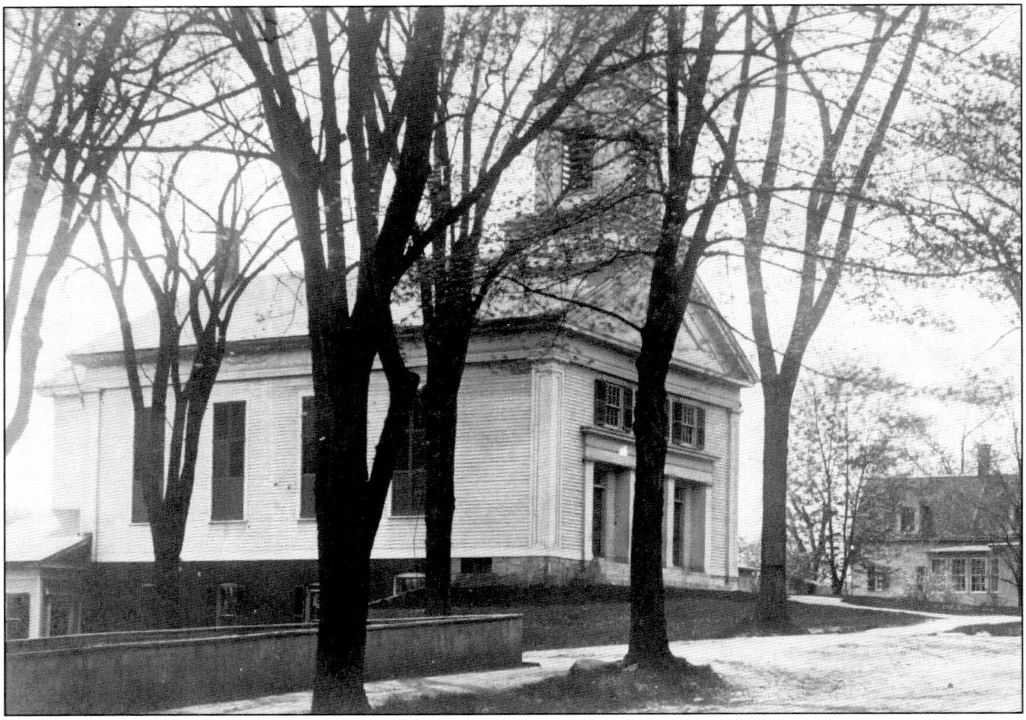

Terryville Congregational Church was built with a subscription of funds dated September 1837 in the amount of $3,558. Additional funds were raised to complete the building. The chairman of the building committee was Wyllys Atwater, and the builder was Riley Scott. The parsonage was donated by Eli Terry Sr. on August 26, 1841. (Courtesy of Plymouth Historical Society.)

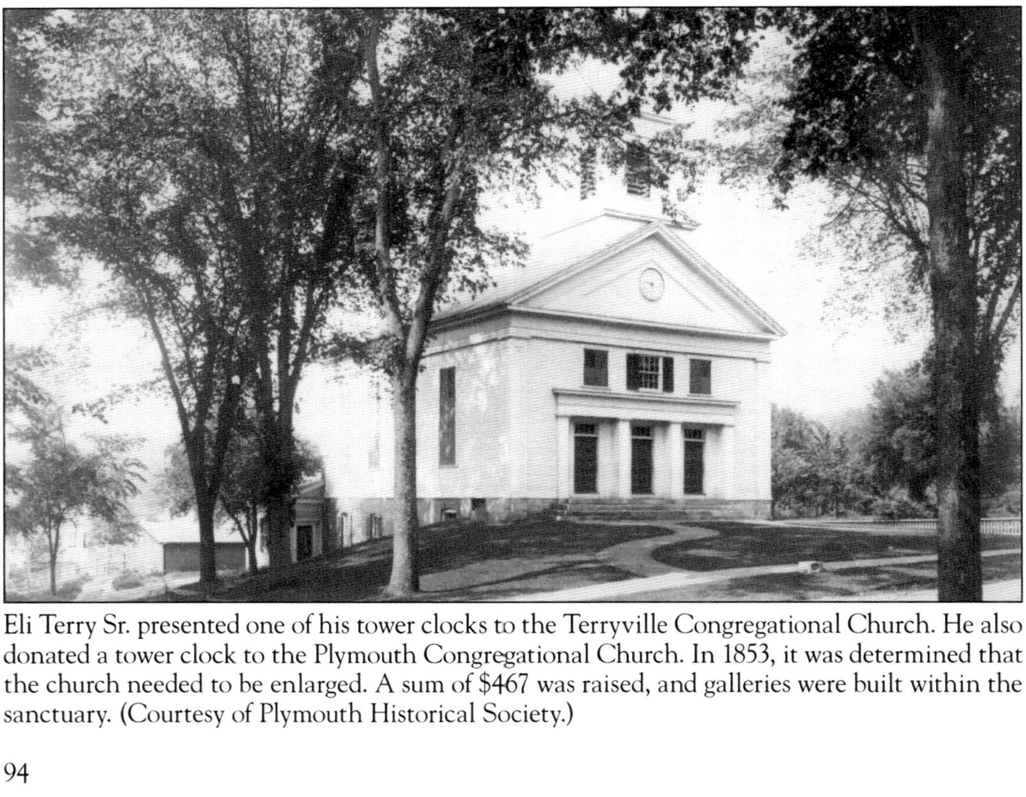

Eli Terry Sr. presented one of his tower clocks to the Terryville Congregational Church. He also donated a tower clock to the Plymouth Congregational Church. In 1853, it was determined that the church needed to be enlarged. A sum of $467 was raised, and galleries were built within the sanctuary. (Courtesy of Plymouth Historical Society.)

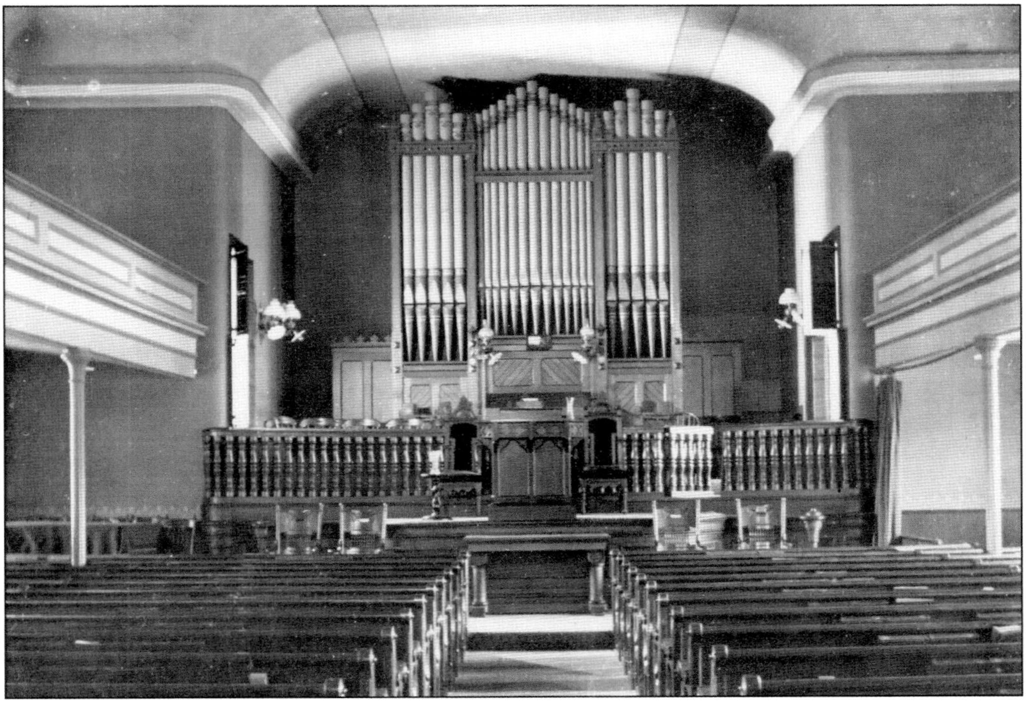

A group of 49 members of the Plymouth Congregational Church left the Plymouth mother church and organized the Terryville Congregational Church. Industries located in Terryville increased the population, and families wanted a church closer to home. August 1838 marked the completion and dedication of this church. Rev. Nathaniel Richardson was the first pastor. This is a picture of the huge pipe organ of the church. (Courtesy of Plymouth Historical Society.)

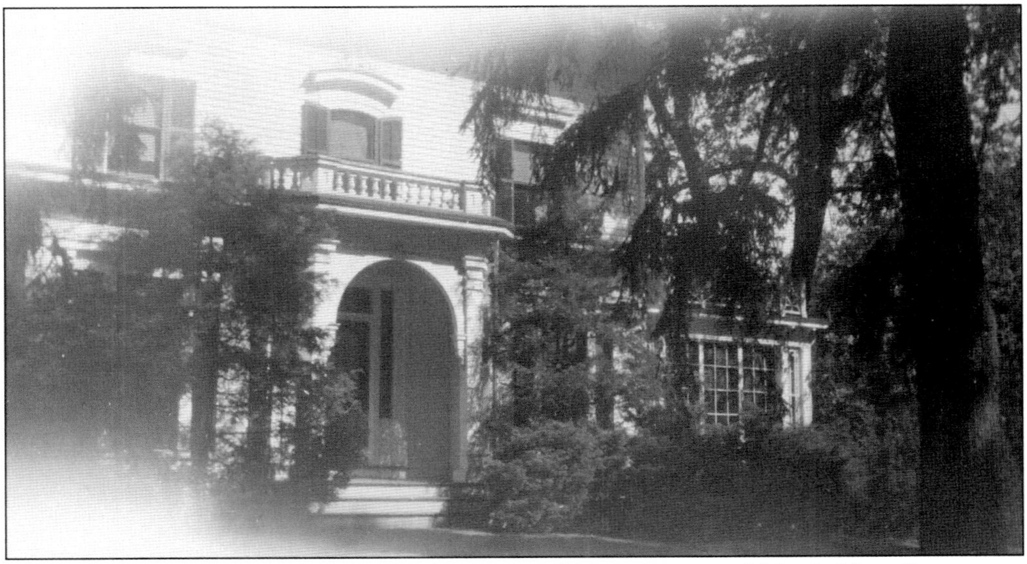

Previously, the Terryville Institute on the corner of Main Street and North Main Streets was used for both grade school and high school. The George Clark residence on North Main Street was demolished to make way for construction of a new building for Terryville High School. Upon completion of the new Terryville High School on North Main Street, the Terryville Institute was demolished. (Courtesy of Plymouth Historical Society.)

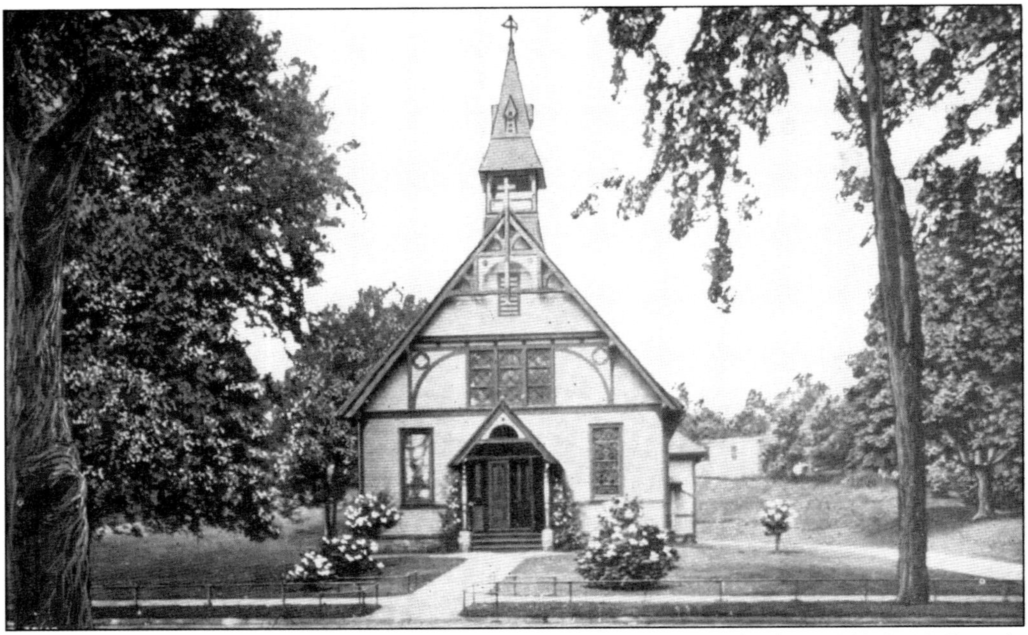

Immaculate Conception Roman Catholic Church on Main Street was built in 1882. In 1848, early Catholics celebrated Mass on an altar made of planks at the home of Philip Ryan. Masses were said in the Ryan parlor until a church was built. Citizens contributed generously to a building fund. The church was completed in 1882 on a lot purchased by John McNamara. (Courtesy of Plymouth Historical Society.)

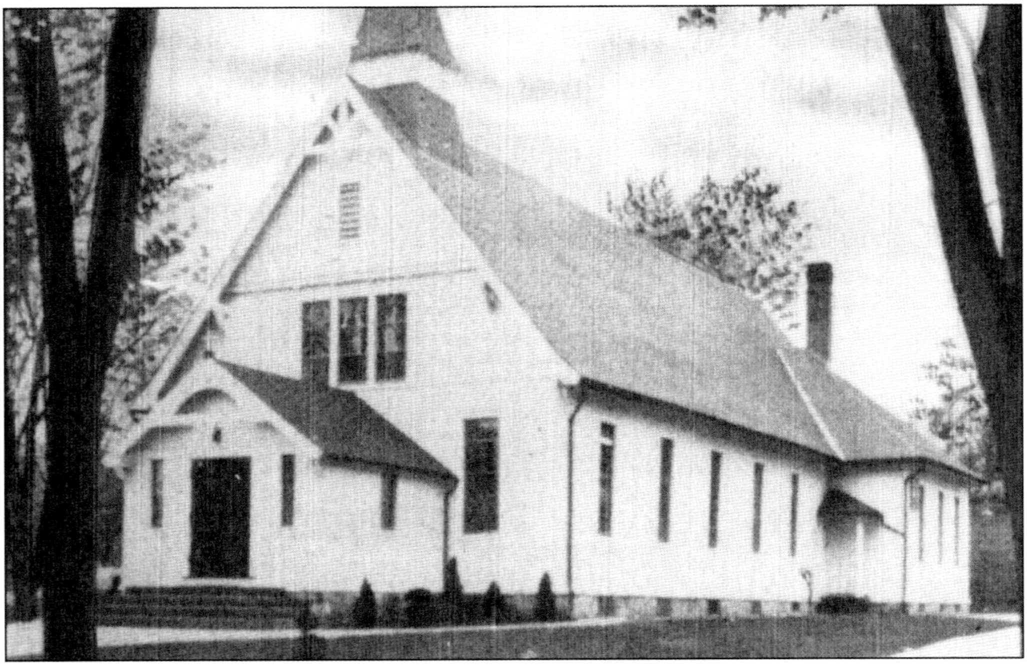

This is a later view of Immaculate Conception Roman Catholic Church on Main Street. It was called the "Little Mission Church at the End of the Park" in the early 1900s. Philip Ryan's family donated the land on South Main Street for St. John's Cemetery in 1858. It is the oldest Catholic cemetery in Terryville. (Courtesy of Plymouth Historical Society.)

Holy Trinity Evangelical Lutheran Church was formed in 1892 by Lutheran immigrants from Russian Poland. It was organized as St. Paul's German Evangelical Lutheran Church, until 1902 when two separate churches were formed. 1902 St. Paul's Lutheran Church was built on Main Street and Holy Trinity Evangelical Lutheran Church was built on Maple Street. (Courtesy of Plymouth Historical Society.)

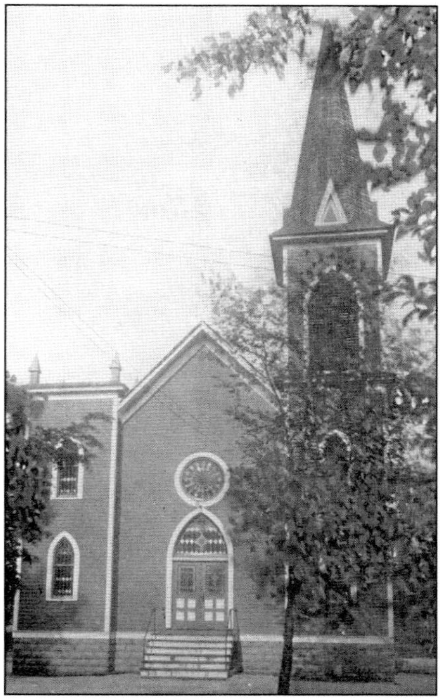

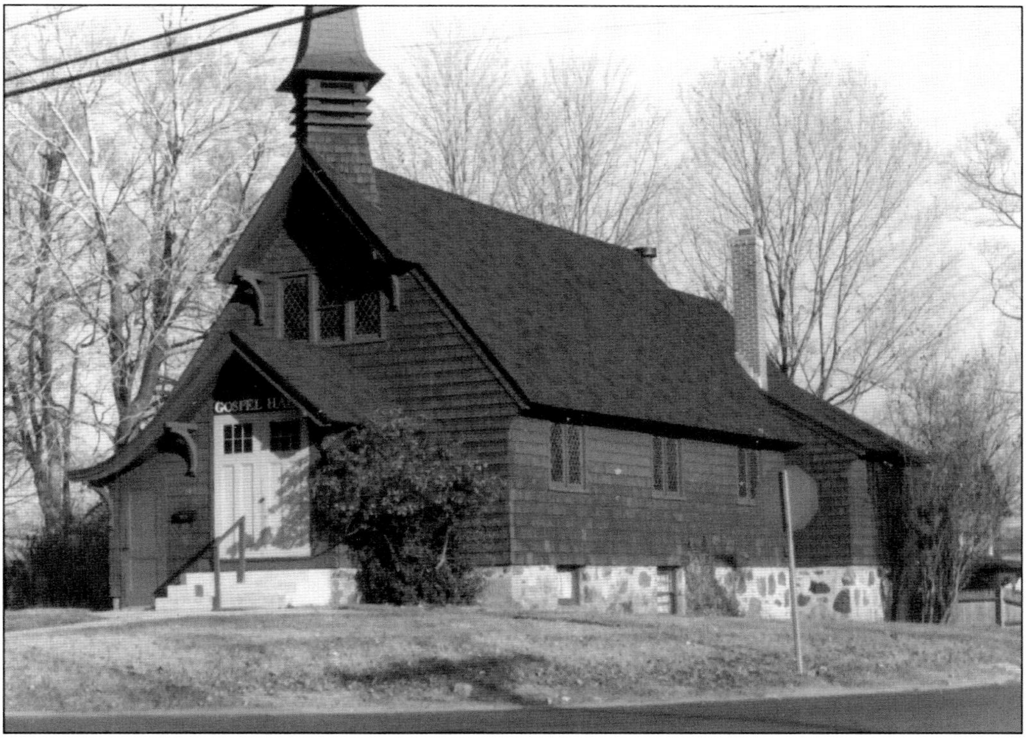

St. Mark's Episcopal Church on North Main Street in Terryville was organized in 1902. Many churches had their beginnings during the horse-and-buggy days, when few possessed a means of transportation. Fundraisers included the sale of shop aprons—as many as 619 in one year. On Labor Day 1911, the cornerstone was laid. The first service was held on December 24, 1911. (Courtesy of Plymouth Historical Society.)

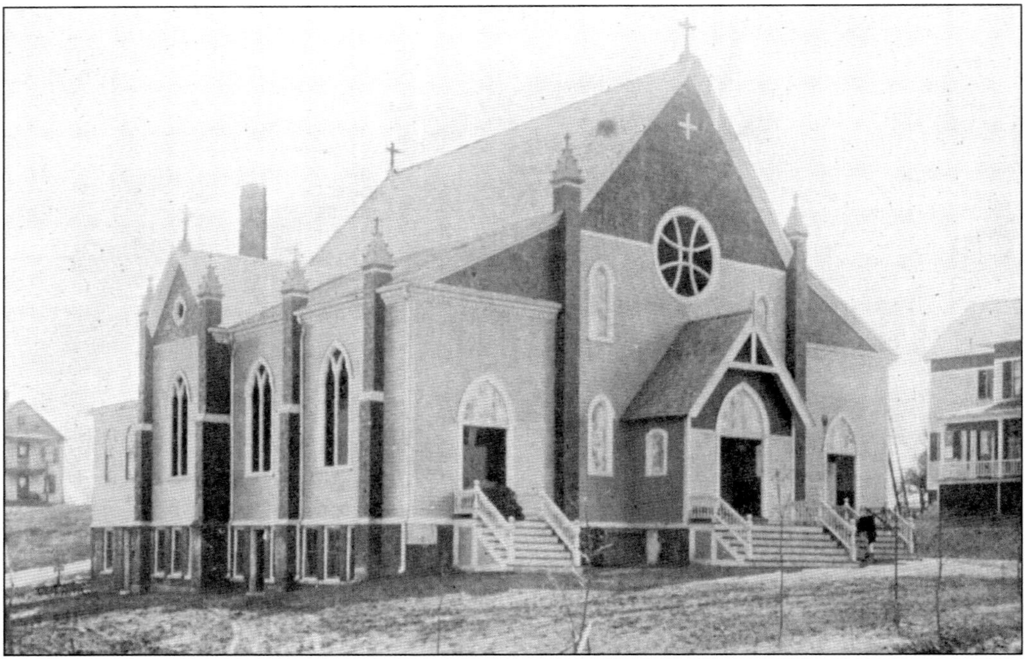

St. Casmir's Church was formed by Polish families settling in Terryville but attending services at the Immaculate Conception Church. The journey began in 1890 when many Polish immigrants came to settle in Terryville to work in the Eagle Lock and Andrew Terry Companies. In Poland, the Catholic Church was the heart of their community and their existence. The faith was closely interwoven with their culture, customs, and traditions. In December 1900, a group met to form the St. Casmir's Society, which became the driving force for a Polish parish. Fundraisers were held and collections taken to raise money for a church. In May 1906, the cornerstone of the church was set. On Labor Day of the same year, the Right Reverend Michael Tierney, Bishop of Hartford consecrated the Church of St. Casmir. (Both images courtesy of Plymouth Historical Society.)

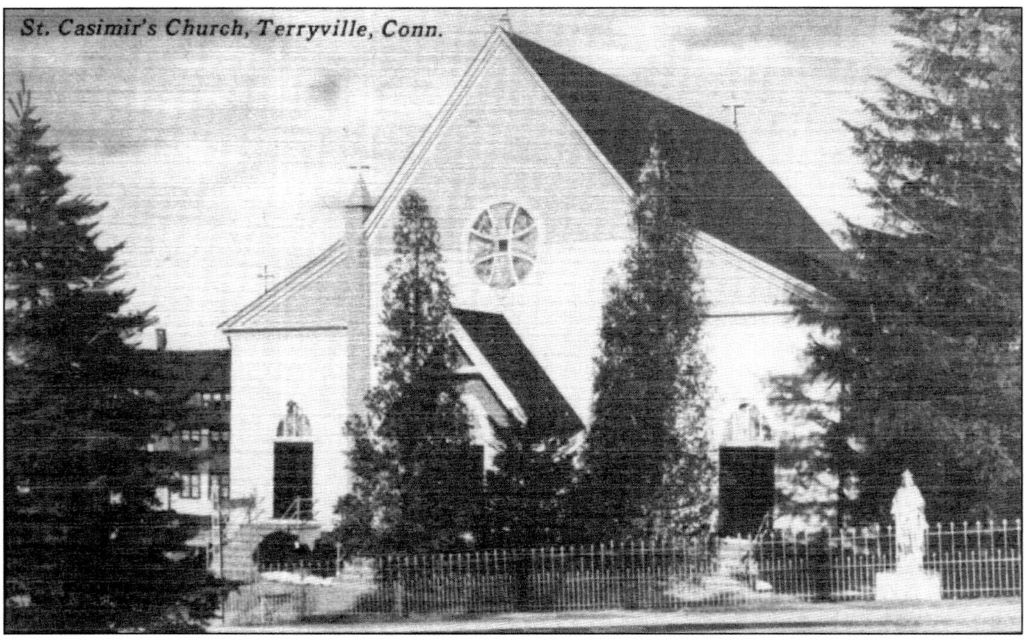

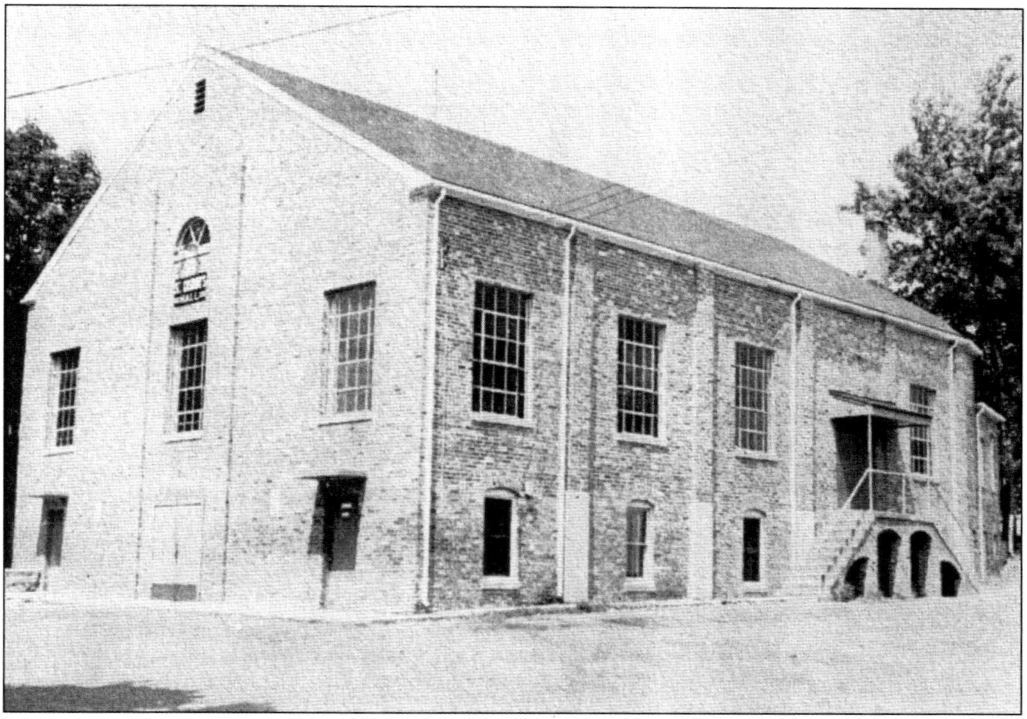

The St. Casmir's Society was formed to preserve spiritual heritage, culture, traditions, and language, but also to provide mutual aid to members in time of illness and death. St. Casmir's Hall, built during the 1930s by donations of labor and funds provided a home for the St. Casmir's Society as well as the building was used for numerous social functions. This landmark was destroyed by fire in 1985 and not rebuilt. (Courtesy of Plymouth Historical Society.)

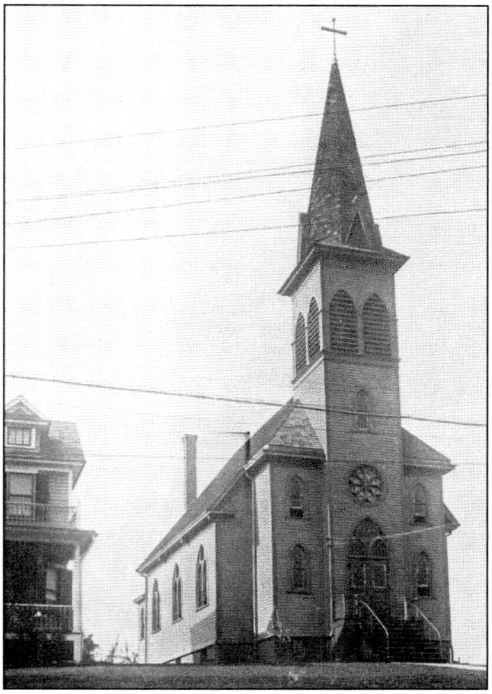

St. Paul's Evangelical Lutheran Church was formed initially by German-speaking Lutherans living in Terryville. Construction began in 1902, and the church was dedicated the same year. In December 1891, German-speaking Lutherans gathered to organize a congregation. The group eventually divided into St. Paul's and Holy Trinity churches, each thriving in their own right. (Courtesy of Plymouth Historical Society.)

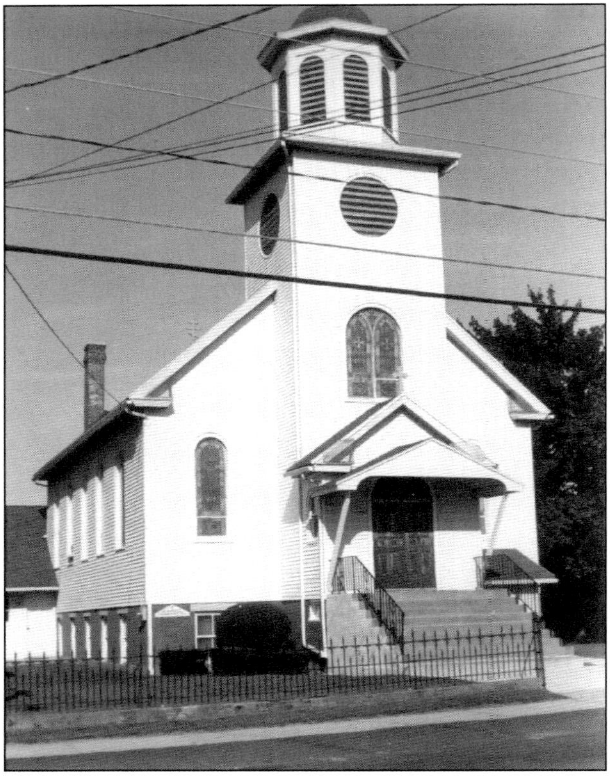

St. Michael's Ukrainian Byzantine Catholic Church on Allen Street was formed for Ukrainian Catholics to preserve their heritage and traditions. The church recently celebrated its 100th anniversary. The exterior of the church is a simple white structure with a domed steeple and distinctive Eastern cross. The interior is known for its beautiful iconostasis artwork. Ukrainian traditions are maintained, including teaching the children "pysanky," or detailed egg decorating. (Courtesy of Plymouth Historical Society.)

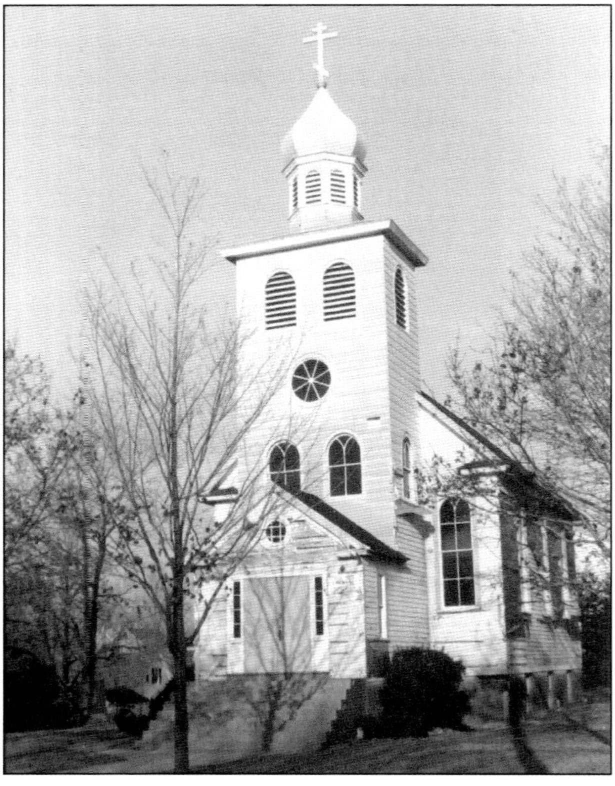

This is a 1958 photograph of Saints Cyril and Methodius Orthodox Church on Fairview Avenue. In 1908, a community of 12 families from the Carpathian Mountain region of southeastern Poland united to form a parish. Ethnically and linguistically, they were Russians. They settled in Terryville because of jobs in local industries. Their goal was a place where their language was spoken and their customs could continue among those also adjusting to life in a new homeland. (Courtesy of Plymouth Historical Society.)

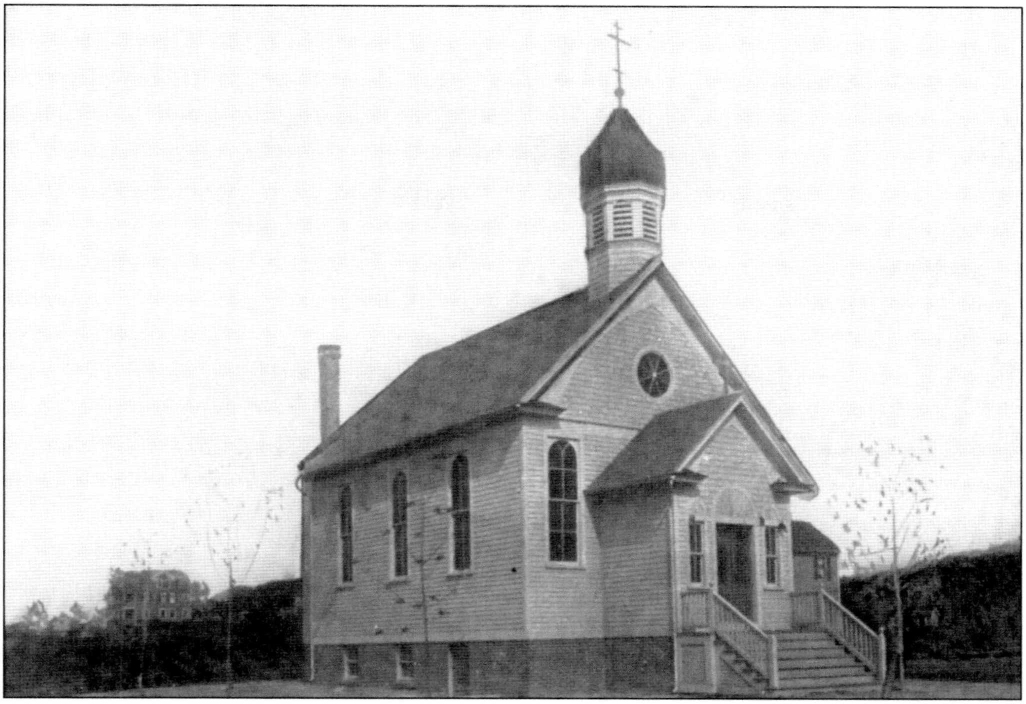

Eastern European Slavs came to America with deep roots in their Orthodox faith. The formation of a church was very important to them. The Brotherhood of Saints Cyril and Methodius bought land for a burying ground and to build a church. The church building was completed in 1912 for the sum of $3,500, which was no small sum to be raised by poor immigrants. (Courtesy of Plymouth Historical Society.)

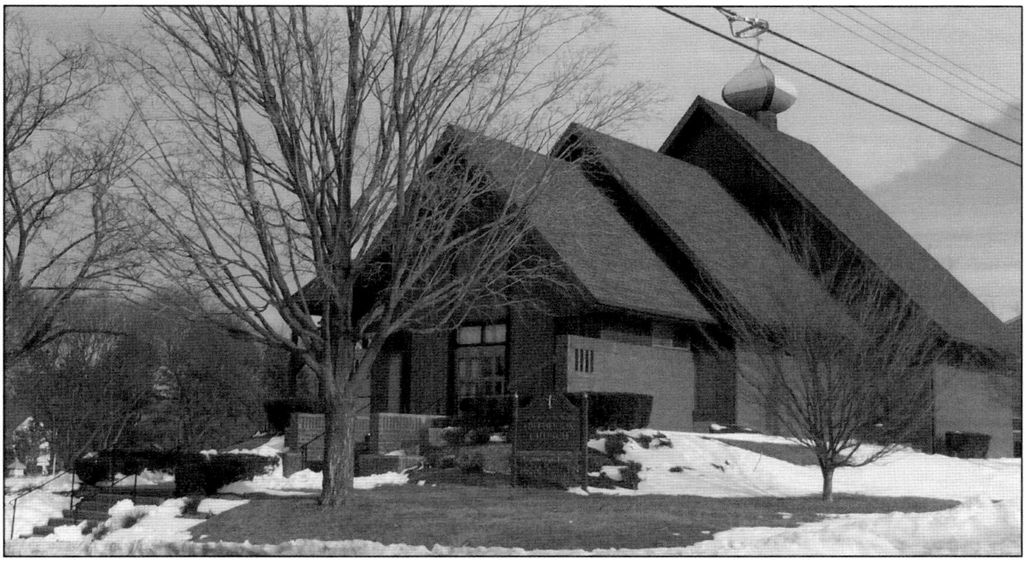

The new Saints Cyril and Methodius Russian Orthodox Church, located on the site of the former building on the corner of Ames and Fairview Avenues, was built in the late 1970s. The interior, a warm butternut wood, is adorned with traditional Eastern Orthodoxy iconography, including several large fresco-like pieces. This beautiful church is the realization of the vision of the earliest founding pioneers. (Photograph by Judy Giguere.)

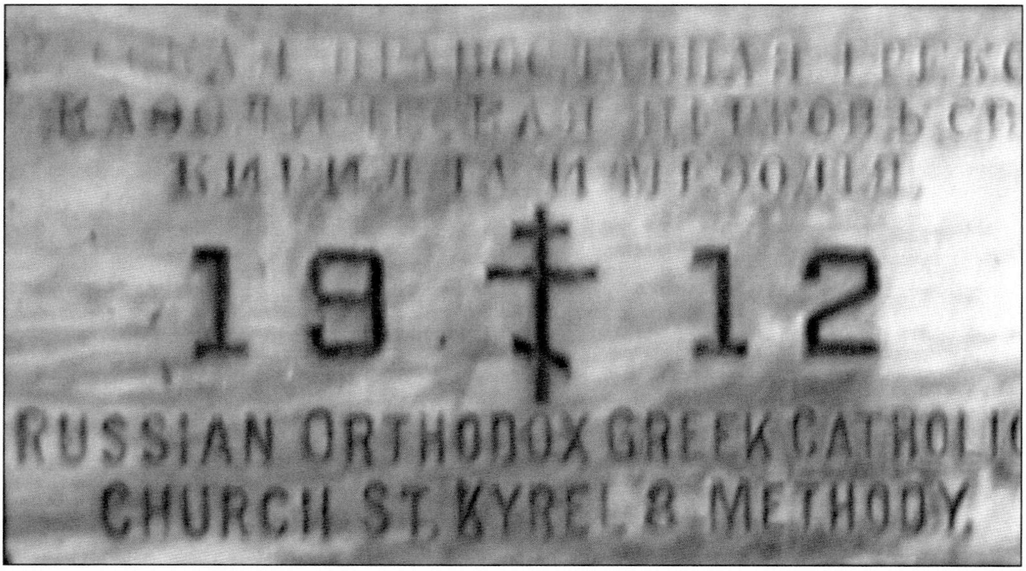

The cornerstone from the original Saints Cyril and Methodius Russian Orthodox Church was laid in 1913. The original building was razed in 1978 for the construction of a new church. This church has been the place of worship for the community on this location at the intersection of Ames and Fairview Avenues since 1908. (Photograph by Judy Giguere.)

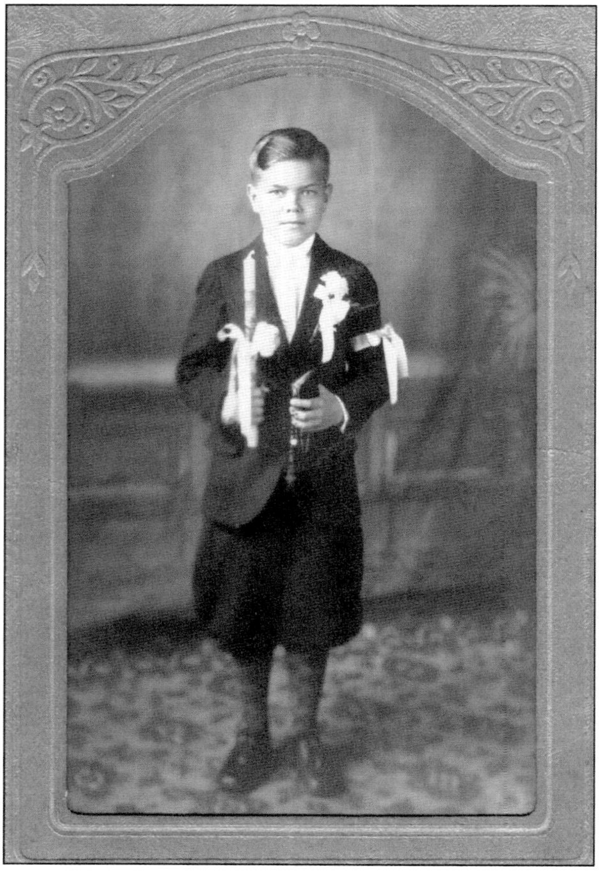

This young man is dressed in his very best knickers for his first communion. Church and religious life were very important as well as attending school. In Plymouth, several neighborhood school districts existed throughout the town. Many had one room school houses with as many as 80 students and one teacher with a mix of grade levels in a single classroom. (Author's collection.)

Pictured is a young girl dressed in her Sunday finest for her first communion. The annual school budget in 1928 was $83,498.59. A class of 22 students graduated high school, and 62 graduated the eighth grade. The Plymouth grand list totaled $156,062.99. The first selectman's salary was $2,000 annually, and the only patrolman was paid $1,500. The town hall budget included $4 for piano tuning, and maintenance of watering troughs was listed at $6 per year. (Author's collection.)

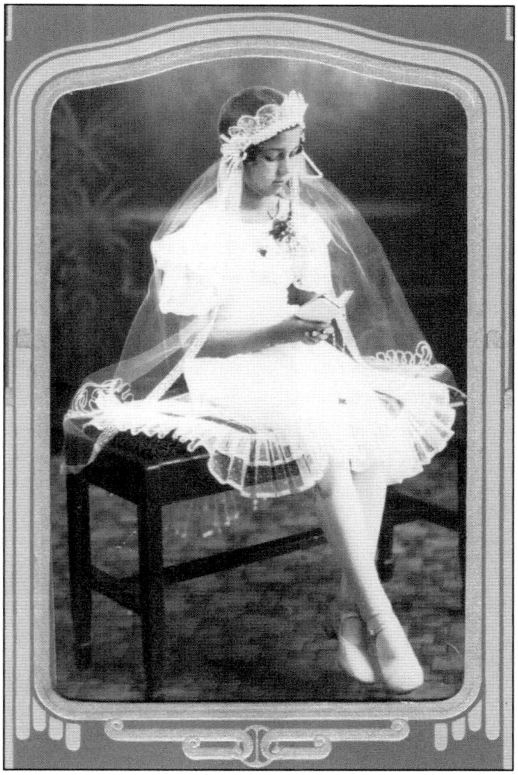

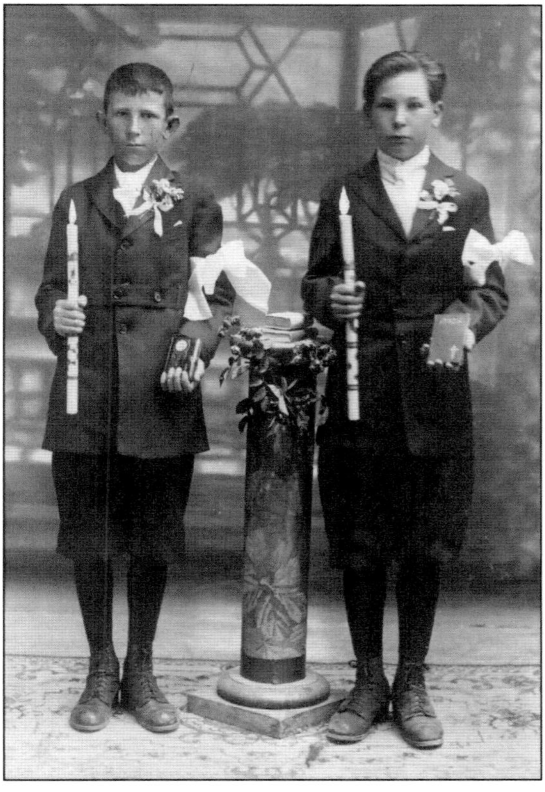

Pictured are well-dressed boys in short pants, ready for church. Several new churches were built during this time, using generous financial contributions and the labor of the parishioners. New churches and new homes, new community growth, approximately 380 new homes were built between 1900 and 1910. (Author's collection.)

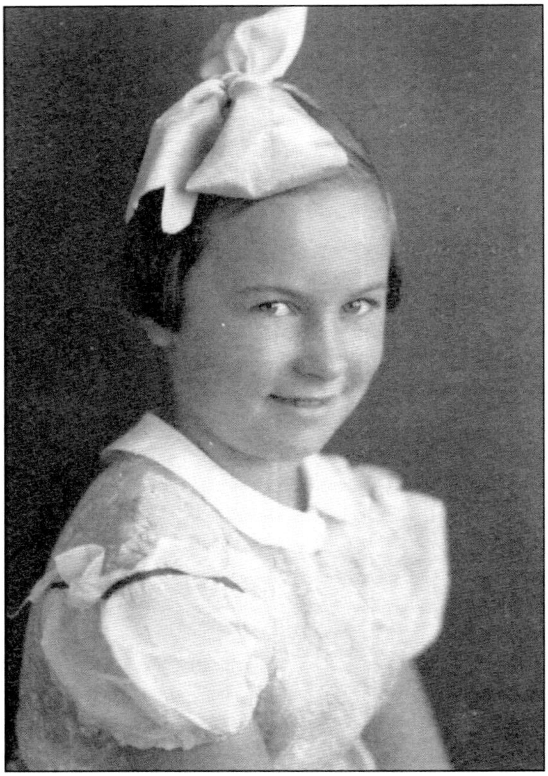

Penicillin was discovered as the first effective antibiotic. Flapper girls, the precursor to the flower children of the 1960s, were common. The girls wore bobbed hair, heavy makeup, and short skirts, danced the Charleston, and smoke cigarettes, flaunting social norms. It was the era of Prohibition, speakeasies, and Elliott Ness. (Author's collection.)

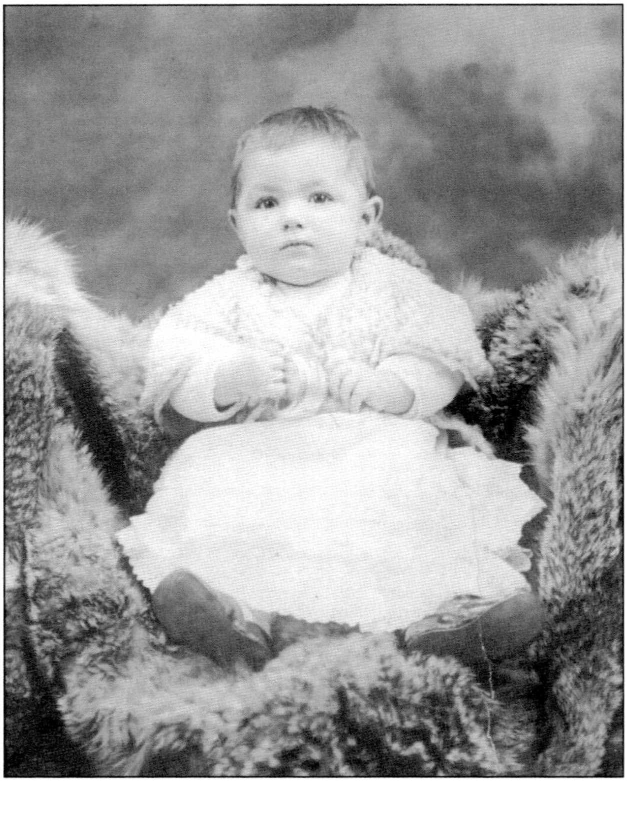

When this child was born, Plymouth's annual budget included such things as maintenance of watering troughs, reimbursement of damage to sheep, and a total budget of teacher's salaries of $6,379 for the year 1900. A new school was built in Plymouth Center at a cost of $4,000. A total of 487 students were enrolled in Plymouth schools, and five graduated from high school. (Author's collection.)

This young woman is formally dressed after the death of her mother in the 1918 influenza epidemic that claimed mostly young adults, leaving broken families, children without parents, and lives forever changed. (Author's collection.)

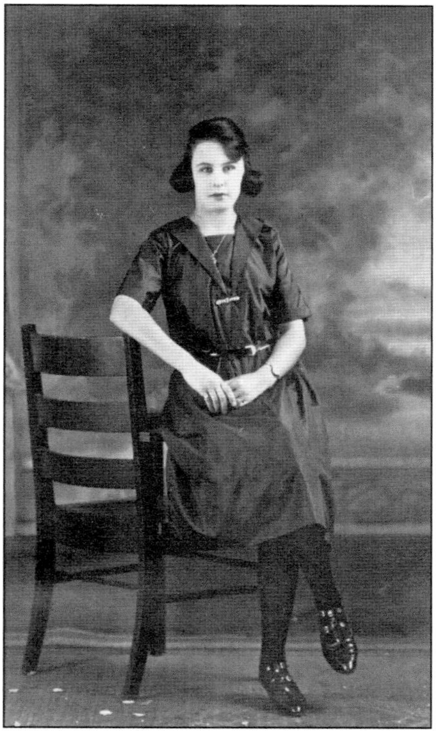

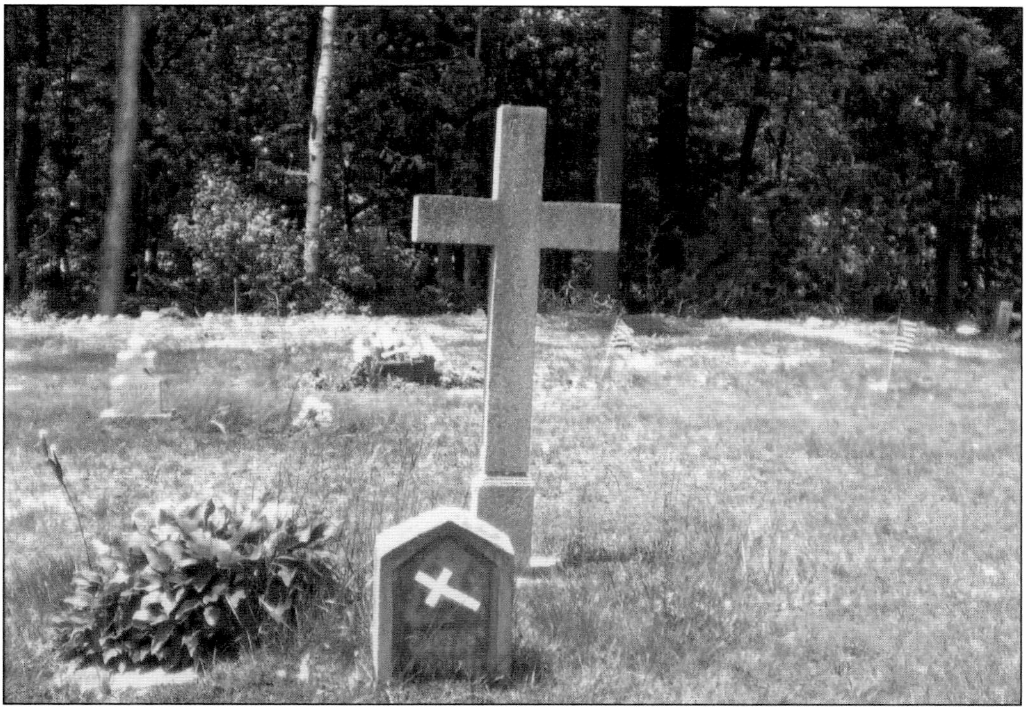

On a tall cross made of cement-like material, the name is carved in Polish on the front of the monument. Although these remarkable homemade grave markers do not follow typical New England symbolism, the intent is clear. This particular section of the cemetery is for individuals that died during the 1918 influenza epidemic. (Photograph by Judy Giguere.)

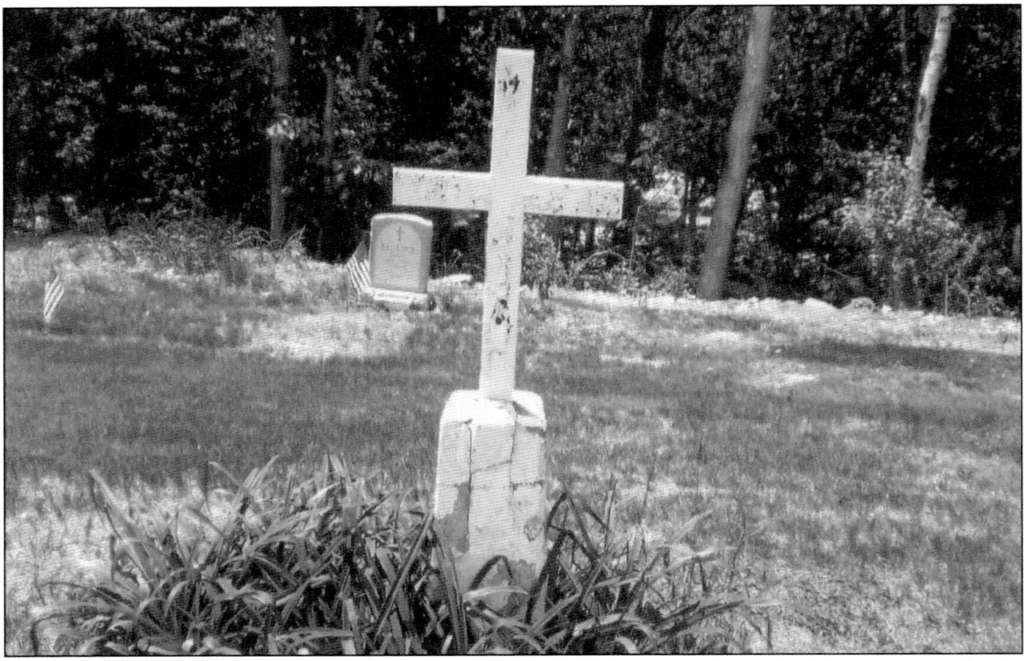

This is a tall obelisk cemetery marker with a metal cross on it and a heart-shaped plaque with the name in Polish. In the autumn of 1918, the Spanish Flu quickly engulfed America. In September 1918, about 12,000 died. In October, another 195,000 died from influenza. Sometimes referred to as "the Spanish Lady," influenza claimed 670,000 lives in the fall of 1918. (Photograph by Judy Giguere.)

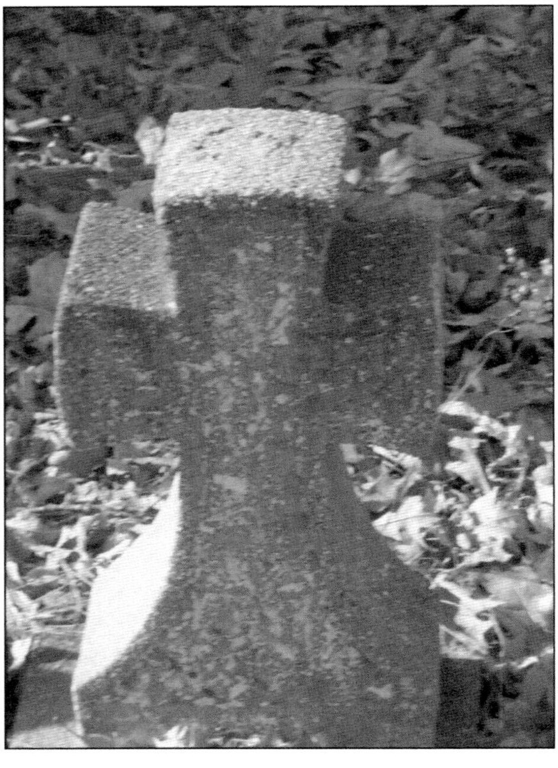

Several of these Celtic-style crosses have been found in Plymouth. No names are inscribed. World War I was dragging on, and the United States had just entered the fray. In the summer of 1918, approximately 1.5 million American soldiers crossed the Atlantic Ocean for war. Conditions were ripe for an epidemic. (Photograph by Judy Giguere.)

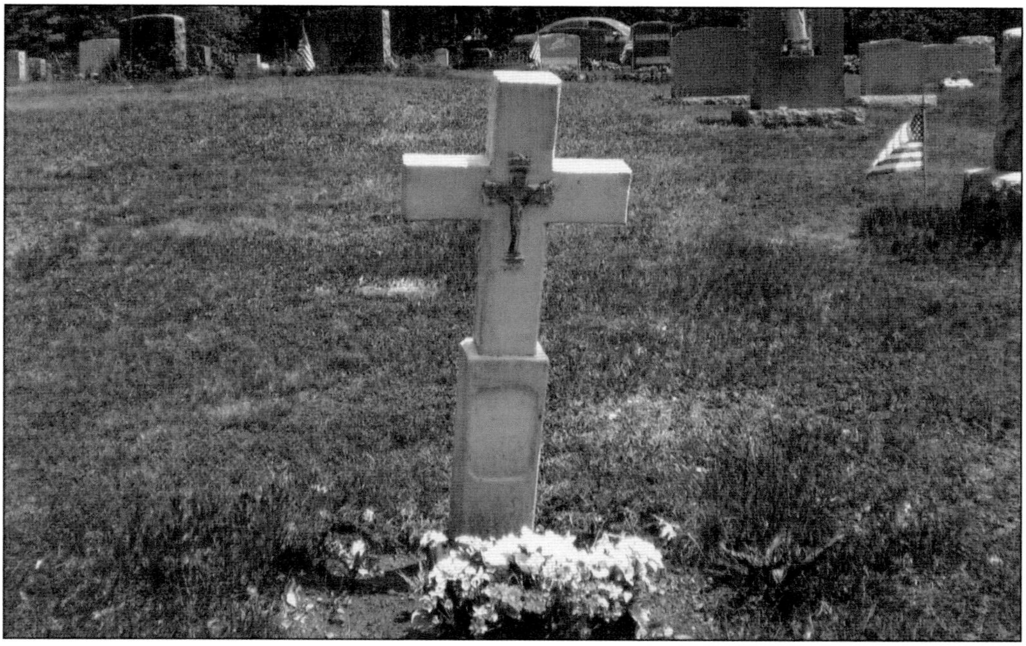

Here is another fine example of a homemade marker bearing an elegant cross. The year 1918 was one of growth, science, and new discoveries. However, despite scientific experimentation and snake-oil remedies, the influenza onslaught continued unabated. (Photograph by Judy Giguere.)

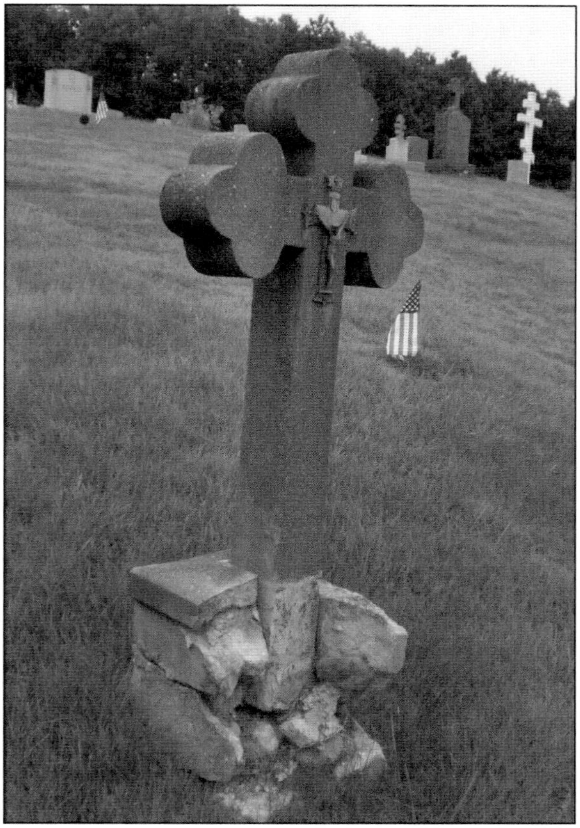

A 1918 children's rhyme went like so: "I had a little bird, and its name was Enza, I opened the window and, In-flew-enza." The epidemic ran rampant for the fall of 1918. And then, as mysteriously as it began, it ended. The Spanish were blamed, with claims of germ warfare, but Spain was equally hard hit by influenza. Plymouth was no exception. (Photograph by Judy Giguere.)

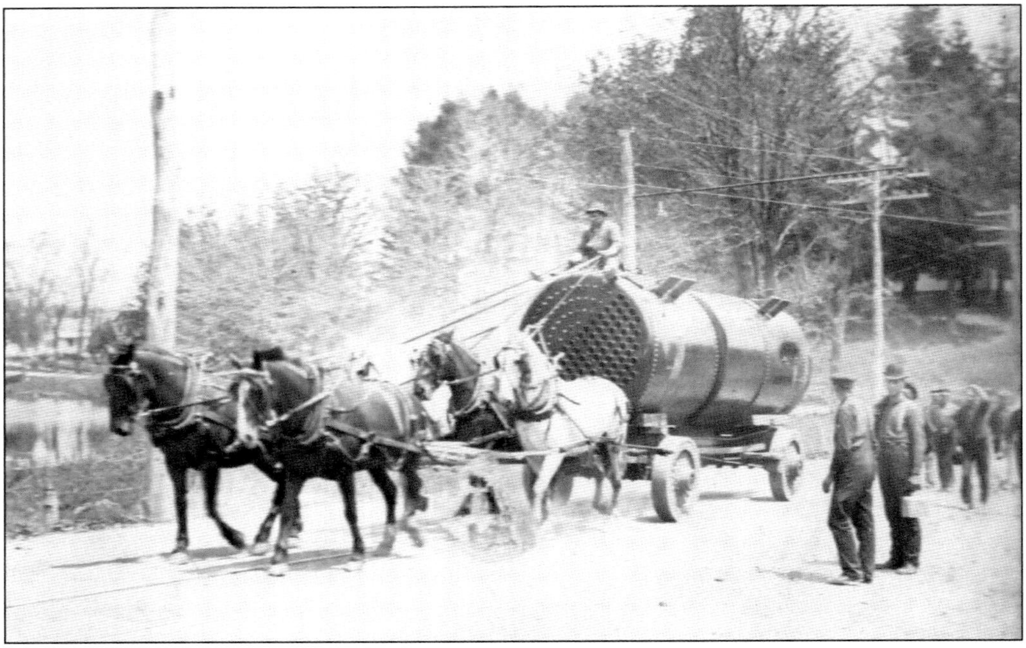

A man drives a four-horse team to pull a boiler unit for the Eagle Lock Company boiler house on East Orchard Street. A group of spectators are ready to assist, if necessary. (Courtesy of Plymouth Historical Society.)

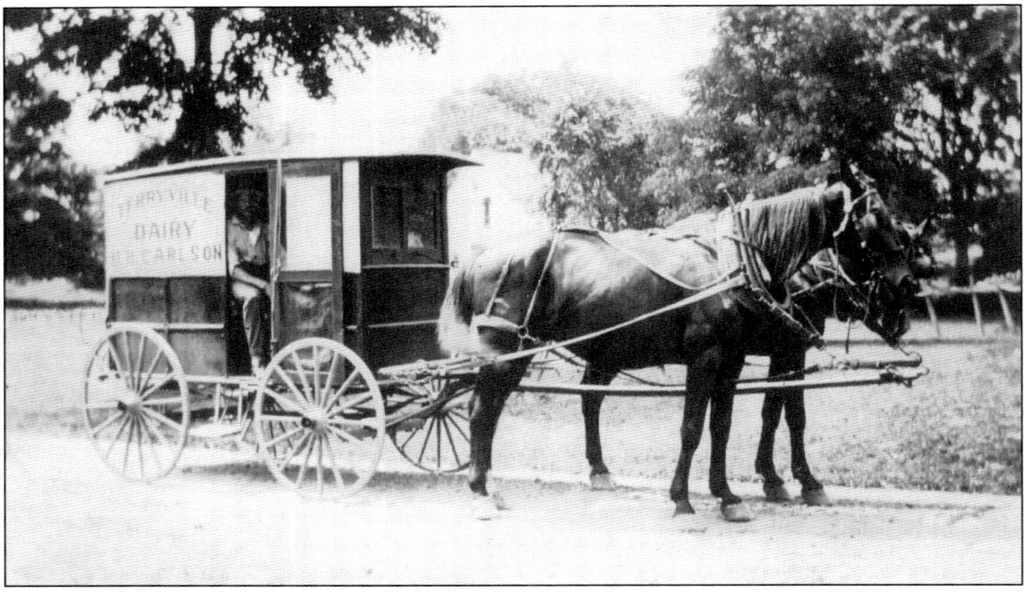

Milk delivery became popular at the onset of the 20th century. The beginning of the century was a mix of old and new. Change was at hand. The first home refrigerator was sold in Chicago, the hand-cranked phonograph, and the washing machine and the telephone began to change old ways. Henry Ford's "Tin Lizzie" sold locally for $950. It was a time of dramatic contrasts. (Courtesy of Plymouth Historical Society.)

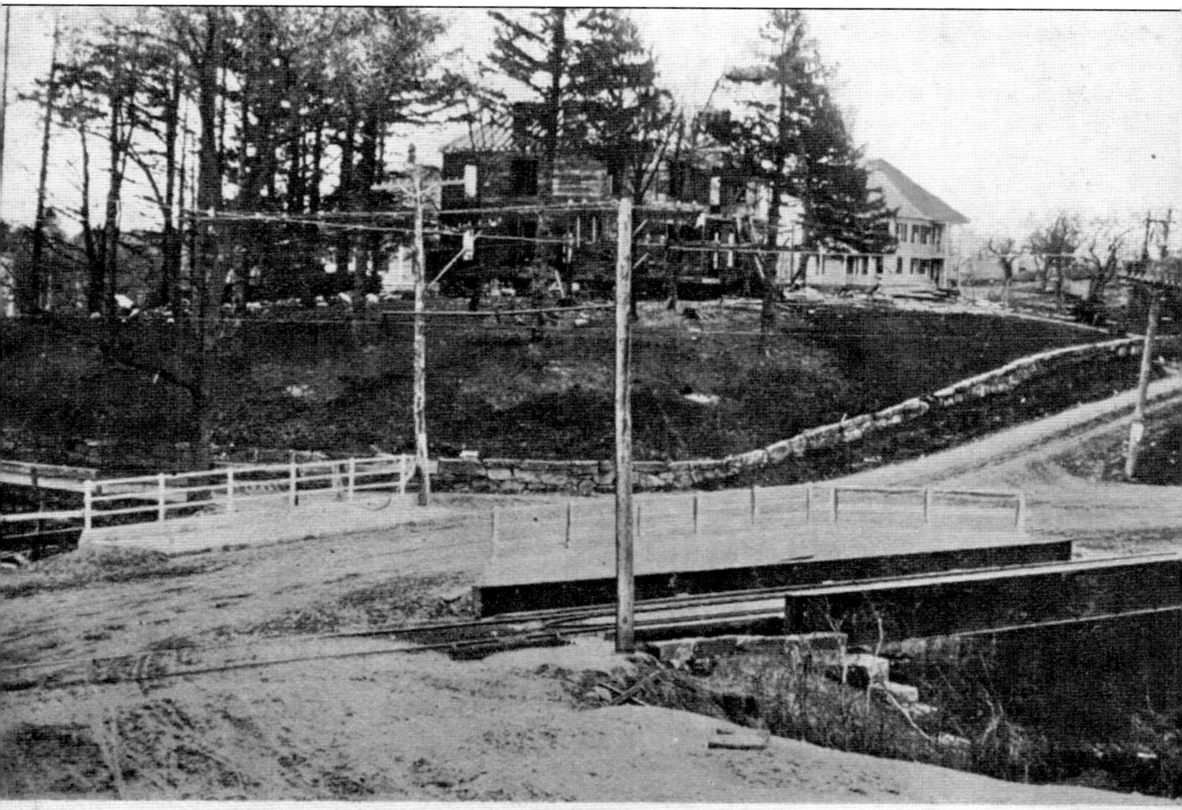

NEW BURNHAM BRIDGE, Terryville, Conn.

A new bridge was constructed at the intersection of Route 6 and Route 72. The road was not yet paved, but early telephone poles and electric lines can be seen. Some of the stonework to support the bridge is still present. The bridge, replaced in the 1955 flood, once had trolley tracks for the line that passed through the center of town. Burnham Pond was located on Bullhead Street, to the left, later known as Riverside Avenue, and included State Route 72. Burnham Pond was filled in after the flood of 1955. (Courtesy of Plymouth Historical Society.)

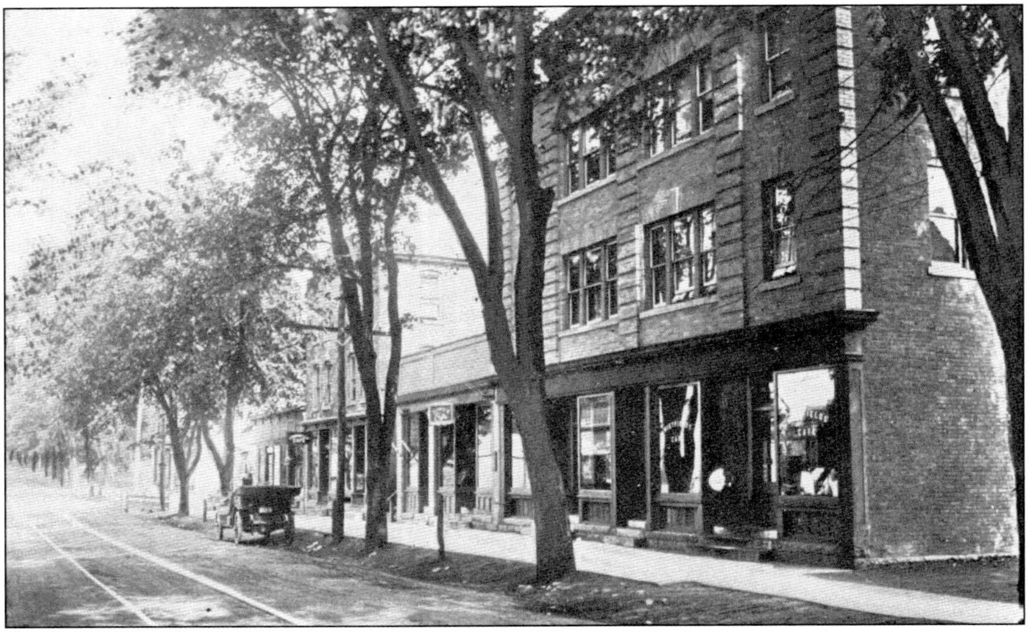

This was Main Street in Terryville at the time of the appearance of Halley's Comet. The comet began to show itself on May 12. On May 18, it passed the sun and was temporarily invisible. It returned to the skies in fabulous fashion for May 20 and 21 with five tails. Incredible sunsets were seen. It appeared as a bright star casting a bright glow with a brilliant tail. (Courtesy of Plymouth Historical Society.)

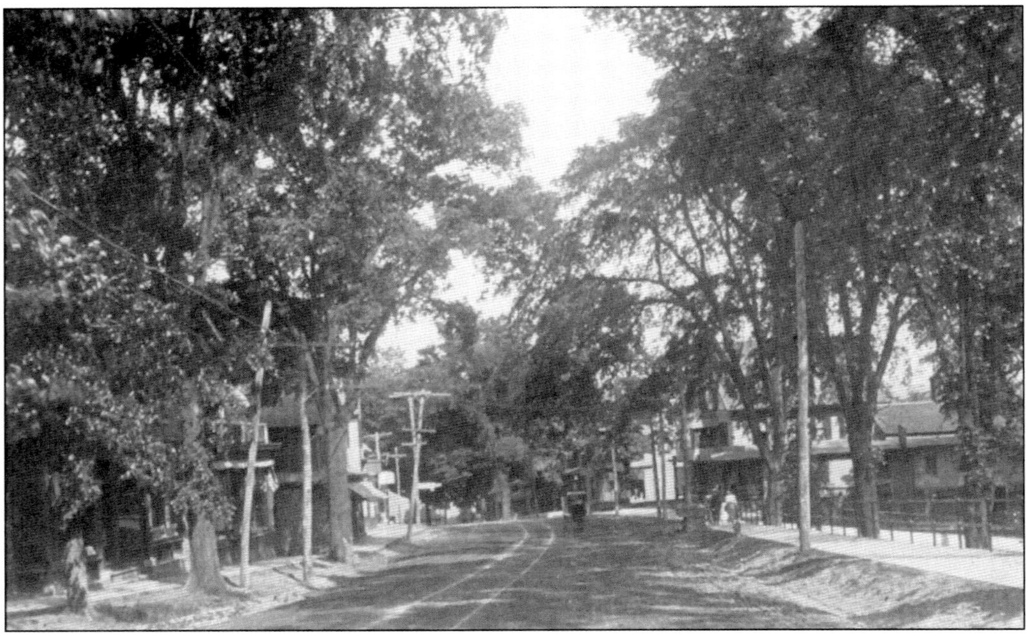

In May 1910, Halley's Comet was predicted to make another appearance. Some feared it was an announcement of the end of the world. Comet pills were supposed to prevent the sickness from the cyanogen gas of the comet's tail. Duly notable was that after the comet had passed, those who had taken the anti-comet sickness pills were still alive—as were those who had not. (Courtesy of Plymouth Historical Society.)

World War I soldiers pose for a formal photograph. Plymouth sent more than 200 young men as soldiers to Europe during World War I, and 12 of them died while serving. Plymouth's soldiers, sailors, and marines served with distinction and those remaining at home participated in home front activities to assist in the war effort. (Courtesy of Plymouth Historical Society.)

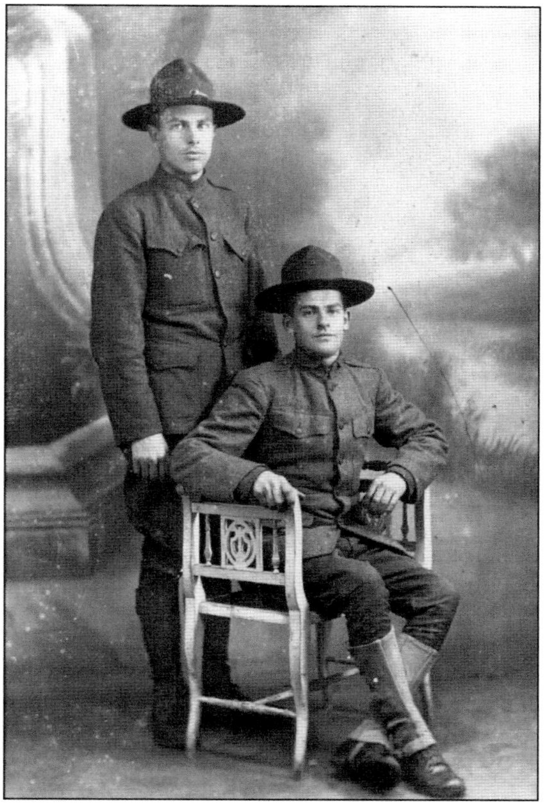

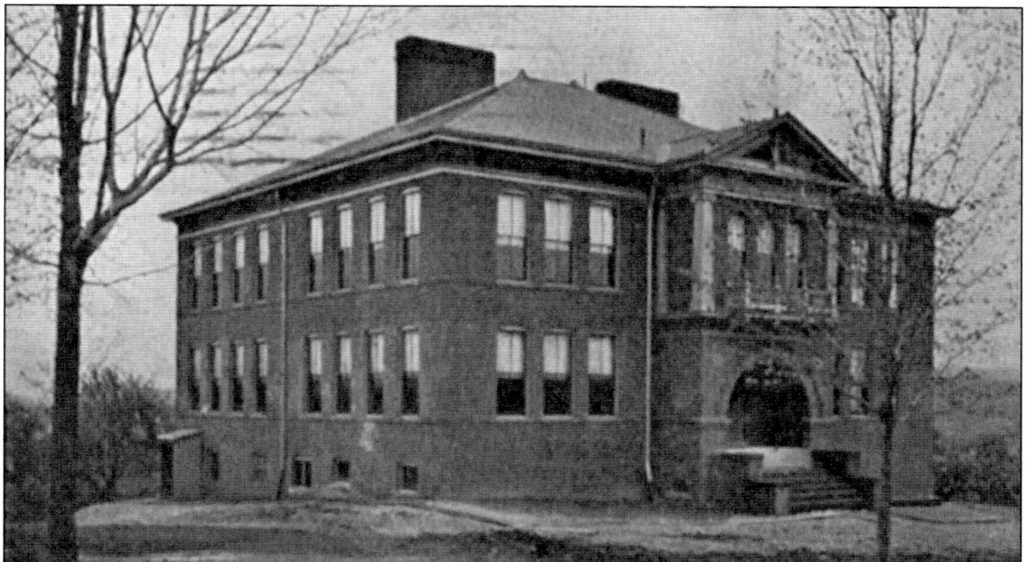

Prospect Street School opened in 1906 to accommodate the increased population of new students brought in by families moving to Terryville and Plymouth for work in the local factories. An earlier, smaller building existed on the site that was destroyed by fire and replaced by a brick building. Later, an addition was constructed on the back of the building to accommodate the increasing school population. (Courtesy of Plymouth Historical Society.)

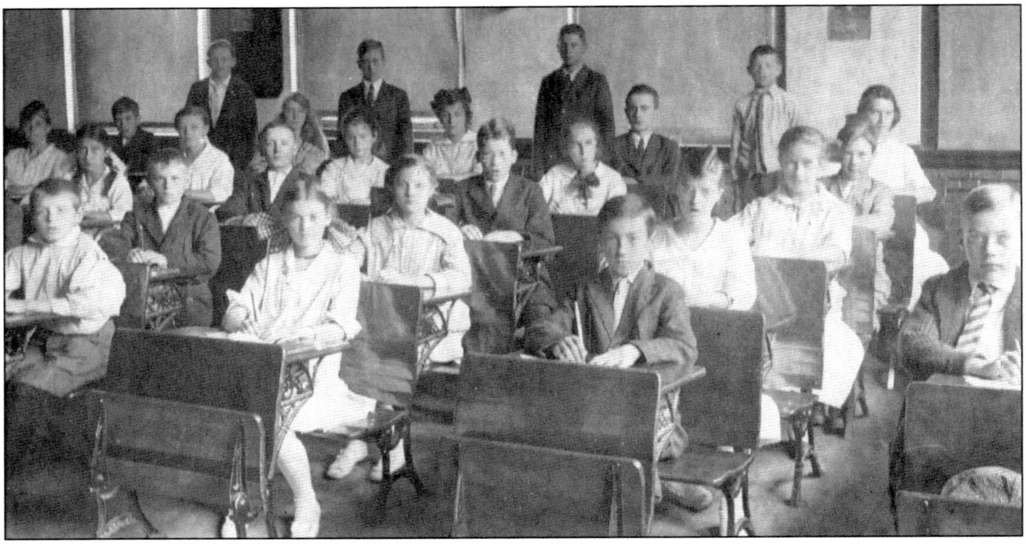

Rules for teachers in the late 19th century included each teacher bringing a bucket of water and scuttle of coal to school each day. Teachers, after spending 10 hours in school, could spend the remaining time reading the Bible or other good books. Male teachers were permitted to take one evening each week for courting purposes, or two evenings a week if they attended church regularly. (Courtesy of Plymouth Historical Society.)

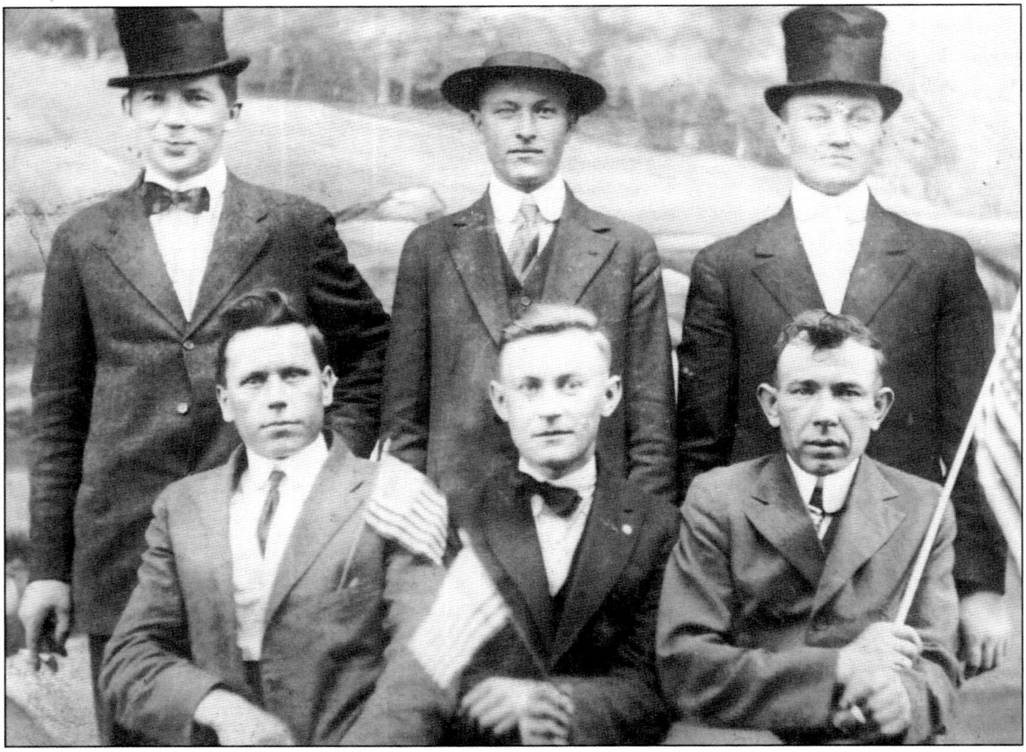

Formally dressed young men pose for a group portrait. As new arrivals to the United States with jobs in local industries, these young men proudly display American flags. America provided a better life and increased standard of living that was not possible in their former homes. (Author's collection.)

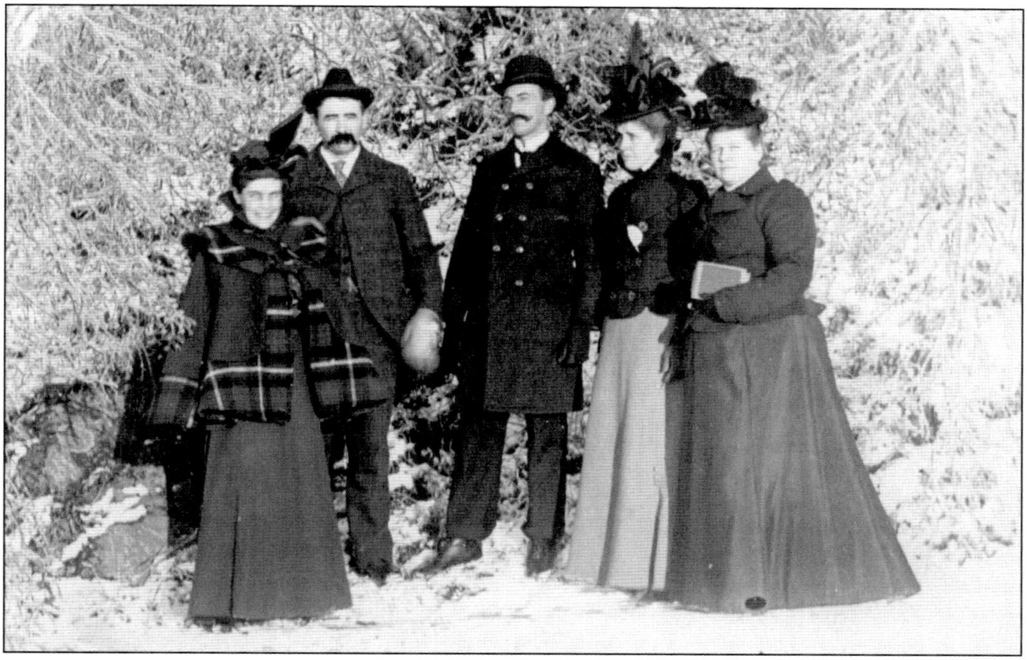

This group is gathered for a winter walk. The trolley was also available for travel, as the first car entered Terryville in 1902. Bristol Tramway Company operated the trolley line. The line extended from Main Street in Terryville, into Bristol with stops in Pequabuck. The fare was 5¢. (Courtesy of Plymouth Historical Society.)

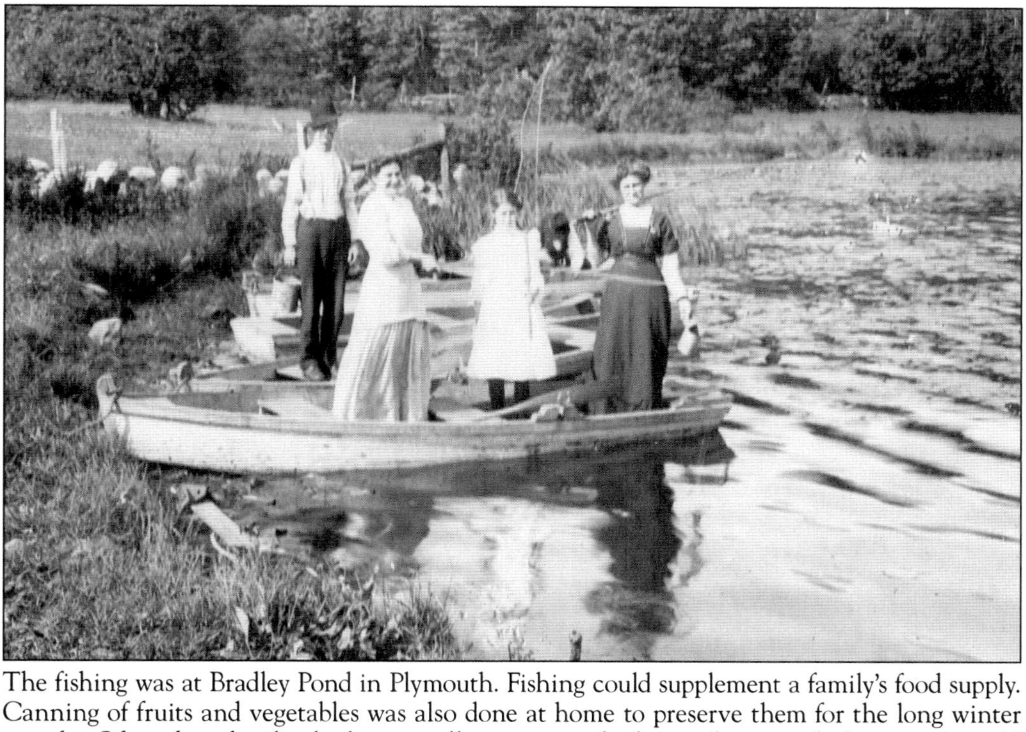

The fishing was at Bradley Pond in Plymouth. Fishing could supplement a family's food supply. Canning of fruits and vegetables was also done at home to preserve them for the long winter months. Often, farm families had a root cellar, or storage built into the ground where goods could remain cool for later use. (Courtesy of Plymouth Historical Society.)

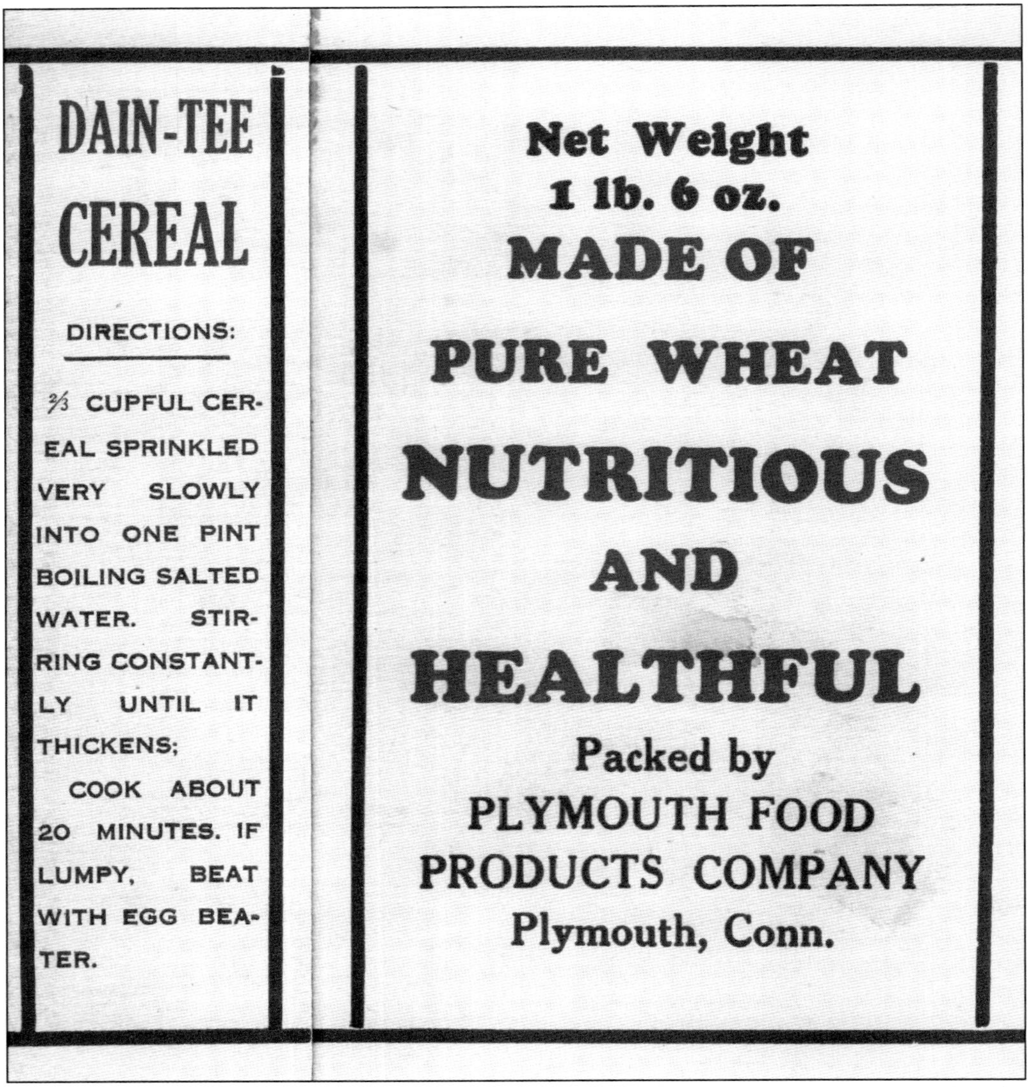

Kellogg's toasted rice flakes sold for 5¢ a package. Twenty pounds of granulated sugar was $1. The local druggists carried such items as Pinaud's Hair Tonic for 35¢, Doanes Kidney Pills were 34¢, sodium phosphate was 9¢ a pound, Atwood's Bitters were sold at 15¢, and swamp root for 35¢. Milk was sold for 8¢ a quart in Plymouth and Bristol, 6¢ a quart in Waterbury, and 7¢ a quart in Hartford and New Britain. Spring was late, and songbirds arrived three weeks later than the previous spring. The winter of 1910 was recorded in papers as the coldest on record. Schools were closed and plumbers rejoiced as the arctic winds burst many pipes, but the opening of spring pastures for milk cows did little to relieve the price of milk for Plymouth families. (Courtesy of Plymouth Historical Society.)

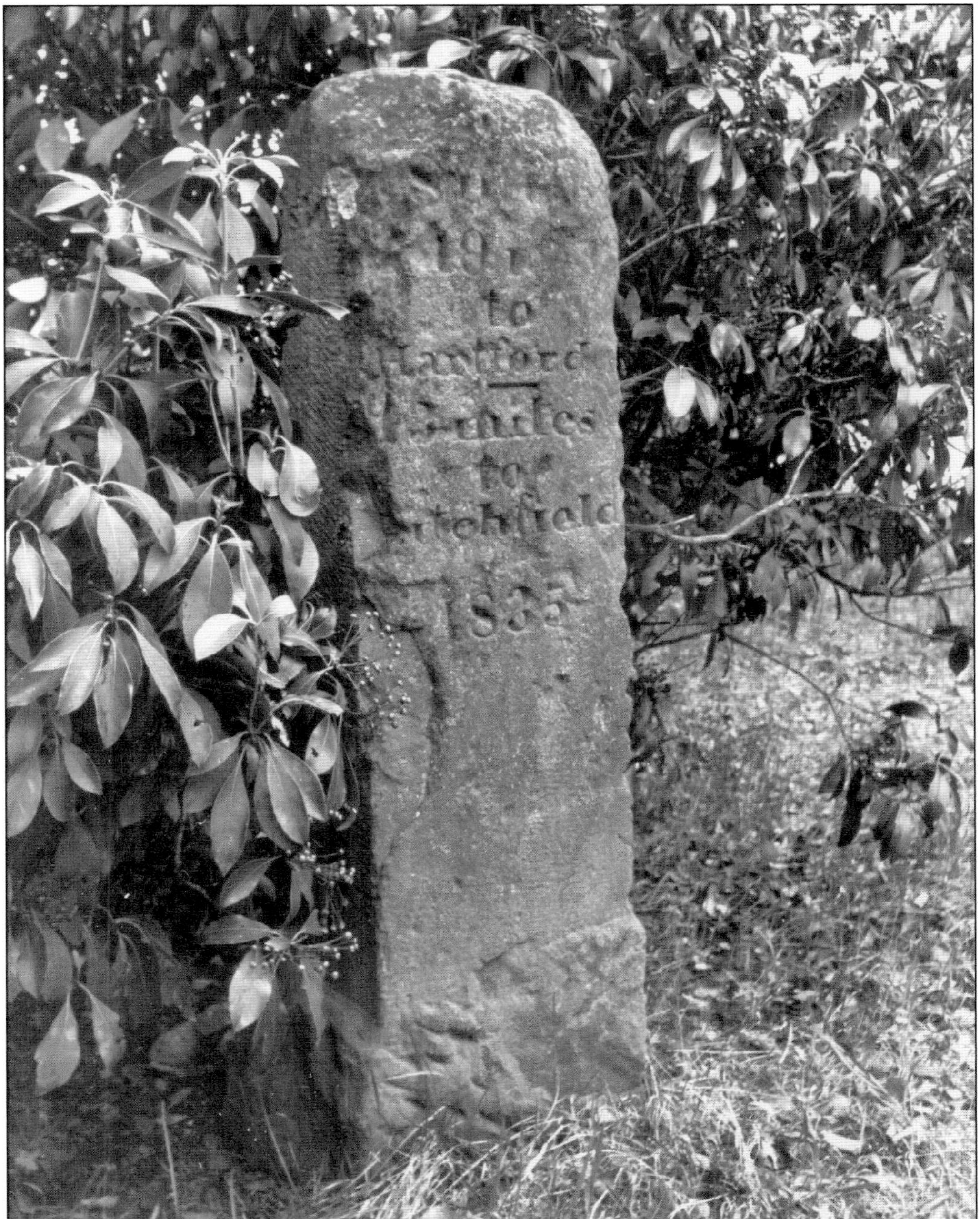

In 1835, a highway mile marker to Hartford was placed on Main Street, near the present Bristol town line, signifying that Route 6 was once a well-traveled roadway. The markers were used to specify the distance from the marker's location to Hartford and Litchfield. The surviving markers are evidence of earlier transportation networks whose history is frequently lost with the passage of time. Some markers in other towns have only a numeral inscribed, implying that the traveler may have known where he was going and where he had been. Considering the rural spaces between towns and civilization of early Connecticut, it certainly seems that one might not have known the specifics of his path. This particular marker has been allotted a special place in the Town of Plymouth with respect to its place in our history. (Courtesy of Plymouth Historical Society.)

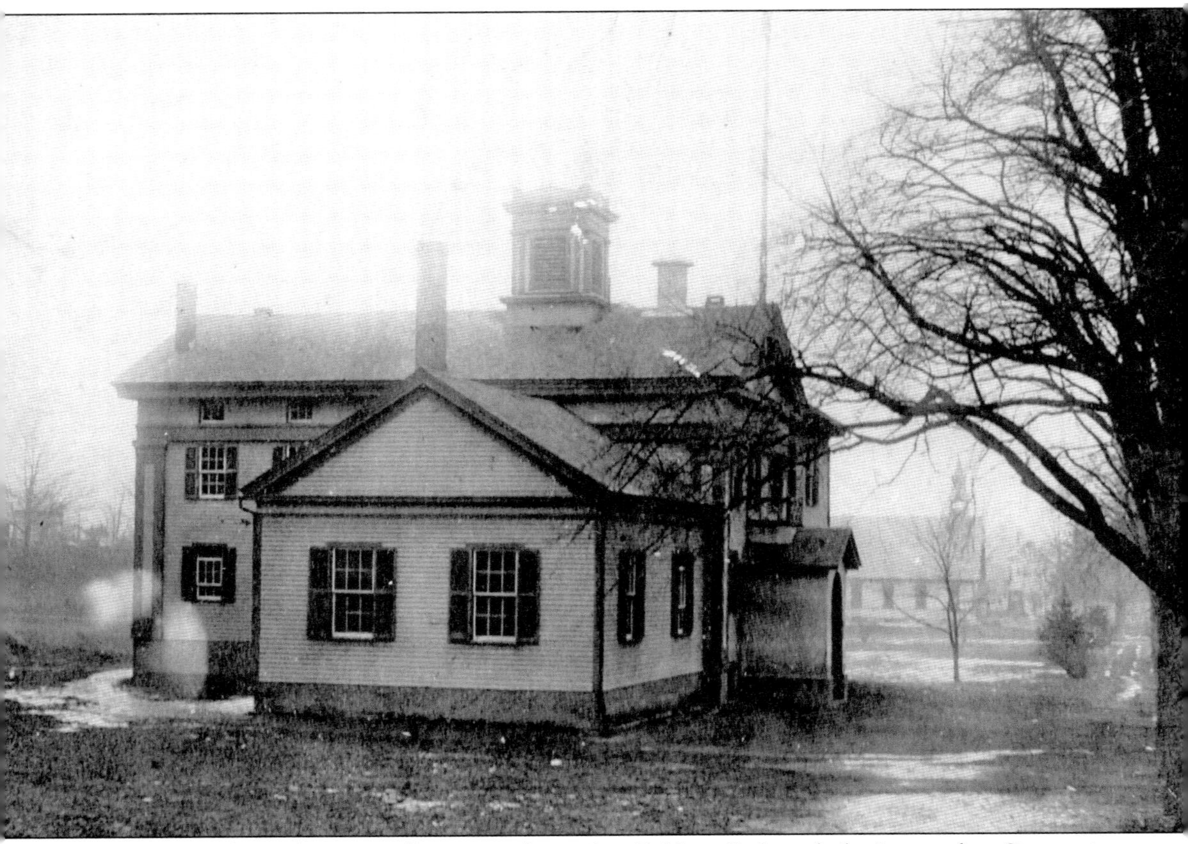

This image shows the Terryville Institute located on Baldwin Park, with the Immaculate Conception Roman Catholic Church shown in the distance. The Terryville Institute, also known as the Main Street School, was a grade school and high school. When Prospect Street School opened, high school classes moved to that location. High School classes continued at Prospect Street School until 1952 when Terryville High School on North Main Street opened. Holt District School, formerly known as District 12, stood on North Harwinton Avenue on Milo Holt's farm. In February 1880, logs were taken to Minor's sawmill, drawn by oxen to be cut into boards for building the school. Holt District School was a one-room schoolhouse that was in use until 1957. It was the last one-room schoolhouse in Connecticut to close. (Courtesy of Plymouth Historical Society.)

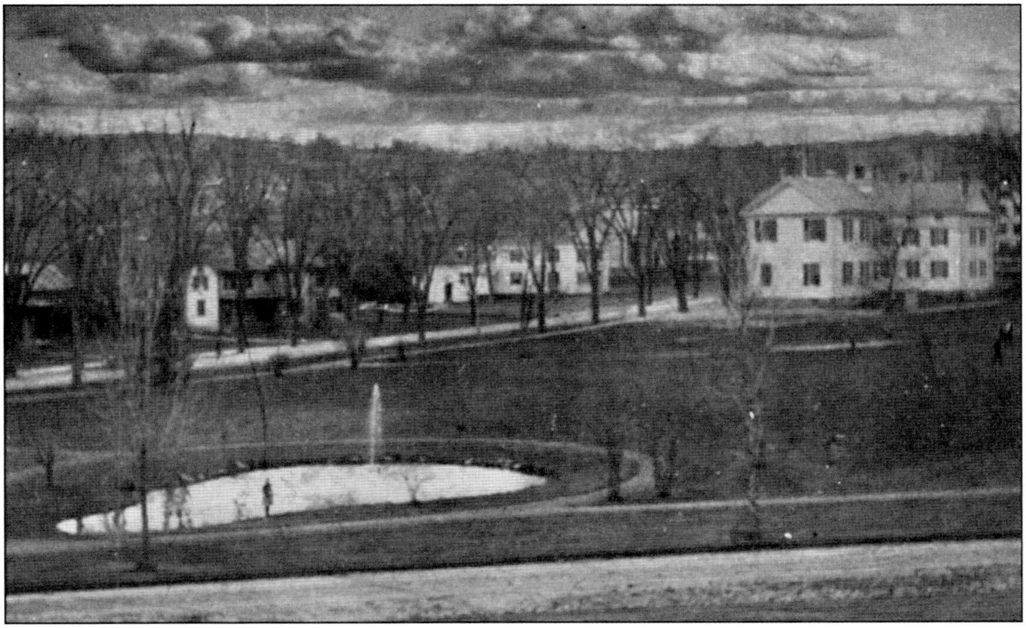

This image shows Main Street in Terryville, overlooking Baldwin Park. Times were changing. The roads were paved, and Plymouth was patrolled by constables. By the early 1920s, the first full-time officer was hired for night patrols. A second officer was added in the 1930s. The new police department had their office in the town hall building that had once been the offices of the Eagle Lock Company. (Courtesy of Plymouth Historical Society.)

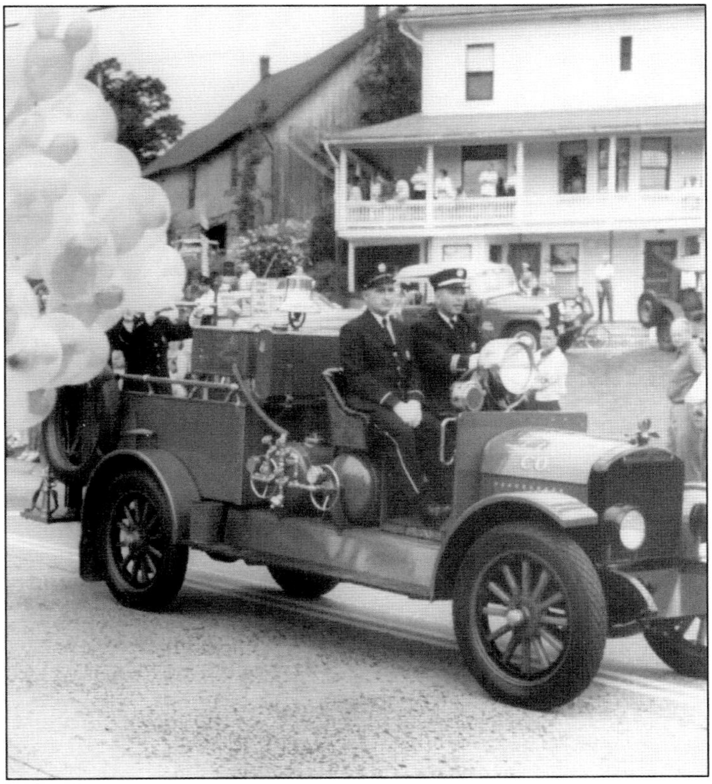

An early fire truck is on display in the Memorial Day parade, with the Austin House in the background. The Austin Livery Stable was located behind the Austin House Hotel. Horses owned by E. Grant Austin available to rent. Scott Funeral Home, one of the oldest establishments in Plymouth, rented teams of horses for funerals from Austin. (Courtesy of Plymouth Historical Society.)

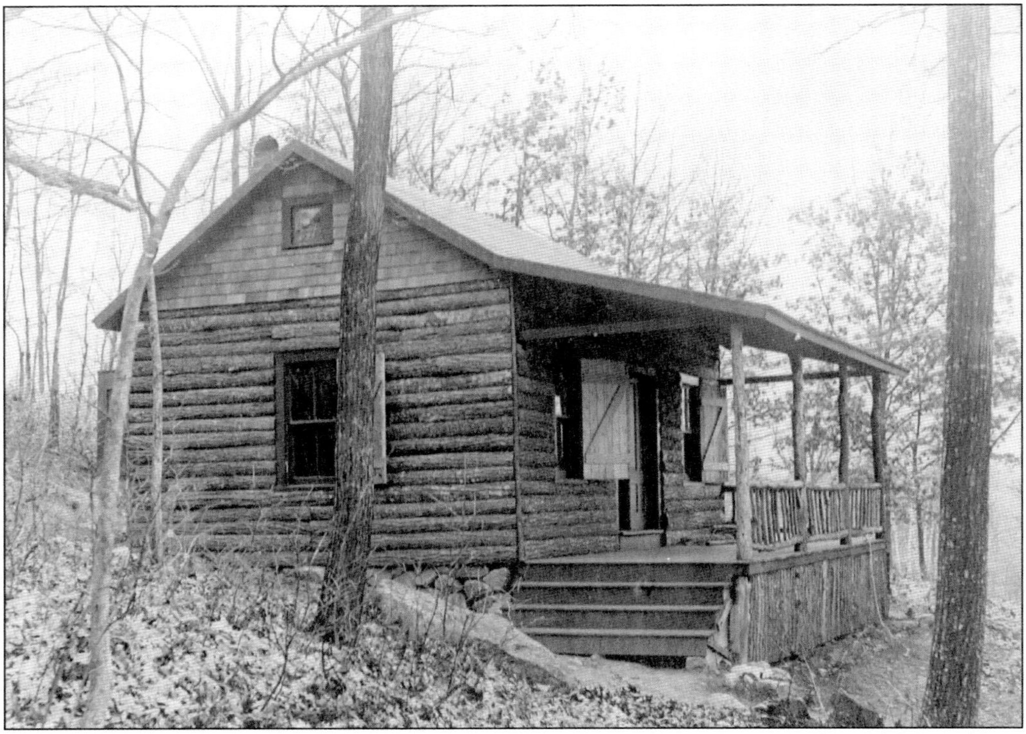

This is an early photograph of the Terryville Fish and Game clubhouse. The clubhouse has a large meeting and dining room with a beautiful stone fireplace, kitchen, and lounge downstairs. The club was founded in 1905. (Courtesy of Plymouth Historical Society.)

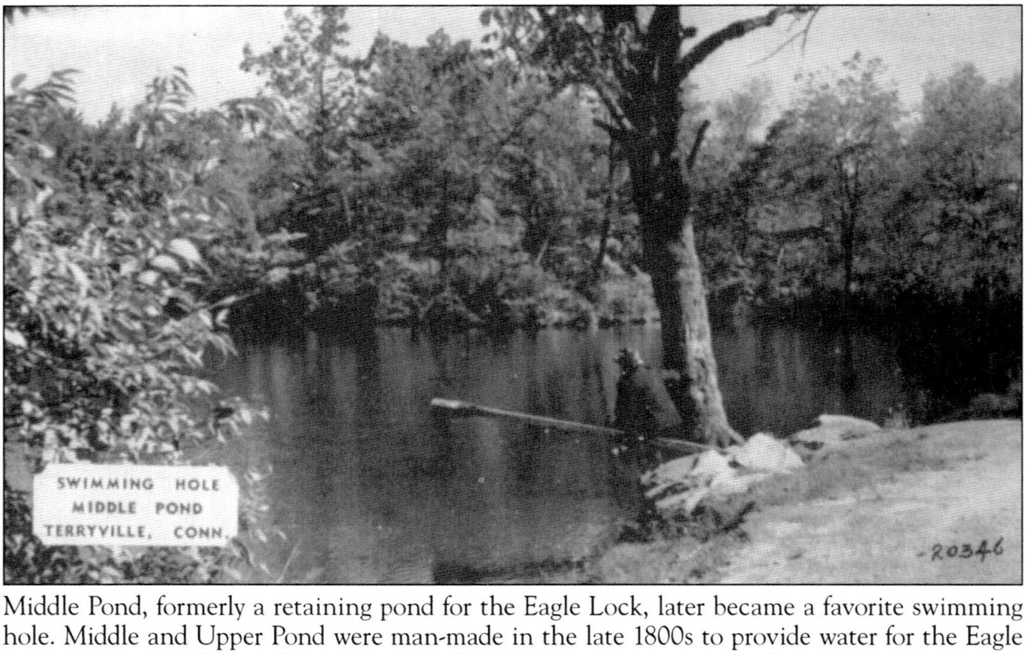

Middle Pond, formerly a retaining pond for the Eagle Lock, later became a favorite swimming hole. Middle and Upper Pond were man-made in the late 1800s to provide water for the Eagle Lock Company. The ponds were used by the Eagle Lock as recreational areas for the company officers and foremen, before the Terryville Fish and Game Club was formed. (Courtesy of Plymouth Historical Society.)

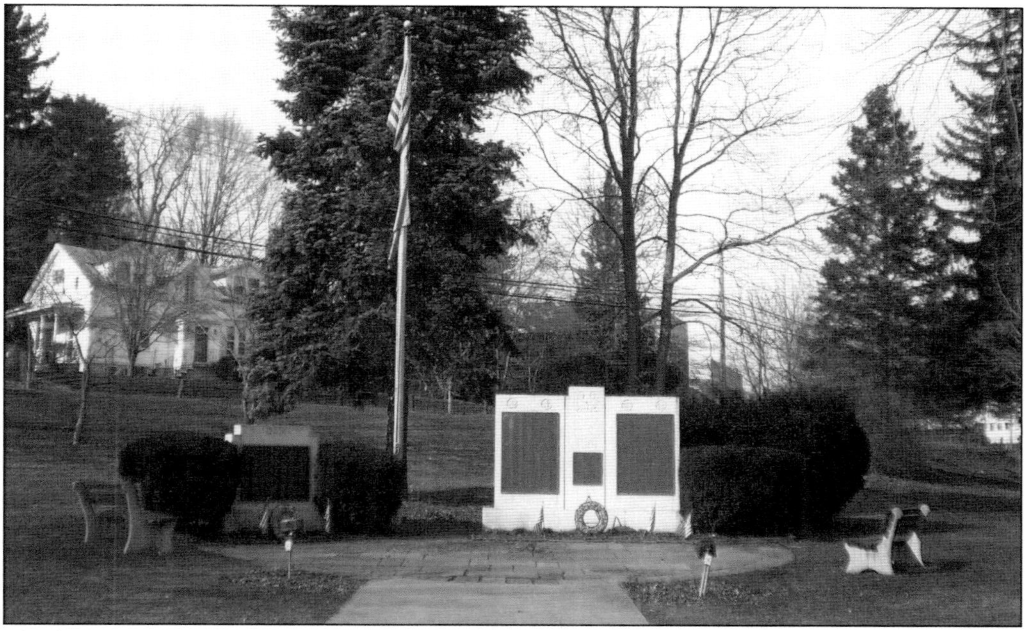

The larger monument is at the end of the brick walkway to honor the town residents who served in World War I, World War II, and the Korean War. To the left is a flagpole with the American Flag and the POW flag, as well as a monument to those who served in the military during the Vietnam War. (Photograph by Judy Giguere.)

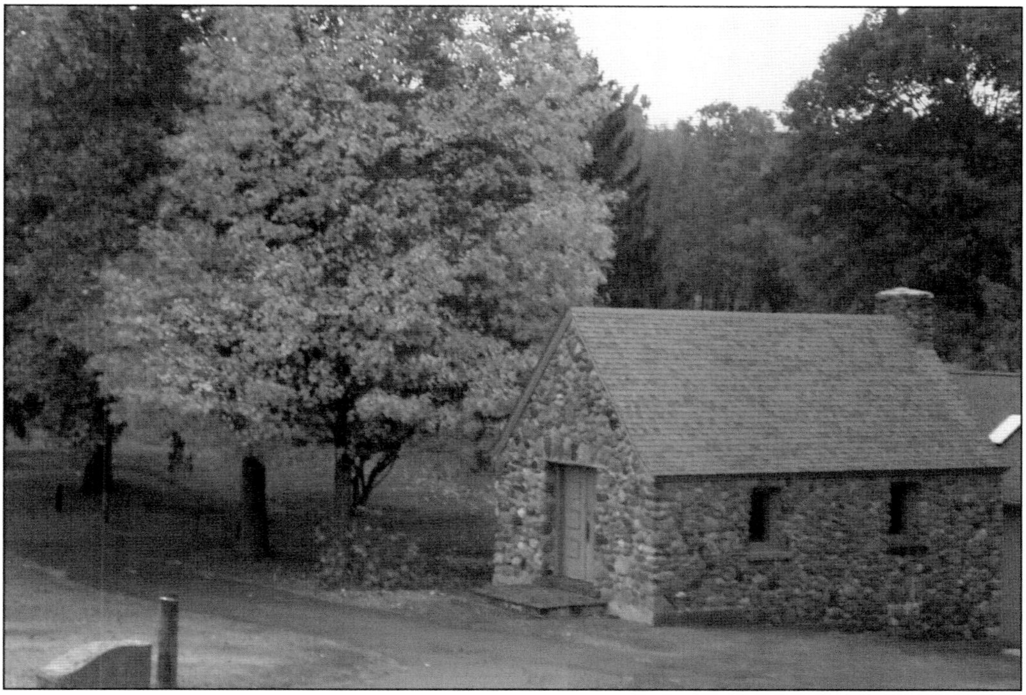

This small chapel was built of local stone and located at Hillside Cemetery. Initially, it provided a place for final services for the deceased on the site of the cemetery property. Hillside Cemetery, located in Terryville, was opened in response to the deaths of local soldiers during the Civil War. (Photograph by Judy Giguere.)

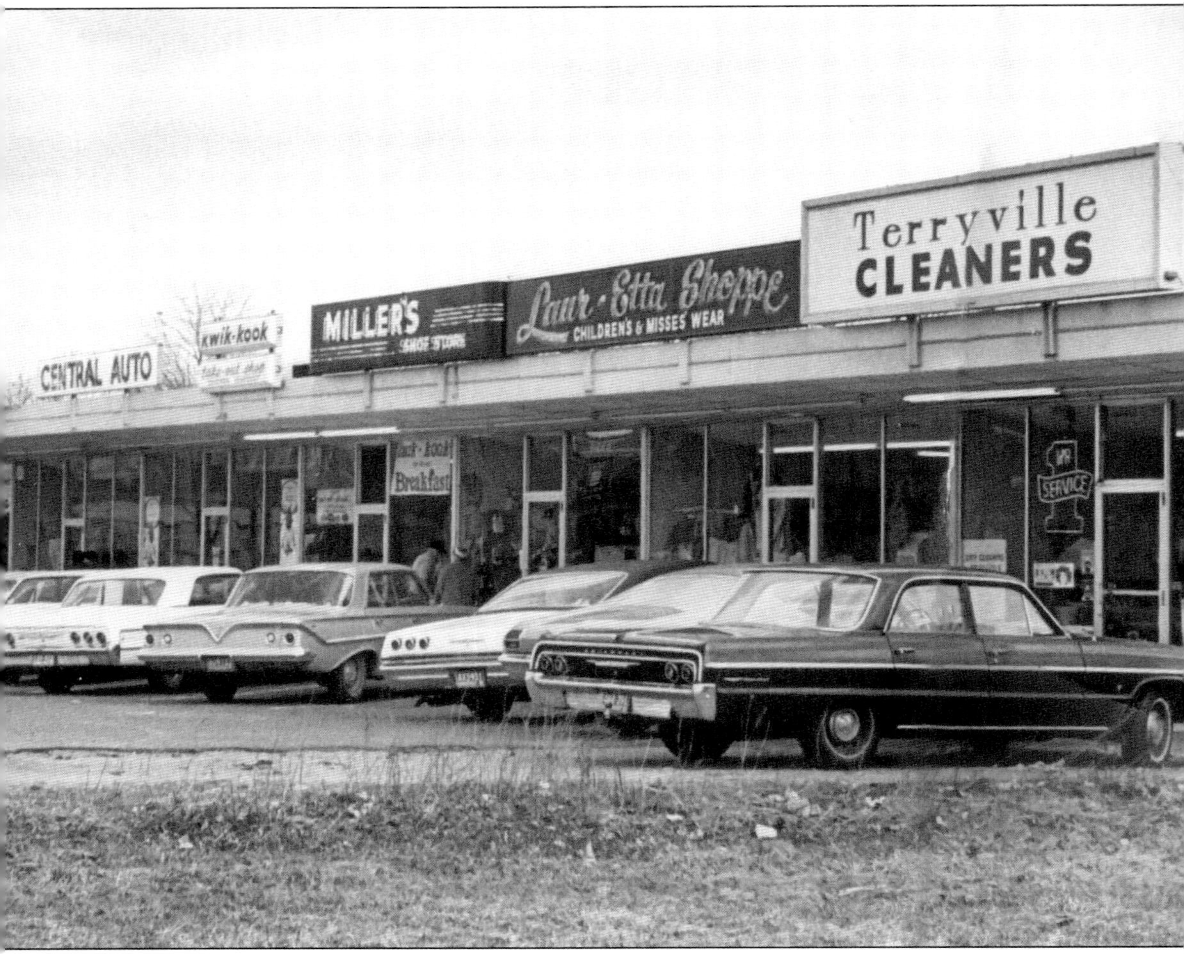

Terryville Plaza on Route 6, Main Street, was still one of main shopping areas of the town in the late 1950s. The Eagle Lock Company closed in 1975; the main building site includes another small shopping plaza. (Courtesy of Plymouth Historical Society.)

The new town government facility was constructed in 1974. Plymouth was incorporated in May 1795. Initially, town government was by a Board of Selectmen and town meeting. In 1976, the town government style changed to a mayor and town council form of government. The mayor is elected every two years and is in charge of the administration of all town departments. (Courtesy of Plymouth Historical Society.)

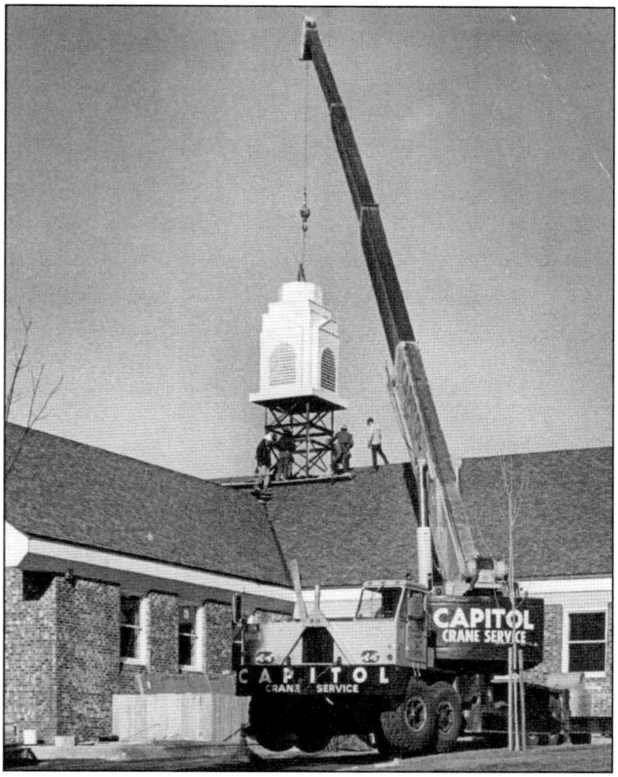

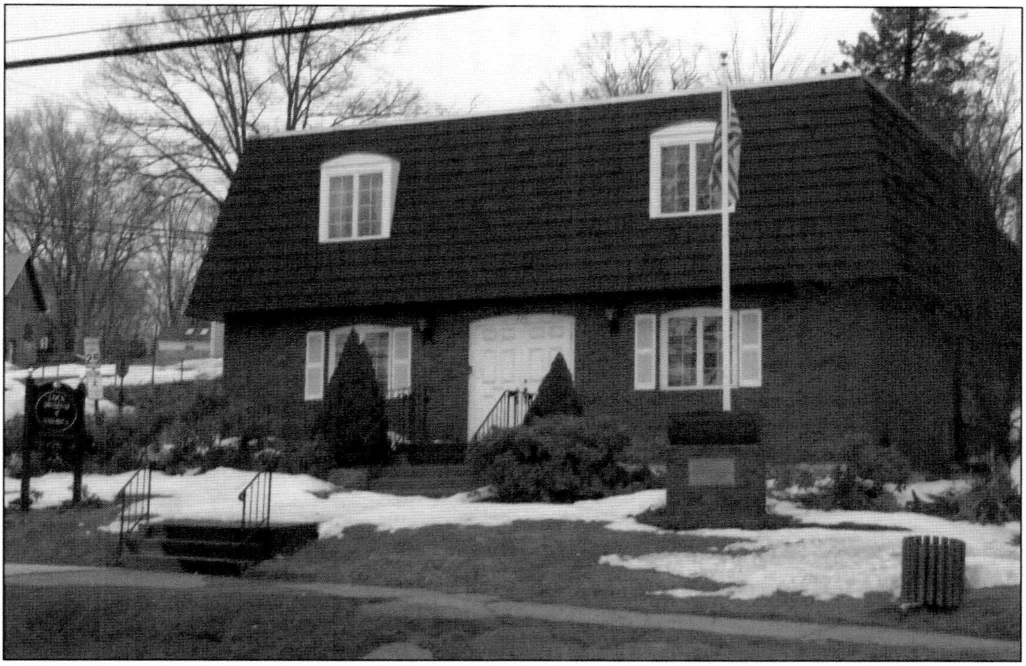

Lock Museum of America was established in 1971 to preserve the history of lock making in Plymouth and nationally. The museum's collection includes an Egyptian lock dating back 4,000 years as well as ornate European locks from the 1500s and collections of the historical contributions of the lock makers of Plymouth. (Photograph by Judy Giguere.)

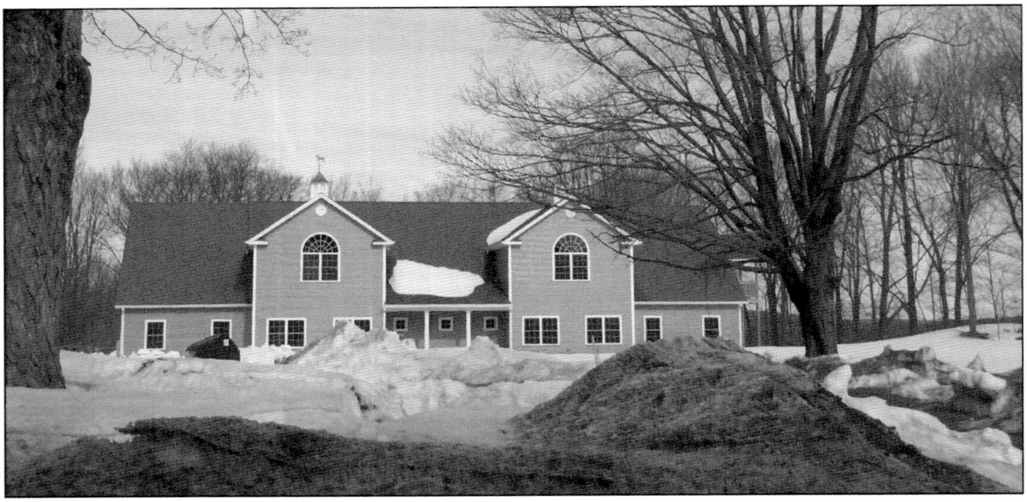

The Animal Rescue Foundation quarters were destroyed by fire in November 2008. Community generosity and hard work rebuilt this home for needy creatures. This volunteer organization devotes its time and energy to placing homeless dogs and cats in good homes. The new facility includes space for training, grooming, offices, and a special room for prospective "parents" to meet potential new family members. (Photograph by Judy Giguere.)

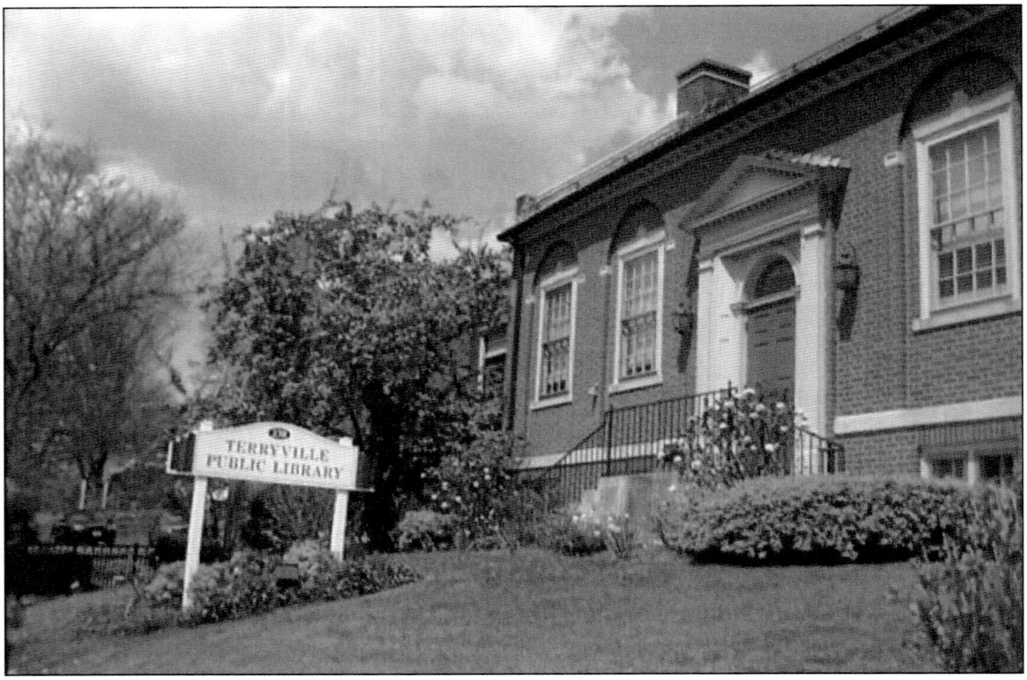

Terryville Public Library was originally instituted in 1839 and is a counterpart to the Plymouth Library. Land for the present site was donated, and Terryville Public Library opened its doors on 132 Main Street in 1922 with thanks to the generous contributions of the citizens of Plymouth and Terryville. (Courtesy of Terryville Public Library.)

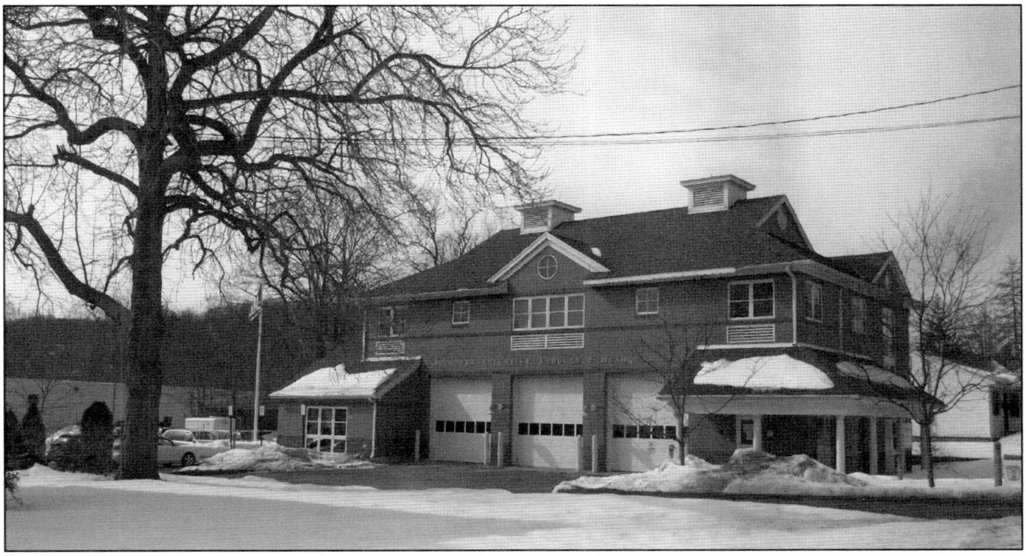

Plymouth Volunteer Ambulance Corps, staffed by volunteers, is ready to serve residents, visitors, and surrounding towns in times of medical emergency. The PVAC Bike Team is a specialized group of volunteers who respond rapidly to outdoor events, such as parades and special events. PVAC is home to Explorer Post 111, chartered by the Boy Scouts for the purpose of training young people to explore EMS as a career. (Photograph by Judy Giguere.)

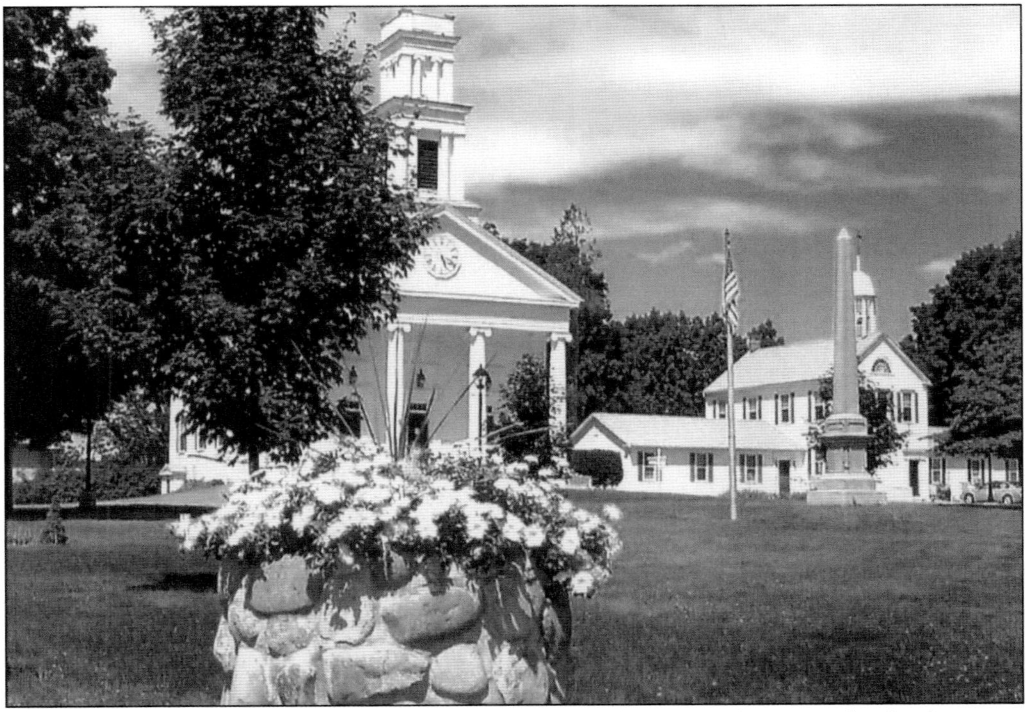

This is present-day Plymouth Green. The field stone and cement planter in the forefront was constructed from an old watering trough. Three watering troughs once existed in Plymouth from the days when horses and oxen were the primary mode of transportation. The watering trough provided a cool drink for the animals and drivers. (Photograph by Jerry Milne, courtesy of Cathy Mathiason.)

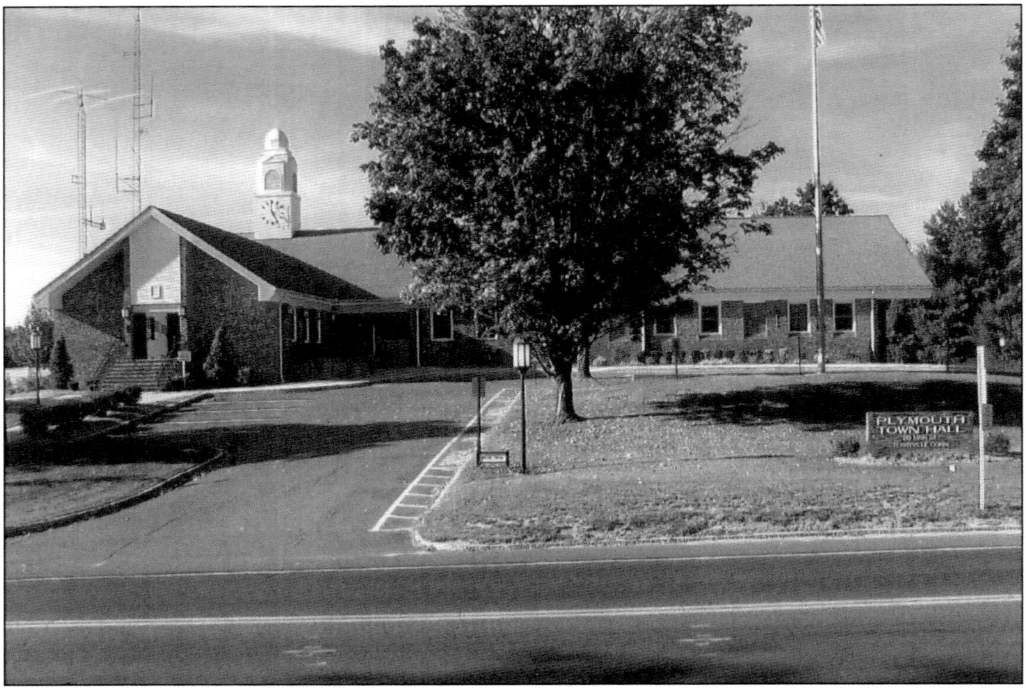

Plymouth Town Hall was constructed in 1974 and is the home of city departments, the mayor's office, and the police department. (Courtesy of Cathy Mathiason.)

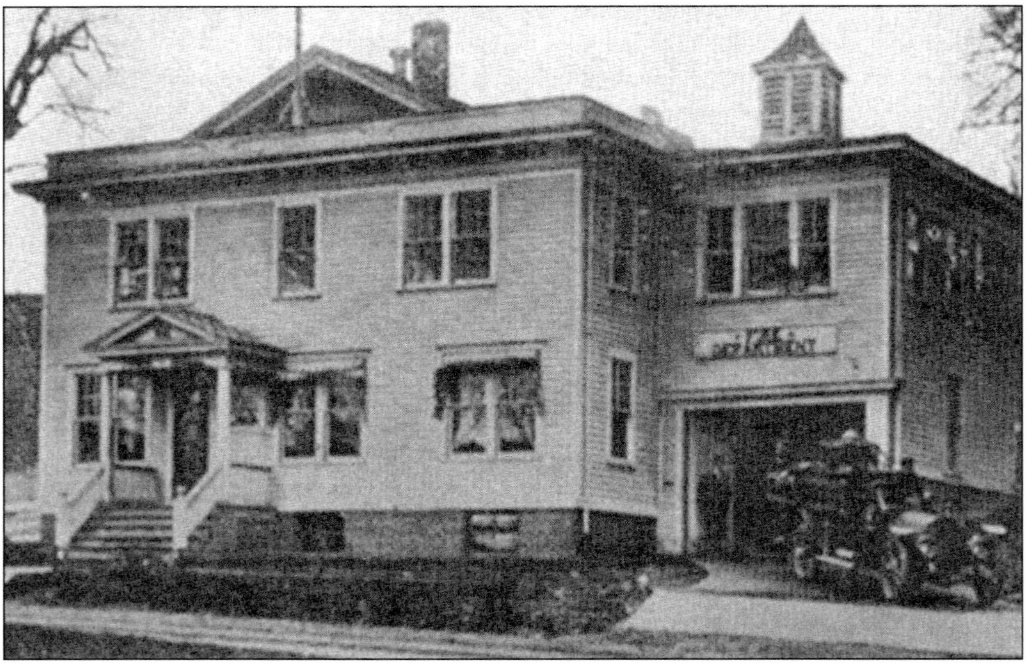

This is an early picture of the former town hall and firehouse structure. Terryville Fire Department was organized in 1911 after a series of devastating fires. A special town meeting was held, and an appropriation of $1,800 was approved for the purchase of the first fire equipment. This image shows one of the first motorized fire trucks purchased and used by the Terryville Fire Department. (Courtesy of Cathy Mathiason.)

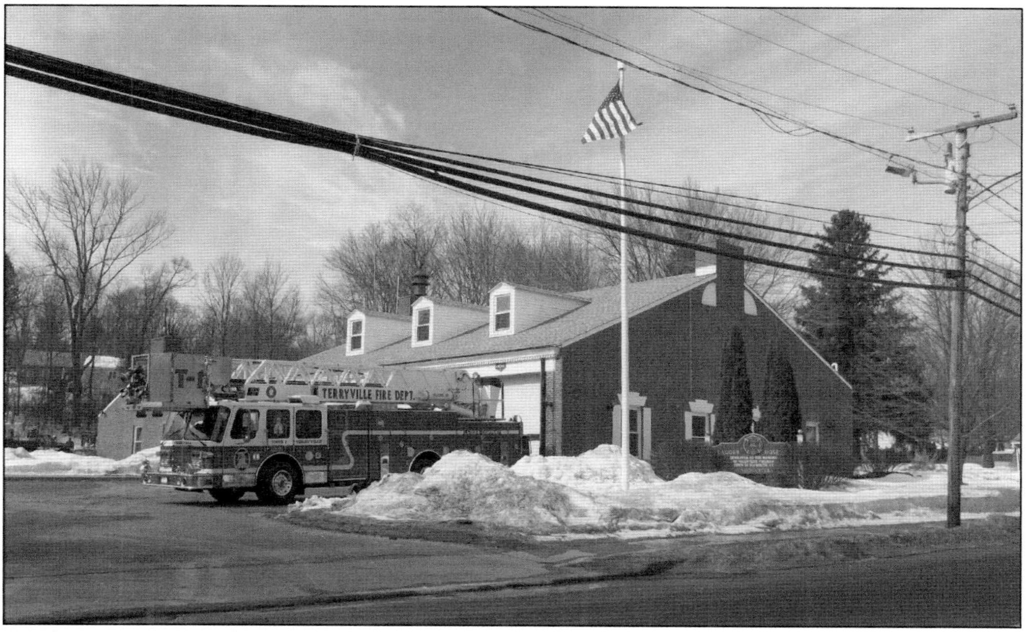

As the town grew, the need for additional fire stations became imperative. The Terryville Headquarters Fire Station was opened in 1969. Plymouth Center station is active, and in 1974 a new station was completed on Fall Mountain. These three stations provide coverage to the entire town as well as support for neighboring towns when needed. The Fire Departments are staffed by volunteers. (Photograph by Judy Giguere.)

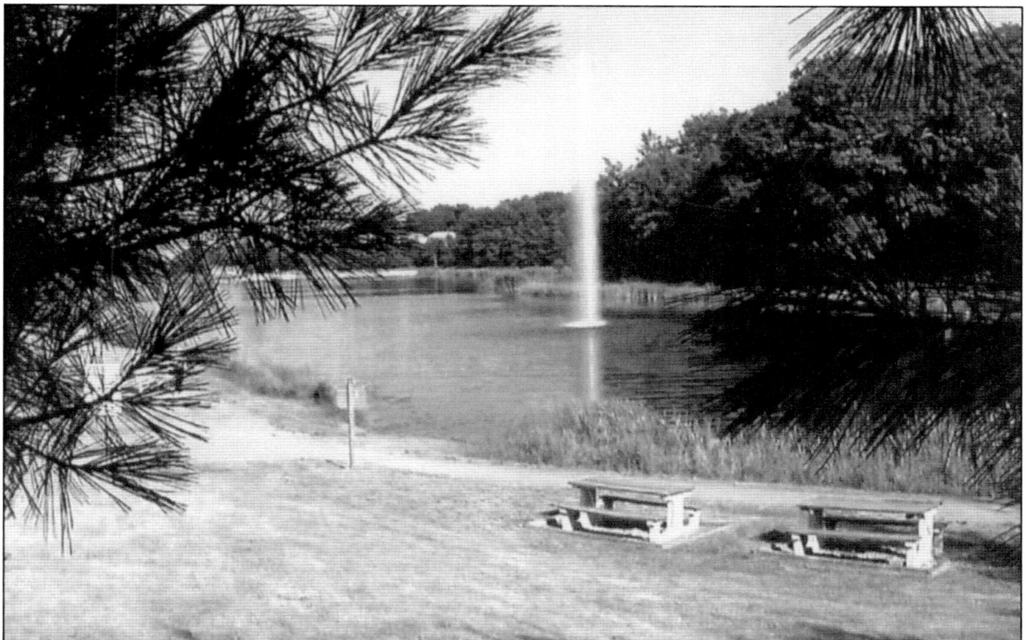

The town-owned Lake Winfield recreational area includes a quarter-mile-long paved walking path around the lake. It is a charming place for summer evening walks. Other hiking areas are sponsored by the Plymouth Land Trust and the Connecticut Forest and Park Association Blue Trail System. (Photograph by Jerry Milne, courtesy of Cathy Mathiason.)

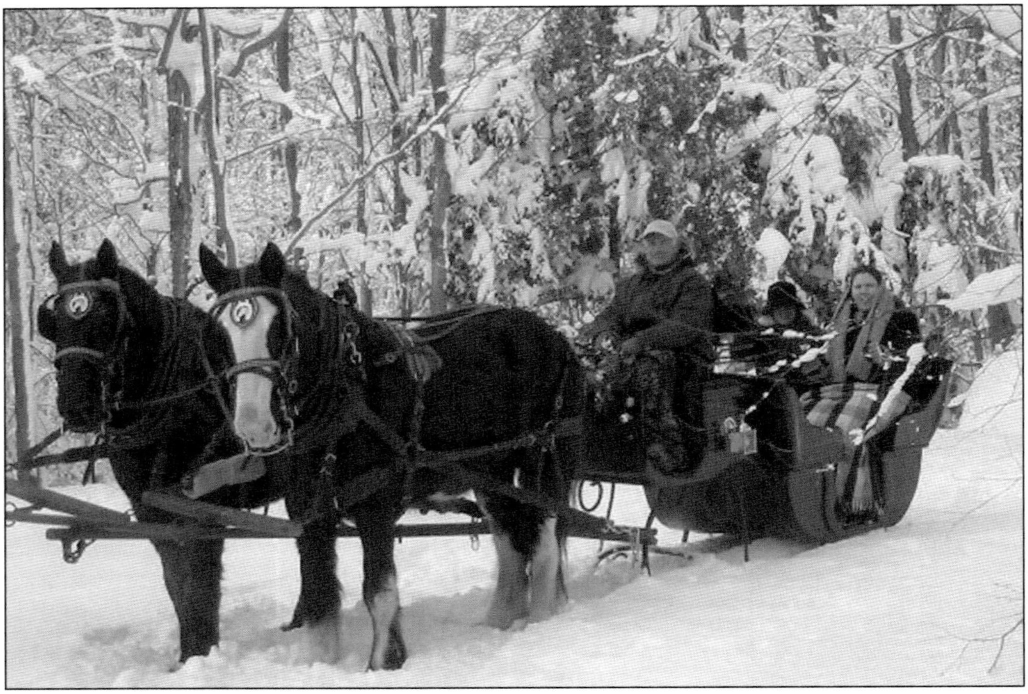

Wood Acres Farm is one of the oldest continuously owned and operated family farms in Plymouth. It specializes in capturing the traditions of past centuries with horse-drawn carriages. Snowy winter days and sleigh bells are made very special in a sleigh of Victorian elegance drawn by magnificent draft horses. (Courtesy of Wood Acres Farm.)

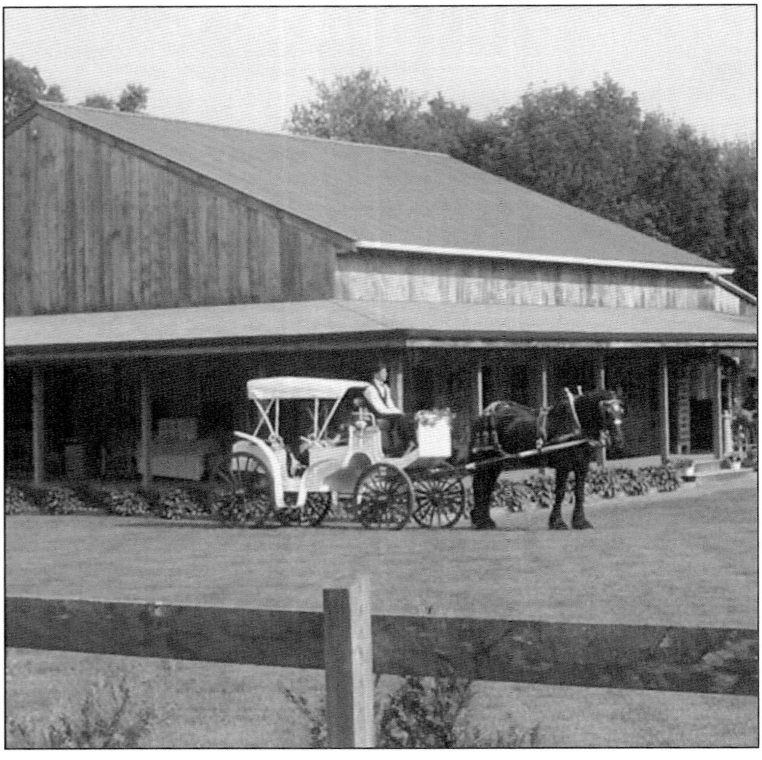

Wood Acres Farm offers a variety of horse-drawn carriages for special occasions. The homestead itself is over 250 years old and is continuously owned by members of the Wood family. An out building has been converted and updated to offer space for hosting special events. (Courtesy of Wood Acres Farm.)

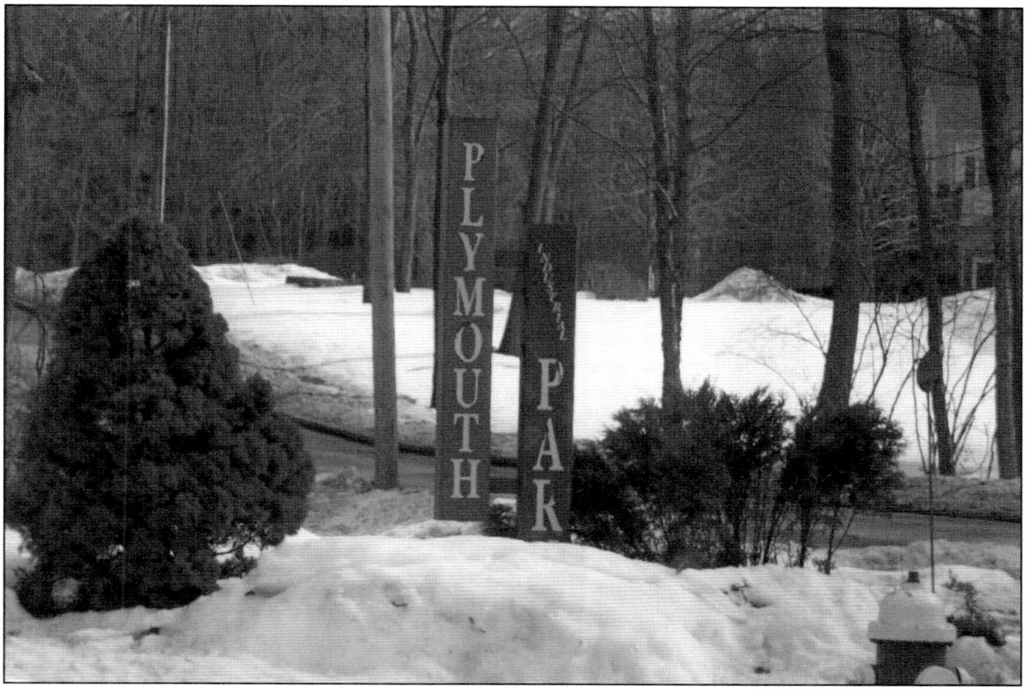

This sign marks the gateway to Phase I and Phase II of the Plymouth Industrial Park. The Park has been so successful that Phase III consists of 40 acres of developable land for new businesses or expansion of existing businesses. It is located on Harwinton Avenue, close to the center of town with access to main roads. (Photograph by Judy Giguere.)

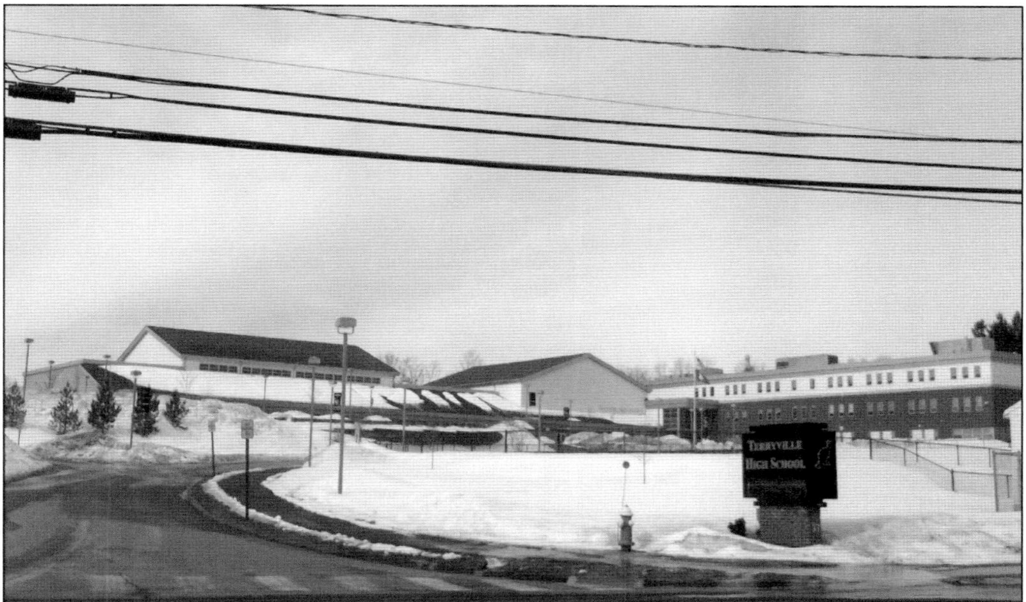

The new Terryville High School is located on the hill above the Plymouth Industrial Park on Harwinton Avenue. It overlooks the Plymouth Industrial Park, the town of Plymouth, and the surrounding landscape. Construction of this new state-of-the-art high school began in January 2006. The school opened its doors in January 2008. (Photograph by Judy Giguere.)